Robert Hayden

A Critical Analysis of His Poetry

Robert Hayden

A Critical Analysis of His Poetry

PONTHEOLLA T. WILLIAMS

WITH A FOREWORD BY BLYDEN JACKSON

University of Illinois Press

Urbana and Chicago

Publication of this work was supported in part by
a grant from the Andrew W. Mellon Foundation.

This book is printed on acid-free paper.

Chapter 1 of this volume first appeared in somewhat different
form as "A 'Life upon These Shores'" in *World Order* 16, no. 1
(Fall 1981): 11–34.

Library of Congress Cataloging-in-Publication Data

Williams, Pontheolla T., 1935–
    A critical analysis of the poetry of Robert
Hayden, 1940–78.

    Bibliography: p.
    Includes index.
    1. Hayden, Robert Earl—Criticism and interpretation.
I. Title.
PS3515.A9363Z95   1987   811'.52   86-6932
ISBN 0-252-01289-5 (alk. paper)

FOR MY PARENTS

JAMES E. TAYLOR, SR. (deceased)
AND
OPHELIA T. STINSON
vis a tergo

Contents

Foreword

Robert Hayden was born in Detroit, Michigan. He died in Ann Arbor, Michigan, less than an hour's ride by modern transportation from his birthplace. Outwardly he lived a relatively uneventful life. He spent virtually all of his adult years, after his formal education in Detroit and Ann Arbor, as a professor of English teaching at only two schools, Fisk University and the University of Michigan. Military service in World War II eluded him completely, however anti-Nazi he may have been. His eyesight was so deficient, from his earliest youth, that he wore glasses almost ludicrous in the thickness of their lenses. The all-too-limited measure of genuine fame he was permitted to enjoy came very late to him. Langston Hughes never made a colossal amount of money, but for forty years Hughes basked in the light of his own celebrity. Such celebrity as Hayden knew was largely confined to the final decade of his rather humble existence in a human guise. It was only during those last ten years, for example, that he became a public lecturer whom people supposedly knowledgeable about American culture were expected to come out to hear. Yet Hayden's inner life must have teemed with a rich and rare eventfulness. Without so crowded and ingenious an activity of his private mind, he could not have written the marvelous poetry, every rift loaded with ore, that he did. How reputable a poet he will remain as posterity assesses him of course it is too soon to say. But that he deserves to endure the exceptional quality of his art undoubtedly proclaims. In the select array of poetry's finest practitioners from every era and every clime, he seems anything but an interloper. He did not want to be merely a parochial phenomenon. And he was not. True, he did often find, always unapologetically, the circumstantial detail of the external world he created to serve as the physical arena for his poetry within the black neighborhoods he tended to inhabit. Of black history and black folklore he was well and proudly aware. But blackness to him was the same sort of incident that the imperialism of Augustan Rome was to Virgil or the bourgeois environment of Emma Bovary to Flaubert, a point of departure into that magic realm where all artists of unmistakably superlative merit do become ecumenical and universal.

It is from an accurate recognition of this quality of Hayden's art that Pontheolla Williams's study of Hayden's poetry derives its original strength and the solid common basis of its many virtues. Professor Williams has neglected none of the obvious duties incumbent upon anyone seriously committed to the task she has so diligently undertaken. She made herself familiar with Hayden's personal history. It was her good fortune, moreover, in doing so, to be able to consult not only written records but Hayden himself—a Hayden with whom she was, to her great credit, able to establish sufficient rapport to receive from him, as to a thoroughly trusted *confidante,* his own musings about his own bisexuality. It was her perhaps even better fortune to possess, and very profitably to exploit, other gifts native to herself, with the result that she could, and did, blend her insights into Hayden's life with her insights into his poetry at levels of perception which permitted her to do a proper job of relating biographically a poet to his poems. One end result of this correlation has been her proof positive that, from whatever perspective Hayden is viewed, his impressive stature as a poet suffers no diminution.

It is not altogether fair to Hayden to say that he abided all his life, as it were, within a cloister. Sometimes, when he thought (always, apparently, with good warrant) an occasion demanded it, he did, to capitalize on the verse of William Blake, grasp his bow of burning gold and mount his chariot of fire. Once at Fisk, for example, conceivably with immediate jeopardy to his job, in his capacity as the faculty sponsor of the *Fisk Herald,* the student magazine of which the undergraduate W. E. B. DuBois in the 1880s had been an editor, he defended the freedom of speech of another Fisk undergraduate who was never to become so renowned as DuBois, but who, nonetheless, had authored a short story, published in the *Herald* with Hayden's full approval but against the vigorous protest of a prominent Fisk alumna. The Fisk faculty, incidentally, rose to Hayden's support in his advocacy for his student, and Hayden, despite the irate alumna, prevailed. But there were other times, at Fisk and elsewhere, when Hayden fought, rarely with accomplices as unflinching and persistent in their allegiance to him as his Fisk colleagues in the instance of his young author, for principles of right that were dear to him. He never played his role of a champion of social justice on a stage so grand and so visible as that granted to the Martin Luther King who spoke of his dream for America in 1963 in Washington. No millions of people ever heard, or saw, him plead the cause of the weak and poor. Even so, enlightened humanitarianism was a part of the creed which made him what he was and entered into the compound of beliefs and attitudes constantly in location as the substratum of conviction for the polemic of his poetry. That compound benefited also from his extensive and profound familiarity with the Negro folk, of his own generation and before; his scholarly knowledge of Negro history; his wide-ranging, highly intelligent, yet also very sophisticatedly intellectual acquaintance with all the world around him, as it was in his own day and as it had been in previous periods of its recorded and unrecorded past; his Baháism; and his passionate involvement with, as well as mastery of, the one thing which meant as much to him as anything he was ever to experience, the craft of poetry itself, the accomplished journeyman's capacity for saying as a poet what he, at moments most crucial to him, did not want to say in any other way.

Professor Williams has sought, in her study of Hayden's poetry, to identify all the elements discernible in the compound described above, to give each element its due, and yet to indicate for all such elements their interaction as well as their sometime splendid fusion into a magnificent whole. So she has chosen well her method. She has availed herself admirably of her own commendable expertise in the complex domain of critical theory. Her skill and her industry have produced an addition to the literature illustrative of Hayden neither meretricious in its value nor minor in its import. Undoubtedly, further studies of Hayden and of his poetic art—various, surely, in their forms and emphases—will be made. To such studies, as to all existing studies of Hayden, of whatever nature, Professor Williams has brought a welcome aid and accompaniment. To a poet of unquestionable worth she has brought, simultaneously, her own token of respect—like this poet's poetry, an achievement much beyond reproach.

BLYDEN JACKSON

Acknowledgments

I am indebted to a number of people and institutions for generous assistance in the preparation of this study. Chief among the individuals are Dr. Robert Bone and poet Robert Hayden. To Professor Bone I am grateful for the guidance he gave in helping me to plumb the Afro-American literary heritage. He gave me sound suggestions and patient counseling in the organization of the manuscript. His ideas concerning emphasis and style are reflected throughout the study.

My debt to Robert Hayden is invaluable and large. He shared with me the biographical facts of his life. He displayed a quite extraordinary generosity in letting me examine his notebooks, journals, letters, and materials in his personal file. He and Mrs. Hayden unfailingly extended warm hospitality to me, which I gratefully acknowledge.

To Dr. Howard D. Langford I am grateful for the interest he manifested in my study. His observant eye has witnessed decades of man's world-wide struggle for human dignity. He led me to see that the Afro-American's struggle, as reflected in his literature, is a significant part of the universal struggle for human dignity.

To Professor M. G. Jacobs, who read portions of the manuscript in draft and gave me helpful suggestions, I express particular thanks.

To Mrs. Sarah Jacobs and to Mrs. Linda R. Mathis, who, respectively, typed the first and second drafts of the manuscript, I express deep appreciation for their careful craftsmanship and patience.

The members of the New York City Public Library Schomburg Collection were helpful, especially Librarian Glenderlyn Johnson. She rendered particular assistance in pointing out Hayden and related materials in the library's possession.

I am appreciative and deeply gratified with the resource services that my former student, Mr. Abraham Wright, provided.

The book has taken me seven years to research and write, perhaps because I write slowly and perhaps because, each time I thought I was finished, new information surfaced. This has been the case especially since 1978, when I became a member of the community of scholars that was developed under the guidance of Dr. Broadus N. Butler, president of the Robert R. Moton Memorial Institute, who also directed the Institute's Independent Studies Center.

During this period, Morris College, Sumter, South Carolina, where I am employed, provided me encouragement in granting me two years of released time for which I am grateful and without which I could not have completed the study.

Grateful acknowledgment is extended to the Robert R. Moton Memorial Institute for its 1978–79 grant to me that enabled me to substantially further this study and to the National Endowment for the Humanities for its 1980–81 grant to me that enabled me to complete the study.

Introduction

Except perhaps for an Indian, to be born an American is to be born without escape or remedy into a pluralistic society. Lacking an indigenous culture of his own, the American paradoxically takes pride in what he considers his own fugitive and individual character, a character fashioned primarily from a multitude of rudimentary experiences and alien influences. His fellow citizens are both aborigines and immigrants, creators and innovators as well as sycophants of distant and remote imaginations. That is not to say, of course, that the American experience is not a cultural marvel in itself, since much of the world's inspired art, invention, and sensitivity springs from this very diversity and paradox, but rather that it is a blend of all that is at once original and mimetic, as well as significant and absurd.

To be born an American and black, however, is to be born more stubbornly aware of the complexity of the American experience. Unlike the white American, who may take temporary intellectual refuge in the social and economic power of his majority, the black American believes himself uncompromisingly forced to accept some sort of simplistic stance toward the paradoxical nature of his American character. Unable to hide in the serenity of numbers, he is led by Caucasians as well as other Afro-Americans to believe that he must either assume the responsibility, and therefore the meaning, of white America—resulting in his rejection by more iconoclastic blacks—or reject that responsibility and meaning—limiting his social and economic horizons in an extremely complex and mobile society. The choice is both fatuous and offensive. It is a limited option born out of more than two hundred years of intellectual guilt and instinctive fear, an option that many black writers have struggled against accepting and a choice that is both crude and artistically degrading.

Both the paradoxical nature of American society and the unique position of the black man within that society have contributed to the peculiar experience of the Afro-American writer in the United States. Believing, on the one hand, that he is forced to reject white tradition in favor of black experience, he is condemned by conservative critics as a limited and inferior craftsman, a writer who deals in propaganda rather than poetic meaning. He becomes the victim of a sterile orthodoxy that ultimately limits his achievement to that of a literary oddity, interesting and cute, but nevertheless amateurish and non-descript. He may be read in college classrooms, but never as an equal to writers such as Faulkner and Whitman. Instead, he is perceived as a heavy-handed moralist who preaches either racial brotherhood or war in rather diffuse tirades, sometimes condescendingly called poetry or fiction. If, on the other hand, he accepts the role of craftsman and poet, embracing the literary heritage of Western civilization, he is condemned by revolutionary critics as the slapstick pawn of a racist society, a society intent upon the subjugation of black consciousness in America. To compose a sonnet instead of a juba becomes a literary analogy to lynching, a rejection of one's own heritage in favor of white masters and suburban cocktail parties.

The distinction, of course, is absurd. It is no more possible for a true poet to reject craftsmanship—sonnet or juba—than it is for a black American to reject his American heritage. That is not to say that the meaning of a poem may not be involved in the revelation of what it means to be isolated in a volatile society or to be poor and black in Alabama. It simply means that the primary duty of an artist is to impose form on his experience, to derive meaning from art and not racial identity. That a poet may remain both a craftsman and a spokesman for a particular experience is clearly evident in the works of every great poet from Homer to Yeats, Shakespeare to Senghor. True poetry transcends time and place, government and issue. It speaks to all of us. It is hardly limited to momentary problems of state. Poetry creates form from formlessness, order from chaos. It demonstrates, if only for a tenuous moment, that the meaning of man's heart lies in his endurance and pride, his triumphs and his failures, and not in the color of his skin or the shape of his skull; and that is true of the white man as well as the black, the Indian as well as the Pole, and the plumber as well as the poet.

Robert Hayden occupies this peculiar, if not too uncommon, place in contemporary American poetry. He published significant poetry from 1940 through 1980, but after four decades his work continued to be labeled as either a mere catalog of racial oppression, separate from and inferior to the American literary mainstream, or as the self-conscious rantings of an Uncle Tom, insufficiently black and given to racial groveling.

While he has emerged as one of America's leading black poets, his work has failed to attract nearly the critical or popular attention granted to white writers of equal accomplishments. He was honored internationally as the recipient of the *Grand Prix de la Poesie* and nationally as a nominee for the National Book Award, as a member of the American Academy of Poets, and as Poetry Consultant at the Library of Congress, and yet not until 1966 was a collection of his poetry available to the general public.

Clearly, much of this rejection is due to his own artistic choices. From the very beginning of his poetic career, Robert Hayden strived to succeed both as a literary craftsman and as an eclectic spokesman for his people. Rejecting the limited notion that a writer must be true to some sort of racial jingoism, he purposely plotted a tortuous and often lonely course of individual and artistic freedom, a course designed at least artistically to blend that which is culturally paradoxical in the American experience with the intrinsic unity of poetic form.

An insistent theme in Hayden's work indicates that the American, both black and white, derives his independence, ferocity, and momentum not so much from his own group identity as from his paradoxical and often vacillating search for artistic and human dignity. Like most American writers, from Cooper to Whitman, Faulkner to Baldwin, Hayden did not reject his cultural or racial identity. On the contrary, he openly embraced it, but as an American, rather than simply a Negro, writer; he transcended mere rhetorical discourse, whether racial or political, in order to comprehend the meaning of his environment in terms of his art. The making of a poem, in other words, becomes a systematic defense against the ambiguity of the American experience. Structure resolves irony, and meaning replaces rhetoric. In this sense, Robert Hayden is truly a poet of the people, black as well as white, laborer as well as congressman. In

Robert Hayden's verse, as opposed to that of many of his contemporaries, there is more poetry than essay, more imagery than argot, and more heart than veneer.

It is my purpose to delineate Robert Hayden's development as a poet, rather than his niche in a racial tradition. He was a poet who refused, at times courageously, to suppress anything relevant—be it the influence of a white poet or a black ritual dance—to his artistic response to his humanistic instincts and perceptions. Hayden was perhaps, like Faulkner, a synthesizer of the elements in the melting pot. He may have been, as is no other poet, a bridge over the socioartistic riptides of American life, and therein the better world to come might recognize his chief value. Perhaps his value as a humanist might someday outweigh his value as a poet, an artist. If so, his commitment will be responsible for such a view, for it is through art that his universal humanism flowered.

Hayden's canon through 1982, including the posthumous *American Journal* (1983), is the concern of this study. For the reader's convenience, in instances where earlier poems are included in *Angle of Ascent: New and Selected Poems* (1975), pagination of the poem being considered is given in *Angle* as well as in the earlier volume being discussed. In instances where poems from those earlier volumes (from 1940 through 1975) are not included in *Angle* or in *Collected Poems*, if it is given, pagination in the volume being considered is, of course, cited. This was done because the publishing company for *Heart-Shape in the Dust* (1940) no longer exists; *The Lion and the Archer* (1948), *Figure of Time* (1955), *A Ballad of Remembrance* (1962), *Selected Poems* (1966) are out of print; and *The Night-blooming Cereus* (1972), a limited edition, was published in London, England, and was not released by an American house.

A final caution is due the reader. The first chapter is a biographical sketch of the poet. Notwithstanding Hayden's hard-won acclaim during the decade of the seventies, he is still relatively unknown, both as a poet and as a man. In view of this fact, and because the shaping influence of his life had great bearing on the direction his poetry took, it is the writer's intention in including biographical information about him to introduce the reader to Hayden, the private man. The "authorized biography" is in process by the writer.

Robert Hayden

A Critical Analysis of His Poetry

A Biographical Sketch

The Early Years: 1913–30

Robert Hayden's mother, Ruth Finn, was born of a racially mixed ancestry. In her late teens she changed her name to Gladys, joined a circus, and ran away from her home in Altoona, Pennsylvania. Eventually she landed in Detroit, Michigan, where she met and married Asa Sheffey, a laborer from Kentucky, by whom she had a son on August 4, 1913. When her son was only eighteen months old, she gave him to William and Sue Ellen Hayden and left for New York.[1]

The near-sighted baby was rechristened Robert Earl Hayden and became the son of the Hayden couple, in name if not in fact. Although the Haydens told the boy otherwise, they never legally adopted him. Perhaps that was the reason they did not take a firm stand against the Sheffeys' visits to their home to see the boy or prevent Robert's visits to his mother's house. Indeed, there were times when Mrs. Hayden herself took Robert to see his real mother.[2]

Hayden recalled Ruth Sheffey as a beautiful woman who was vivacious and fond of dancing. She introduced him to the theatrical and cultural advantages of Buffalo, where she had relocated after she left Asa Sheffey and married Albert Moore, cabaret owner. The boy, who had known only a lower-class life in Detroit, was thoroughly enchanted. He vividly recalled his times with his mother—the quiet boat rides, the theater excursions, the aptly chosen gifts—as experiences which immediately and indelibly captured his imagination. Such glimpses of culture and refinement played a part in putting his life on a track that would later result in a less ethnically centered view of art than that espoused by many black artists.[3]

But mixed with his memory of these happy holidays from life in the ghetto were bitter recollections of "a certain amount of jealousy" that arose between his adoptive parents and his real mother. Mrs. Sheffey told him that, contrary to what the Haydens claimed, he had never been legally adopted, that he was *always* to be "her" son. Consequently, the Haydens and Mrs. Sheffey were trapped in a tenacious battle for Robert's affections, while the helpless object of their struggle suffered traumas that affected him until his death.[4]

Asa Sheffey, meanwhile, sometimes came from Gary, Indiana, where he had found work after Ruth left him, to visit his son. In an effort to make his visits occasions that would impress a boy of ten or twelve, he took him on shopping tours and appealed to his affections through gifts. When Robert visited his father in Gary, however, his stay was stormy. Between the good times, when his father displayed what Hayden recalls as "his outrageous humor" and lavished the usual gifts upon him, there were drinking bouts during which he disparaged his estranged wife. Hayden, who adored his glamorous mother, resented the attacks and developed an indignant attitude toward his father. Decades later, Hayden revealed that he simply could never develop a genuine feeling of love for the man, who never really understood the "queer sort of boy" he had fathered.[5]

The child's nearsightedness was a pronounced handicap. Because of it, he could not engage in athletics or other activities usual for one of his age.[6] His answer was to withdraw, and in his isolation he developed an abiding passion for reading. According to Hayden himself, he became a nonathletic, bookish little boy, one who would understandably appear strange to a man with his father's virile energy.

William Hayden, on the other hand, led a life of quiet, if troubled, poverty. A laborer, he was able to afford his family only a hand-to-mouth existence even when he was working. When he was unemployed, his family accepted public welfare. His existence was further troubled by his dissatisfaction with his uncertain status as an adoptive parent and the fact that he and Mrs. Hayden did not get along very well. As a devout Baptist fundamentalist, he ruled his household sternly and frowned upon any display of frivolity. For example, he pronounced that Bessie Smith's "low-down songs could not be played on their 'victorola' [victrola]."[7] This dictum pleased neither his wife, who was fond of the blues, nor Robert, who was later to pay tribute to the famous blues singer in his poem, "Homage to the Empress of the Blues."[8] William Hayden was, however, the father to whom, many years later, the poet offered a poignant, if belated, tribute in "Those Winter Sundays."[9] He was also "Pa," who, though uneducated himself, undertook to finance his adopted son's college education.

Sue Hayden, uneducated, was the "handsome woman" who haggled with Italian and Jewish butchers to provide choice cuts of meat for her family. It was she who regaled Robert with Afro-American folktales, stories of southern racial atrocities, and her own post–Civil War experiences, when she was a chambermaid on Ohio River steamers. Her first marriage had been to Jim Barlow, a handsome man who perhaps was white and who had, at one time, worked on the same river steamer. She could never forget him and, unfortunately, never let William Hayden forget him either, thus feeding the fires of discontent in their household.[10]

Her memories of life in the South provided a rich fund of inspiration and material for Hayden's poetry. It is her relationship with Jim Barlow, overlaid with Hayden's impressions of his real mother, that he fictionalized in "The Ballad of Sue Ellen Westerfield."[11] Hayden was deeply affected by the fact that his real mother looked white. Additionally, he was impressed by Mrs. Hayden's accounts of her marriage to a man who looked white. His concern with racial appearance was thus awakened. He asserted, for example, that he was almost as fair as his white playmates. One can imagine the effect that such a situation would have on a young boy.

These, then, are the basic elements of the "terrible love-hate relationship[s]" that Hayden could not forget.[12] He described them in "Those Winter Sundays" as the "chronic angers of that house" (line 9). He remained in this household, however, until he was twenty-nine,[13] and here he began his retreat into the private world of the poetic imagination. In his interview with Paul McCluskey, formerly his editor at Harcourt Brace Jovanovich, he recalled that "the conflicts, the quarreling [and] the tension kept [the family] most of the time on the edge of some shrill domestic calamity" which consequently "turned [him] upon [himself]."[14] His family situation, he said, left him with "a feeling of apartness, noninvolvement . . . half in and out of things." He attributed his "nervousness" to this troubled household also and became upset at any mention of those painful experiences.[15] Yet, in a softening of his description of Pa Hayden, the poet later said "he did like fun." Sometimes he even joined the jovial group in the household, including Ma Hayden and Aunt Roxie, her daughter by Jim Barlow, who cajoled him to tell some "tales."[16] Moreover, it is out of both the positive and negative aspects of his ordeals that he created some of his most poignant lyrics, such as "The Whipping"[17] and "Those Winter Sundays."

"Sunflowers gangled there"

If the Hayden household was penurious, insecure, and explosive, the larger world of their neighborhood was no less so. Just as life in the Hayden home fed his poetic imagination, so did the ghetto around it.

The neighborhood in which Robert was born, and where the Haydens lived, was a central-city slum. By 1918 the area had rapidly expanded to some twenty city blocks and was becoming predominantly black, as Jews, Italians, Irish, and others moved away.[18] Hayden recalled that the area, from 1928 through the early 1930s, was "the most notorious part of town."[19] Beacon Street was in the old East Side section near downtown Detroit, where lived those "who feared alarming fists of snow / on the door and those who feared the riot-squad of statistics."[20] Here, too, the real-life counterparts of the personae of " 'Summertime and the Living . . .' "[21] made their home, those who were plagued with "quarrels and shattered glass" because they were "so harshened after each unrelenting day / that they were shouting-angry" (lines 7, 12–13). They endured, he wrote, because they were strong and had Pan-Africanist dreams of "Ethiopia spreading her gorgeous wings" (line 32).

"Incense of the Lucky Virgin"[22] furnishes a particularly poignant expression of this ethos. The subject is a deserted wife and mother who tries magic and prayer to bring her husband back and is finally driven to infanticide as an alternative to watching the children starve:

Incense of the Lucky Virgin,
High John the Conqueror
didn't bring him home again,
didn't get his children fed,
     get his children fed.

I prayed and what did prayer avail?
My candles held no power.
An evening came I prayed no more
and blew my candles out,
     oh blew my candles out.

. . . .

Garland was too quick for me
(he didn't yell once as he ran);
Cleola, Willie Mae
won't be hungry any more,
     oh they'll never cry and hunger any more.

(Lines 1–10, 21–25)

These people could be devoutly religious as he shows in "Mourning Poem for the Queen of Sunday,"[23] where the cathartic effect of the "Queen's" fundamentalist church ritual eases their despair:

     sing Jesus down
to help with struggling and doing without and being colored
all through blue Monday?
Till way next Sunday?

(Lines 10–13)

Yet they could be quite worldly, temporarily banishing the grimness of ghetto life through the magic of the "Homage to the Empress of the Blues" with her secular song:

She came out on the stage in yards of pearls, emerging like
a favorite scenic view, flashed her golden smile and sang.

(Lines 5–6)

And despite the prevailing harshness of conditions, they were quite capable of feeling vicarious joy when the lucky few—for example, the "big splendiferous / Jack Johnson in his diamond limousine"— achieved success in the world beyond the ghetto.[24]

Until the early 1930s, when a new wave of southern black immigrants flooded the area, the neighborhood had a multi-racial character. Hayden recalls these times in several poems, notably "The Rabbi,"[25] which reflects the Afro-American influx and the widespread departures of the Jewish people, many of whose children were his playmates. The poem treats the distance between the world of the child and the adult, between innocence and experience (none of the children understands the religious rituals performed by the Rabbi), and explores the relationship between belief and prejudice. Thus, to the perception of the child, who had not yet learned the differences perceived by adults, the departure of his friends can only be understood in terms of a mysterious religious ritual: "the Rabbi bore [his] friends off / in his prayer shawl" (lines 23–24).

Some blacks who were financially better off began to move away, too. Among them were some of Hayden's friends from the Second Baptist Church. Because they were fortunate enough to move to the more affluent West Side while he remained on the East Side, they began to "patronize" him. Their condescension left scars on his memories; yet they did not deter him from recalling his old neighborhood as one of the most colorful parts of the Detroit of that era. Indeed, he said that he could go on for the rest of his artistic life drawing on those memories.[26]

In response to a question on racial prejudice in his neighborhood, Hayden said that instead of bigotry there was a feeling of victimization. Some landlords refused to repair the houses of their tenants, for example, but neglect was not universal. Jews and Italians did extend credit to his family. He had white playmates. No doubt his memories of them inspired "The Rabbi." Later, Hayden was to recall that his own parents cautioned him against "running around with so and so," reminding him that he was "colored." He said, when he reached puberty, whites warned him, "You're colored and I don't want you playing with my girls."[27] Perhaps, however, it was the memory of the crucially important services Jews and Italians extended to his family and his pleasant memories of his playmates on which he based his claim that his childhood was relatively free from hard prejudice.[28] The insight and compassion gained from his own interracial experiences and mixed ancestry inbued him with a warm, humanistic worldview that became a significant asset in his art.

"Who will sing Jesus down"

The Afro-American church was a key feature in Hayden's neighborhood and was a vital factor in the lives of most of the people. As early as 1917, there were thirteen major black churches on Detroit's East Side. According to George Edward Hayes, the churches were powerful forces that served socio-economic and cultural as well as religious needs.[29] Their force was recalled by Hayden, who remembered that in the twenties and thirties, when he was growing up, the church was the center of his family life. His adoptive father was a member of the Second Baptist Church, one of Detroit's largest.[30]

It was to this church that William Hayden took his adopted son. Here Hayden said he experienced a genuine, even near-mystical, conversion and became a member while still a child. He was involved in both the Sunday School and the Vacation Bible School and became president of the Baptist Young People's Union. More important to his literary development, he acted in the dramatic group, wrote for the church paper, and spoke at various programs.[31] These activities gave him an enriching proximity to the ceremony, pomp, and splendor of the practices and rituals of the Afro-American fundamentalist church, and these experiences would later be transmuted into poems, such as "Mourning Poem for the Queen of Sunday."

It is interesting that Hayden's first religious vows were made to a church that approves the doctrine of the elect—that is, that only those who are baptized by immersion may be saved. This doctrine, of course, stands in ironic contrast to his adult relationship with the Bahá'i faith, a religion that is inclusive rather than exclusive. Nevertheless, his early response to Baptist fundamentalism instilled the "God consciousness" he continued to feel until his demise[32] and created a depository of feeling and symbology for verse that, while it is free from proselytizing, as perhaps his Bahá'i verse is not, is flavored with the fundamentalist Baptist convert's idiomatic speech rhythms and Biblical allusions.

Toward the World beyond the Ghetto

After completing elementary school, Hayden attended classes briefly at the predominantly black Miller High School, located on Detroit's East Side. Because his sight was so severely impaired, it was determined that he should be in a "sight-saving school." Hence he was transferred to the predominantly white Northern High School in Northeast Detroit. Despite the prejudice "we kids felt" in being "shut out of things," Hayden said, he "got on well there." He said he even won the high school award for "Gold" (1934), a short story he wrote.[33] His high school experiences helped lay the foundation for his later rejection of black literary iconoclasm, his acceptance of crafts-manship and artistic freedom, and his wish, in his own words, for "acceptance as a writer . . . not as [a writer] with a particular racial identity."[34]

Even before he enrolled in high school, however, his interests in literature, creative writing, and the fine arts had crystallized. He recalled that he had read some books on scenario writing when he was in the fifth or sixth grade, though he did not mention any specific titles. He told me he tried to rewrite the stories of plays and movies he had seen.[35]

He was sixteen years of age when he discovered modern poetry. It was, he continued, a dual discovery—that is, the discovery of the existence of both a modern Afro-American literary tradition and a modern mainstream American literary tradition. In his own attempts to write poetry he used Elinor Wylie and Countee Cullen as models. The title of his first volume, *Heart-Shape in the Dust*, comes from Wylie's "Hospes Comesque Coparis," and his first published poem, "Africa," owes much to Countee Cullen's "Heritage." Carl Sand-burg, Langston Hughes, Sara Teasdale, Edna St. Vincent Millay, and Stephen Vincent Benet were other poets he read. Thus, his first impressive experiences of poetry crossed the lines of ethnic tradi-tions.[36]

During this period, Hayden briefly attended the Detroit Institute of Musical Arts and took violin lessons with money made available by Aunt Roxie, Ma Hayden's daughter by Jim Barlow, and Mrs. Sheffey, who was, of course, determined to maintain her influence on her son's life. He continued these lessons until his adoptive father, who eventually had to assume the expense, could no longer afford them. At the same time, his congenitally impaired vision deterio-rated to such a degree that he was forced to sit so close to his music that it interfered with his playing and obstructed the view of the other musicians in both the high school and the Sunday School orchestras. Soon he had to quit these cherished activities. Hayden told me that his interest in music was so important to him that it proved to be the decisive attraction of the woman he married. She was a concert pianist and delighted him then and later with her playing. Allusions to music form a minor thread that runs through his poetry. As early as 1942 Hayden gave tribute to the force of music in "Beethoven"[37] from his 1938 award-winning Hopwood collection:

> Above the nervous bulletins of war,
> The fingered-over rummage ends of talk,
> This music builds its huge, superior
> Energy . . .
>
> (Lines 1–4)

Clearly, Hayden's secondary-school experiences were a decisive force in motivating him to become a serious artist. He gained competitive exposure to the dynamics of racially integrated learning; he was introduced to the dual traditions of Afro-American and American literature; he began his study of the Spanish language, a study he pursued in college and used in the creation of his Mexican poems. In short, by 1931 Hayden had begun laying the foundation for a poetic stance that both partakes of and crosses ethnic lines.[38]

The Depression Years: 1930–40

Nineteen thirty, the year of Hayden's graduation from Northern High School, was the beginning of a cataclysmic decade in this country's history. America had been economically ripped apart by the stock market crash of 1929, and the ensuing Great Depression had affected not only the economic and political spheres but American letters as well. Hayden's entrance into this tragic world as a young adult marks him as a member of the Depression generation.

He was interested in continuing his education in college, but at the time of his high school graduation his family was on welfare. His adoptive father, he said, "never questioned the value of [his] going to school, but . . . could not obtain the necessary sixty-five dollars tuition fee." He did, however, manage, with his father's consent, to attend postgraduate classes at Cass Technical High School. Hayden diligently sought work, and he accepted what was available. He worked in a grocery store. He set himself up as a public typist, using the typewriter that Albert Moore gave him. He typed letters for people, and for twenty-five or fifty cents, he said, he typed songs for the choir at Second Baptist Church. To his adoptive parent's displeasure, he issued numbers for a policy slips man, a procedure in the poor man's gambling game, and he ran errands for people, including some who were of ill repute.[39] Hayden continued to read, to write creatively, and to "try to come to grips with [himself]."[40]

The Second Baptist Church continued to provide a public outlet for his talent. He remembered writing didactic short stories for the church paper, and he recollected a poem on the American Legion for which he was able to develop a marching rhythm. He was both energetic and imitative at this time, ready to try his hand at new things. For instance, after reading Paul Laurence Dunbar's poems in high school, he was inspired to try to write verse in dialect.

Because of his energy, talent, and education, the church elders decided to groom him for a leadership role, and their specific suggestion was that he prepare himself for a career as an African missionary. Even though he participated in church activities, Hayden had known since the days when a bespectacled boy bent over books while other children were wrestling in the streets that he was incapable of a real commitment to the group spirit. As to the missionary suggestion, he commented, from the perspective of his years: "Now what would have become of me? I probably would have stood there and said the Hell with it all . . . would probably have become a voodoo doctor, a dancer . . . a medicine man."[41]

At about this time, he submitted to "Harper Brothers" a manuscript of poems he thought he entitled *Songs at Eighteen.*[42] Most of these poems treated the Afro-American history of the period. The manuscript was rejected, but at about this time, "Africa," a poem that treated what was to become his major poetic theme, the Afro-American experience, was accepted by *Abbott's Monthly.*[43] Publication in this popular ethnic magazine introduced him to the national Afro-American audience.

The poem, "Africa," echoes the primitivism of Countee Cullen's "Heritage"[44] and reflects, therefore, Hayden's tie to the waning Harlem Renaissance. Cullen's speaker in "Heritage" considers and questions the Afro-American's unique roots in Africa and expresses his need in the Western world for a black God who could better understand his anomalous position in America:

What is Africa to me?

. . . .

One three centuries removed
From the scenes his father loved,

. . . .

Jesus of the twice-turned cheek,
Lamb of God, although I speak
With my mouth thus, in my heart
Do I play a double part.
Ever at Thy glowing altar
Must my heart grow sick and falter,
Wishing He I served were black.

(Lines 1, 60–61, 96–101)

The speaker in Hayden's "Africa," on the other hand, extols the Afro-American's tie to Africa and his pride in that continent as the "cradle of his race" (line 40). He, therefore, gives an affirmative answer to the question Cullen poses and answers in the negative in "Heritage":

Though Freedom's light upon me shines,
My heart is native; my soul pines
For sight of thee, and all day long
I mourn and sing my fitful song:
"Dear Africa, you're more to me
Than reeking jungle—ebon sea!
In thee I take undying pride—
Dark cradle of a race denied!"

(Lines 33–40)

As far as prosody is concerned, "Africa" initiates Hayden's traditionalist period. The poem is formally structured—that is, it is composed of five stanzas, each consisting of four couplets, some of which are closed, some open. The lines are octosyllabic, closely patterned on the Cullen model.

Cullen's influence transcends that of a particular poem. From the outset of his career, Cullen had insisted on being accepted as a "poet" rather than a "Negro poet." He had refused to be restricted to racial themes, preferring the universality of human consciousness to the tribalism of racial consciousness.[45] Cullen was locked into the restrictions of the traditional English forms he had chosen, and his deepest poetic response was to the lyricism of Keats rather than to the

social issues of his day: lynching of blacks, housing and labor problems. Hayden, in his turn, argued against the tendency of American
critics to label the established black writer as a spokesman for his
race, and he criticized them for their habit of judging black poetry by a
different standard.[46] Unlike Cullen, however, Hayden responded to
social issues during the Great Depression, as he would later to World
War II, the upheavals of the sixties, and the Vietnam War. But however much they may resent being called "Negro poets," both writers
in fact often treated racial themes. Some of Cullen's finest verse
suggests, in an unimpassioned way, the dilemma of being black in
America, while Hayden's poetry passionately evokes the historic
plight of the black man in America.

   Hayden was not to publish again, at least nationally, until
1937.[47] In the interim, his public audience was still restricted largely
to church groups. His education and poetic growth, however, continued and were given a boost by a welfare case worker.[48] In his
McCluskey interview Hayden recalls that during a visit to the welfare station, his family's case worker expressed curiosity about two
books he was carrying. He showed her copies of Cullen's *Copper
Sun*[49] and told her that he, too, would publish a volume of poetry
someday. His sincerity apparently was very impressive, for she eventually helped him obtain a college scholarship.

   He left his postgraduate high school studies at Cass to become a
freshman at Detroit City College (later Wayne State University),
where he majored in Spanish with a view to a teaching career. He did
not take poetry courses because he could not fit them into his sched-
ule. He read T. S. Eliot, Ezra Pound, and others, however, indepen-
dently, and he continued to write. In 1936 the *Detroit Collegian* of
Detroit City College published "Epilogue," his brief reminiscence of
Keats.[50]

   Early in his college years Hayden began an association with a
group of young writers including John Malcolm Brinnin, Kimon Friar,
and other local writers in the arts. He credited his association with
this group as a significant factor in his development as a poet. Some of
the group espoused Marxism, identified with the labor movement
and the class struggle, and wrote realistic didactic poetry. Hayden
stated that their models as revolutionary poets were Sol Funaroff,
Lola Ridge, Carl Sandburg, and Langston Hughes.[51]

Langston Hughes was at this time president of the League for the Struggle for Negro Rights, a leftist front organization. A key figure in the Harlem Renaissance, Hughes already had articulated its literary philosophy in "The Negro Artist and the Racial Mountain." Later, during the thirties, when the Harlem Renaissance was petering out under the onslaught of the Great Depression, Hughes proclaimed a new revolutionary image for the Negro. In 1935, in a document which predated Richard Wright's influential manifesto, "Blueprint for Negro Writing," Hughes declared himself solidly grounded in the working-class struggle.[52] At the same time he said the Negro writer should reveal his ethnic qualities in order to destroy the white man's stereotypes. He should expose bigotry in the unions, the "sick-sweet lies" of organized religion, and the false leadership of Negro opportunists. This philosophy clearly flavors the proletarian protest poems in Hayden's first volume, *Heart-Shape in the Dust*.

Hughes was not only an influence on Hayden's political and social views but a literary mentor as well. When Hughes came to Detroit during the late thirties to see his play *Drums of Haiti* performed, Hayden, an actor in the play, met him. Over lunch, Hayden gave him some of his poems to examine. Hughes encouraged him to continue writing but cautioned him against imitating others.[53] This criticism was apparently justified, considering the nature of many of the poems in *Heart-Shape in the Dust*.

Decades later, Hayden acknowledged a debt to Hughes, but stated that he grew to regard his verse as "too simplistic, very often careless in construction and development." This judgment was foreshadowed when Hayden gave Hughes a sonnet to examine, and Hughes commented that he had never been able to write one.[54] No doubt Hayden saw Hughes's failure as an indication that he was unwilling to submit to the necessary rigors of the discipline or was caught up in social concerns to such an extent that his prosodic development was crippled.

By the time Hayden left Detroit City College in 1936, one credit hour short of graduation, to enter the working world as an employee of the federal government, his admiration for Countee Cullen and Langston Hughes, no less than Lola Ridge and Carl Sandburg, had firmly anchored his work in both the Afro-American and white literary traditions.[55]

The Writers Project Years

Forced now in the midst of the Great Depression to earn his own living, he was faced with the almost impossible task of finding a position, let alone one in which he could use his poetic talent. What he found, however, was the grim reality of America's unemployed—the world of hunger and exile. But he was not merely one of the millions of unemployed Americans; he was black into the bargain.

One result of economic desperation was the Works Project Administration, a relief program. One aspect of it was the Federal Writers Project, a haven to which Hayden, among 6,686 other writers, fled. The necessary declaration of pauperism was humiliating and distasteful,[56] but indignity was not new to Hayden. His family had submitted to this requirement since at least 1930. So he made the declaration and was hired by the Detroit branch of the Project.[57]

Hayden said that among the projects he completed on the Detroit Writers Project was an essay on the anti-slavery movement in Detroit and an essay on the anti-slavery movement in Illinois. As he remembered, his most important undertaking was to supervise research into local history and folklore.[58] His group attempted to gather letters and journals that had historical significance. It investigated, for instance, the papers of a prominent Afro-American family in Detroit, the Lamberts, with antecedents dating back to the slave era. At one time, John Brown had presented a sword to William Lambert, who was associated with the Underground Railroad. It was thought that the documents might include a few interesting letters, but Hayden and his group found nothing. They were successful, however, in compiling and publishing a calendar of the John Dancy–Booker T. Washington letters.[59] Hayden believed that none of these materials were ever used.

While the Lambert project was a failure, working on it and developing the substitute Dancy-Washington project probably furthered Hayden's interest in Afro-American history—an interest that lasted beyond the topical concerns of the thirties. He soon explored the poetic possibilities of such knowledge in *Heart-Shape in the Dust*, in which he included a ballad about a slave hanged for leading a revolt. He declared in "What is Precious is Never to Forget":[60]

> This is the spirit's true armament,
> Heart's true program of defense—

That we remember the traveled roads of our history.

(Lines 7–9)

The Project also gave Hayden and his black colleagues the opportunity of communicating with other Project writers; the result was an interracial exchange that eroded the insular world that, in many cases, was the black writer's lot. Moreover, the contacts established by Afro-Americans within the group led to the exposure of their work to white audiences. Thus they reaped practical as well as artistic benefits from this exchange.

Though there was interracial contact, there was also a coterie of Afro-American writers, most of whom were in the Chicago, Detroit, Cleveland, and New York projects, that grew up around the influential figure of Richard Wright. The members of the Wright generation were born within the same decade (1908–17).[61] Very youthful though they were in some cases, they shared, to some degree, memories of the end of World War I and its aftermath of bloody race riots and lynchings.[62] They were adolescents when the Harlem Renaissance flowered in the 1920s. They were shaped by the Great Depression, and their initiation rite into American society was the emasculating horror of the Scottsboro case, a *cause célèbre* in those years.[63]

Affected by their generational ties, their shared heritage of childhood poverty, and their common employment on the Writers Project, Hayden read Wright's work and was influenced by his politics and literary style. Too poor to purchase a copy of *Uncle Tom's Children*, he recalled that he read a library copy and was struck by its "daring and unprecedented subject matter."[64] In creating his short stories, Wright had blended the techniques of social realism with his perceptions of the violent black-white confrontation in the South. Hayden takes his literary cues for *Heart-Shape in the Dust* from Wright's short stories and his poem "Between the World and Me." Like Wright, he denounces lynching and attacks capitalism. Hayden probably would have written about the lynch victim irrespective of Wright's work, but Wright's treatment of racial and social grievances provided him with a contemporary Afro-American model that was written in the mode of realism. Wright's influence on Hayden was not transitory; much of his work is socially realistic, and his forte was protest.

Hayden's immediate response to *Uncle Tom's Children* was a

congratulatory note to Wright. Later, he occasionally sent him good-will messages through mutual friends who were going to Chicago. Unfortunately, Hayden missed an excellent opportunity to see Wright in Detroit when a lecture Wright was scheduled to give was cancelled.[65]

The Project years allowed Hayden to learn more about Marxism. Exploiting the exigencies of the Depression, the American Communist party had succeeded in gaining the acceptance, although sometimes passive, of a substantial proportion of the nation's most gifted writers. They expressed their conviction, through organizations established and controlled by the party, that radical change based on Marxist theory was imperative. According to Wilson Record, the party's objective was to encourage the writers, without regard to race, to create a realistic literature, based on the facts of Negro life, that would develop Negro cultural nationalism for the immediate purpose of establishing a Negro nation in America, as well as promoting the working-class struggle.[66]

While Hayden was not a member of the American Communist party, or even its associated organizations, he was exposed to its ideology in his college discussions and through his Project contacts. One of these contacts was the John Reed Club. It was through the discussions and activities of its Detroit branch that he came to understand party ideology and developed strong reservations about communism as a possible solution to the "Negro problem." In his words, he developed an abhorrence of communism because of its suppression of creative freedom, its rejection of artists, and persecution of those who did not follow the party line. Too religious as well as individualistic to join the Communist party as Richard Wright had done,[67] he remained on the "periphery of the radical movement." He gave the John Reed Club credit for his "understanding" of what the political issues were in the United States and the world in general, as well as the inspiration to consider cultural questions in his works. Above all, it gave him the "chance to write and to be involved in a literary circle."[68] The endorsement of Marxist strategy evident in *Heart-Shape in the Dust* is mild in contrast to Wright's in *Uncle Tom's Children*. Whereas Wright makes a direct call for revolution and gives clear-cut strategy for its execution,[69] Hayden limits himself to an appeal for black and white worker solidarity. His mass chant,

"These Are My People,"[70] gives his most direct appeal to the working class:

> O white brother,
> won't you march with me?
>
> **Marching, marching, marching, marching**
>
> Toward the day that is to be.
>
> (Stanza 9, lines 25–28)

Though he later turned away from Marxist ideology, his interest in it represented his first decisive step toward expanding his political consciousness—that is, his evolution from race to class consciousness, a departure that moved him toward the internationalism that begins to appear in *Heart-Shape in the Dust* and becomes abundantly clear in the Mexican, Jewish, and World War II poems of *A Ballad of Remembrance*. His later disillusionment notwithstanding, the early interest in Marxist ideology was no more than a logical outgrowth of his background, which had, in his case, de-emphasized racial differences in the leveling influence of his pluralistic neighborhood and in his experience of integrated schools.

At bottom, Hayden was a cultural assimilationist rather than a Marxist. That is, Marxism simply offered him an opportunity to fuse his sense of racial identity with a broader historical movement. His reference point was no longer merely ethnic but ideological as well; instead of striving exclusively for limited racial advancement, he could participate in the larger struggle for social justice.[71] This assimilationist tendency became a permanent part of Hayden's philosophy and art. Although he rejected communism's *political* promise of brotherhood, he was later to accept the *religious* vision of world brotherhood of the Bahá'í religion.

Jerre Mangione, from his vantage point as national coordinating editor of the Federal Writers Project, maintains that "Blacks were [its] greatest beneficiaries." In support of this position, he discusses the insights they received from their in-depth investigation of Negro history, myth, and folklore.[72] The immediate benefit Hayden enjoyed, however, was the signal opportunity for national exposure. His

poem "Autumnal" was one of four works by Afro-Americans included in *American Stuff: An Anthology of Prose and Verse by
Members of the Federal Writers Project*, the official anthology of
works by writers on the Federal Writers Project.[73]

He wrote "Autumnal" while he was gaining his reputation as a
proletarian-protest poet and while he was writing in a direct, hortatory style that was often only sparsely symbolic. At the same time,
however, he was developing in some poems a literary realism and a
more effective use of symbolism. For instance, "Autumnal" points
toward his later mastery of poetic craftmanship. It is ostensibly a
nature lyric, but it may also be read as a protest poem against lynching and a moving plea to pity its victim. It accomplishes this through
symbolism taken from nature:

> Pity the rose
> With death for root
> And bleeding boughs
> Bereft of fruit,
> Pity the pheasant
> In the gilded wood
> And the buck lying stark
> In a snare of blood.
>
> (Lines 1–8)

In the first part of the poem, he develops a disturbing inversion of
a pastoral scene. Taking the rose, a Christian symbol of love, the
pheasant, and the deer, he inverts their usual pleasant connotations.
The rose suffers blight and death; the pheasant and the entrapped deer
lie dead, in contrast to the "gilded wood."

In the last half of the lyric, nature itself is made to reflect these
disturbances, as what should ordinarily be a joyous time of thanks-
giving for the natural harvest becomes the occasion for a harvest of
blood. Ominous "Medusa trees," "hollow skies," "winds that rock,"
a "bloody moon," and reapers who gather sheaves that tear their
hands characterize the scene.

Although Hayden does not mention race *per se*, his choice of
"buck" lends itself to the interpretation that it represents a black
male lying bloody and trapped in the wood. Such a view is strengthened by the repeated references to blood, the trees that harken up

visions of the hangman, reapers of this kind of harvest who have blood on their hands.

During the late thirties, Hayden's proletarian-protest works caught the attention of officials of the United Auto Workers Union, who asked him to read at an organizational rally of a UAW local in Detroit. His verse so impressed the group that they proclaimed him the "People's Poet."[74] His participation was not without a real element of danger. At that time the city was divided into warring elements—capital against labor and white against black. It was not just a war of rhetoric, as news items of the period in Detroit and New York papers indicate. The Ku Klux Klan, the Black Legion, and other white supremacist groups, supported by a sympathetic police force, repeatedly perpetrated violence against blacks and others who actively supported union organization.[75]

At this time Hayden was writing drama and radio scripts. One of these, a social protest one-act play titled "Many Mansions," treated the housing situation for blacks in Detroit. Making use of the biblical theme explicit in the title, he drew his plot material from the infamous Sweet case that had shaken the Afro-American national community in the twenties.[76] The cast was made up of whites as well as blacks, and in its denouement the play had blacks and whites working together toward a solution. Ironically, Hayden was scathingly criticized in the black press for "airing [our] dirty linen," a reaction easily understood in the light of the audience's desperate middle-class pretentiousness. His published reply affirmed his determination not to be an escapist and proclaimed his intention to deal with social issues. He entered "Many Mansions" in a competition sponsored by the Delta Sigma Theta sorority's annual Jabberwock. Although it did not win first prize, he was consoled when, later, his poem "These Are My People" was choreographed by Margaret Burroughs and given a performance.[77]

From 1936 to 1939, while he was still employed on the Project, he wrote scripts using Afro-American history for various radio stations. He recalled that his subjects were Ira Aldridge, Harriet Tubman, and the slave's love of freedom. In 1938 he was a member of the writing staff for the exposition held in Detroit that observed "Seventy-Five Years of Negro Progress." His responsibility was to write a weekly script on Afro-American history and culture to be presented over radio station CKLW in Windsor.[78] Thus, not only in his Project responsibilities, poorly paid for as they were, but in his "moonlight-ing," he was able to maintain and develop the interest in Afro-American history that he had begun in his first published poem, "Africa."

The Decisive Years: 1940–46

As the decade began, the Detroit Project was being phased out, and Hayden was forced to find other employment, which he did, on the *Michigan Chronicle*. His job as rewrite man and music-drama critic helped him to maintain his ties with the fine arts but did not help his financial situation much, for his salary was a subsistance-level six dollars per week.

His first important decision of this period was to marry, and he did so, though not without opposition from his prospective in-laws, who raised objections to his East Side ghetto origin, his fundamental-ist Baptist background, and his poverty. The fact that he had to borrow fifty dollars from Mr. Hayden to pay expenses connected with the wedding did not, probably, serve as much of a recommendation.[79] The publication of *Heart-Shape in the Dust* in 1940, however, im-pressed his fiancée's parents sufficiently to dispel their middle-class, West Side, Episcopalian reservations, and they gave their consent for their lovely, talented daughter to marry him.

Erma Inez Morris was an ambitious woman, a concert pianist and a music teacher. Her elders and peers, as well as her parents, considered her too good for Hayden, but they were married nonethe-less in June of 1940. From this union, which lasted until his death, one child, Maia, a daughter was born.[80]

Unpleasant gossip and censure of Hayden's lack of financial security shortened the couple's stay in Detroit to only one year. Their first effort to flee was in the summer of 1941. They stored their belongings with friends in Detroit and spent the summer in New York City. It was a period when he began his life-long enchantment with that city as well as his use of its offerings for the promotion of his art. He spent much of his time in research for materials on "Middle Passage"[81] at the New York City Public Library Schomburg Collec-tion. Meanwhile, Erma studied the piano at Julliard and sometimes was the accompanist for the Talley David Dance Company. She sometimes played for dances in the city. Erma's earnings were a welcome supplement to their meager funds.[82]

When Hayden left New York City in the fall, it was to travel directly to Ann Arbor to resume graduate studies that he had begun in 1938 at the University of Michigan. Erma, who wanted him to be a success, made the decision that he resume his studies, and, to insure his financial support, she kept her teaching post in Detroit and commuted from Ann Arbor. Soon he was awarded a teaching assistantship and was better able to support himself. The couple was even able to "get a small house," and in 1942 Maia was born.[83]

Because he had left Detroit City College short one credit hour and therefore without a degree, he was not allowed official matriculation in the university. The situation was corrected, however, and he was awarded his degree when he notified officials at Wayne State of his provisional acceptance at the University of Michigan.[84] The fact that he had published a volume of poetry and had two First Prize Jules and Avery Hopwood Awards to his credit probably militated in his favor.[85]

Hayden did not continue his undergraduate Spanish major at the university; he majored, rather, in English and continued his association with aspiring writers: he knew John Ciardi and Arthur Miller at the university. He recalled that he played a part in a production of Miller's play *The Great Disobedience* and that, when Miller departed for New York City, he "had the nerve to wish him good luck."[86]

Of much more significance, however, was the opportunity, in 1941, to participate in a class taught by W. H. Auden. His return to the university and enrollment in the Auden poetry class occurred at a crucial point in the development of Hayden's career as a poet. This was a time when political disillusionment might have silenced him as it silenced many members of his generation.[87] He had responded psychologically as well as artistically to the failure of government to ameliorate the plight of black Americans, and he had become disillusioned likewise with the Communist party. The Great Depression was being eased by social reforms and the prosperity of a wartime economy. Civil rights gains fired the hopes of millions of Afro-Americans. A literature of protest no longer seemed necessary. Consequently, the members of the Depression generation either faded into silence, took up other pursuits, or left the country.[88]

As Auden's student, Hayden's perspective was broadened so as to discourage his identifying himself completely with black writing; certainly he strengthened his ties to the general literary currents of the time. Moreover, through Auden, who was a recent English expatriate, he benefited from the contemporary European literary crosscurrent. During his formative years, Auden had been influenced by Thomas Hardy, Gerard Manley Hopkins, W. B. Yeats, and T. S. Eliot. In England during the thirties, he was the principal poet in a group of socialist writers including Louis MacNeice, Cecil Day Lewis, and Stephen Spender—poets Hayden read as a graduate student at the University of Michigan. However, Auden had come to repudiate his political stance before he taught Hayden.

Perhaps Auden's most valuable contribution to Hayden was a view of poetry that led away from racial and political rhetoric, from the direct statement to the view that poetry is best when it is oblique, conceptual—a view that gave him a sense of direction that other black protest poets did not find. Hayden recalled that once, when he gave Auden two poems to examine, he rejected one with the comment that it was like arithmetic and preferred the other because it was like algebra.[89] Auden makes this analogy clear in his essay "The Virgin and the Dynamo," which includes the idea that algebra deals with concepts and exists as potential on the poetic level of raw experience, whereas arithmetic deals with the positive, the routinely demonstrable.[90]

Although Hayden makes no mention of it, techniques for creating the kind of poetry Auden preferred probably were the concerns of the poetry class. Auden's promotion of Gerard Manley Hopkins's prosody, his own demonstration of multiple techniques in a variety of verse forms, and his experiments with off-rhymes probably were some of the details the class studied. Hayden reluctantly indicated that about the time he came under Auden's influence, he wrote "Frederick Douglass,"[91] demonstrably a Hopkinsean sonnet. Moreover, whether or not the influence is direct, subsequent to his class with Auden, Hayden's poetry makes frequent use of off-rhyme.

The poetic philosophy Auden expressed in his caution to Hayden (to avoid racial and political rhetoric) is treated in his "In Memory of W. B. Yeats,"[92] in which he defines his concept of art and the poet's role. Written, of course, after his period as a social poet, the elegy makes two points: that poetry is inconsequential in advancing social

causes because the interpretation posterity will give it is uncontrollable, and that the real value of art is that it can "teach the free man how
to praise" (line 65)—that is, how to begin to value order above disorder, even though the order is artistic rather than political.

Yeats was likewise a crucial influence on the maturing Hayden.
Of the Irish poet's impact on him, Hayden remarked, "It is Yeats's
ability to handle the Irish question of nationalism without propagan-
dizing," that impressed him.[93] It is evident, too, that Yeats exercised
a thematic influence on Hayden. For example, in title and theme,
" 'Lear is Gay' " continues to explore the poetic materials of Yeats's
"Lapis Lazuli."[94] Furthermore, in "Kodachromes of the Island," dedi-
cating himself to the plight of the oppressed and alluding to Yeats's
"The Circus Animal's Desertion," Hayden pays a significant tribute
to the Irish poet:[95]

>   I roamed
>   the cobbled island,
>
>   and thought of Yeats,
>   his passionate search for
>   a theme. Sought mine.
>   (Stanza 3, lines 8–12)

In *The Night-blooming Cereus*, Hayden's commitment to classic
philosophy, as treated in Plato's "Parable of the Cave," parallels
Yeats's neoplatonism to the extent that it promulgates the doctrine
that the real world behind the everyday material world can be reached
only by the imagination.[96] One critic goes so far as to imply that
Hayden's "verbal dexterity" is directly attributable to the influence
of Yeats.[97]

Whether Auden introduced Hayden to Stephen Spender, C. Day
Lewis, and Rainer Maria Rilke is not clear. In his McCluskey interview, Hayden mentions reading Auden, Spender, and Lewis at about
the same period. Hayden says he was impressed with their "tren-
chancy of phrase . . . imagery-daring which opened up new vistas for
[him]."[98] It was at that stage of his poetic development, too, when he
had become critical of those poets whose verse was "synonymous
with propaganda."

Concerning Hayden's link to Rilke, it is not improbable that

Auden led him to Spender, who translated Rilke into English. In any case, it is demonstrable that Hayden's "Dance the Orange" owes its title and theme to Rilke's "Sonnet 15."[99]

Meanwhile, having got her husband back into graduate school and thus assured of his intellectual opportunities as well as a certain measure of financial security, Mrs. Hayden turned her attention to his spiritual well-being. Although his decision to convert to her faith was neither hasty nor easy, by 1943 he had read the literature she offered him and decided to become a Bahá'i. A serious commitment, it had a lasting effect on the philosophical direction of his thought and thus on his poetry as well.

Hayden became a Bahá'i, he said, for several reasons: the belief in progressive revelation (i.e., revelation that is not limited historically to the appearance of a unique prophet, but rather is augmented by the insights of a succession of great religious figures, the latest of whom was Bahá'u'lláh); the belief that the Bahá'i world order could effect the relationship between religious thought and scientific discovery necessary to a unified physical and metaphysical outlook; and, most important, the belief in the transcendentalist principle of universal brotherhood. The Bahá'i religion, as a basic principle, recognizes no bounds of race, creed, or color and, unlike communism, offers the added comfort of a religious sanction.[100]

Hayden's conversion may indeed have been an inversion of the old concerns that motivated his interest in communism, as well as a response to the disillusionment with its failure to build one world, one people. The Bahá'i faith presented the opportunity to participate in "the long hard struggle toward freedom,"[101] in a matrix where "freedom" becomes a generic term describing a universal necessity. Thus the struggle of the Afro-American becomes a symbol of the larger yearning and struggle that has developed through the ages of human history.

David Galler observes that Hayden's quest for solace and purpose in religion was a "turn a white man would not take."[102] This statement is made without further clarification, but I can only assume that he failed to recognize Hayden's conversion as part of a trend that whites had begun. T. S. Eliot embraced Anglo-Catholicism in the twenties, as Auden did in the thirties. Hayden, in 1943, anticipated what Stephenchev notes as concern for other-worldliness in the fifties, resulting in poets becoming Zen Buddhists, Roman Catholics, Jungians, Black Muslims, and so on, and what Robert E. Spiller elsewhere calls a search for love.[103]

In 1946 Hayden was preparing to leave his home state. He would take with him a philosophical confidence rooted in the Bahá'i religion and the experience of having studied with Auden, who influenced him in the belief that art was a concern more timeless than race or social condition. It should be noted, however, that while certain white poets were cognizant of his worth Hayden was not able to move quickly toward the public stature of his white contemporaries. Whatever optimism he derived from the Bahái beliefs and whatever white poets recognized the quality of his work, for the establishment the artist himself was still the wrong color.

The Pilgrimage Years: 1946–69

When Hayden left the University of Michigan, he had reason to believe that his master's degree, his teaching experience, and his publications would constitute considerable bargaining clout in securing an estimable position. Indeed, when he was hired by Fisk University in Nashville, Tennessee, he was informally led to believe that he would fill the writer-in-residence position. He did; but his actual duties turned out, for the most part, to be those of an overloaded English instructor assigned a teaching load of fifteen to sixteen hours. Under such conditions his creative writing class, in which he helped to develop several important writers, was the one saving grace of his new position.[104] As if the work load were not enough, the Fisk of those days, as Julius Lester, one of his students, puts it, was a "miasma of black bourgeoisie gentility," which Hayden indicted as a stronghold of pre-civil-rights-legislation satisfaction with the status quo.[105]

Hayden, however, was not about to accept the status quo. Within two years of his arrival at the university, he had articulated his new literary and political stance. He became the guiding spirit of a group of young writers including William Demby, a World War II veteran and a student in Hayden's writing class; Myron O'Higgins, a visiting research consultant at the university; and Ben Johnson, also a veteran and one of his creative writing students. With Demby and the others, he developed a polemic that they privately published as the first of a series planned to attack what the group felt to be discriminatory practices of the white literary establishment. *Counterpoise 3* is a position statement that sets forth four points critical of both the nationalist school of black writers and the white publishing world. In essence these points are (1) opposition to the chauvinistic, the cultish, [and] special pleading; (2) support and encouragement for the "experimental and the unconventional in writing, music and the graphic arts"; (3) opposition to criticism of their works "entirely in the light of sociology and politics"; (4) opposition to "criticism of their works by coterie editors, reviewers and anthologists who . . . refuse encouragement or critical guidance because [their work dealt] with realities." The manifesto avows belief in the humanistic and spiritual value of poetry and concludes, "We believe in the oneness of mankind and the importance of the arts in the struggle for peace and unity."[106] This declaration of literary independence indicates a position from which Hayden did not waver from that day—a position that black nationalists in 1966 were to find objectionable because of its rejection of a social-racial concept of artistic values.

Yet another influence on Hayden's poetic philosophy is evident in the statement, "We believe in the oneness of mankind." This declaration is a restatement of Bahá'u'lláh's and 'Abdul Baha's principles concerning the unity of the human race, the artist's role, and the function of his work: "Of the Tree of Knowledge the all glorious fruit is this exalted word: Of one Tree are all ye the fruits and of one bough the leaves. . . . In the Bahá'í cause, arts, sciences, and all crafts are counted as worship. . . ."[107]

Accordingly, immediately after *Counterpoise 3*, Hayden began to effect its philosophic principles in *The Lion and the Archer*, written in collaboration with Myron O'Higgins. Taking literary cues from the poets mentioned previously and from the French surrealists and the baroque poets, he created an ensemble of six poems that vividly evoke, in non-didactic terms, the nightmare world he perceived. He followed this brochure with another, *Figure of Time*, which continued his new literary techniques and introduced both his nostalgic poems and his Bahá'í poems. In the early sixties, no doubt still disenchanted with American publishers, he turned to a European house for publication of his award-winning *A Ballad of Remem-*

brance, and only after twenty-six years had passed did he again locate an American firm for publication of his *Selected Poems.*

While Hayden was gaining recognition for himself as a poet, he was increasing his knowledge of the Deep South. A few months before Hayden began his tenure at Fisk, William Dean Pickens of the U.S. Treasury Department wrote and asked Hayden to participate with other writers in a U.S. bond rally in New Orleans. In addition to the opportunity it gave him to see that historic city, his trip, undertaken for a patriotic cause, ironically brought him face-to-face with raw racial prejudice—open and abrasive segregation at a coffee shop. That traumatic incident in New Orleans was followed by another when, in 1951, accompanied by his friend and Fisk colleague, Arna Bontemps, he journeyed by auto to Jackson State College in Jackson, Mississippi, to participate with other well-known Afro-American writers in a literary festival celebrating the college's seventy-fifth anniversary.[108] When they stopped at a gasoline station, he experienced what he felt was an atmosphere of latent racism.[109] In time he objectified and recorded these experiences in his arresting poems, "A Ballad of Remembrance" and "Tour 5."[110] These experiences, between 1946 and 1951, in the heartland of the Deep South, heightened his perception of black-white dynamics, both historic and contemporary, and informed the brilliant series of poems about the pre-civil-rights-legislation South he began in *The Lion and the Archer.*

During the middle fifties, Hayden had an opportunity to gain new experiences with the economically oppressed when, through the sponsorship of Dr. Charles S. Johnson, he was awarded a Ford Foundation grant for travel and writing in Mexico. The grant enabled Hayden to sojourn in Mexico for several months in 1954 and several more months in 1955. Thus, he learned firsthand about the plight of the Mexican peon.[111] His experiences provided the background for the Mexican poems that he wrote between 1955 and 1962 and included in *A Ballad of Remembrance.*

Meanwhile, during the fifties, Hayden's personal life was saddened by the death of his natural parents, and it was made even more insecure by an identity crisis. Having lost both of his adoptive parents (Sue Ellen Hayden in 1941 and "Pa" Hayden in 1938), with whom he lived until they died, he lost his natural father between 1950 and 1955 (exact date unknown), and in 1957 suffered his most traumatic loss when his natural mother died. Prior to her demise and free of the Haydens' presence, he enjoyed a closer relationship with her—a relationship in which she irrevocably secured his kinship and artistic ties to her family and to her forebears. She convinced him that the Haydens did not legally adopt him, and she declared that his true name, the name she and his father gave him, was Asa Bundy Sheffey. It was the name he wished to legally adopt.[112]

Burdened by the bereavement and disquietude he suffered in his private life during the fifties, Hayden experienced an even more unsettling new decade. Just as his private crises had taken their toll on his sense of personal well-being, so did the social upheavals of the sixties wreak havoc on his professional security. Indeed, the very nature of his dual professions as poet and professor of English in a leading black university made his positions vulnerable. It was a black college, the Agricultural and Technical College of Greensboro, North Carolina, that nurtured the spirit of revolutionary civil-rights protest in four students who began the wave of sit-in demonstrations that swept the South and the North. Also, it was at certain black colleges and universities that black nationalists publicized their political views and strategies for black writers. By the mid-sixties that "bastion of middle-class respectability," Fisk University, no longer offered Hayden security; as a poet and teacher he was attacked as never before.

Nineteen sixty-six was a year of extremes. On the one hand Hayden was accorded important approbation from his admirers: at the First Negro Festival of Arts in Dakkar, Senegal, in international competition, he won the Grand Prix de la Poesie; he was made poetry editor of *World Order*, the official and international organ of the Bahá'í faith; his poetry was being published in important little magazines and was being noticed in important American literary circles; and his latest volume, *Selected Poems*, was just off the press and was reviewed in *Poetry*. On the other hand, he was severely attacked by a group of militant black nationalists who had convened at Fisk University for the first Black Writers' Conference.[113] Having achieved some status in American and international literary circles, he incurred the active displeasure (and perhaps jealousy) of the black militants who raised the political issue of the black writer's role during the "searing sixties." They espoused the Maoist-inspired philosophy. decreed by Ron Karenga and other black nationalists, that black literature should be didactic and propagandistic for the purpose of indoctrinating the masses in their revolutionary cause.[114]

When Hayden resolutely held to the artistic stance that he avowed in *Counterpoise 3*, the initial pamphlet in the series that followed, they countered with a new attack: they censured his long-standing refusal to be categorized as a black poet. Again Hayden, having found a place and a voice in the grander cause of world building that the Bahá'i religion afforded, refused to capitulate. As he saw it, his refusal to be categorized as a black poet was not a rejection of his biological inheritance or the black struggle but was rather a refusal to be restricted in subject matter to "race" or to be identified with second-class craftmanship. In adhering, at this time, to his stand to be "unalterably opposed to the chauvinistic, the cultish and to special pleading," he made a final turn away from jingoism and propagandistic didacticism.

Contributing to Hayden's role in the confrontation was the fact that his maturation took place during the 1930s and 1940s, when the growing assumption was that the Afro-American writer could and would be merged into American literary life, losing the pejorative aspects of the literary identity that had been assigned to him. He said, "My generation was working hard for acceptance as writers, as artists and *not* [emphasis mine] as writers with a particular identity."[115] Indeed, he had achieved enough status in places where it counted to believe he was a part of the literary mainstream.

The militants were responding to the disappointing fate of the Supreme Court civil rights decisions of the forties and fifties and the generally slow progress (or seeming non-progress) of integration as a means of insuring constitutional freedoms. Hayden, shaped by the forces of the integrationist thirties, forties, and fifties, was under-standably reassured by the new civil rights laws. But the black nationalists and the new generation of Afro-American writers pointed to the indefinite timetable the Court had set for implementation of the laws and the South's delaying tactics. In their view, integration, if it were to be accomplished, would become a mere merging of blacks into the polluted stream of American life.

Confusing artistic aims with political activism, they espoused political separatism and encouraged the rejection of traditional aesthetics and literary standards as monuments of a degenerate, racist culture. It was this artistically naive failure to recognize the necessity of individual integrity, demanding that the artist subordinate his creative talents and perception to the socio-political goals of the group, that Hayden would not condone. But Hayden, too, had misgivings about the civil rights laws. He had a difference in method. He did not feel that bigotry was going to get rid of bigotry.[116]

He had felt himself beleaguered at Fisk even before the time of the conference. From the time of his arrival he had been obstensibly the writer-in-residence, but the university had seen fit to appoint the novelist John O. Killens and to superimpose him on what Hayden had been given to understand was his own official post.[117] That Killens organized the 1966 conference must have seemed the unkindest cut. Killens was also responsible for a series of conferences which followed. Hayden, though he was invited, did not choose to attend.

Julius Lester, who saw Hayden shortly after these events, says that the immediate response was a verbal tirade against the black nationalists. His rage is understandable, as is the sorrow he felt. He had been the admired literary "father" of the young black writers at Fisk from the days when he had inspired and co-authored the Counterpoise series. He realized that, having been identified as an "Uncle Tom," he would not see those days again. He had to live with the knowledge that a group of people whose heritage he shared, and indeed had celebrated powerfully in poem after poem, were attacking him simply because he believed that any artist should feel free to approach his materials as a man of unique sensibility and a craftsman of integrity. The events of 1966 were such an emotional trial that it was four years before he could give them objective poetic consideration. Meanwhile, however, all was not gloom.

The demand for his poetry was growing impressively. In 1967 he recorded his poems for the Library of Congress and was poet-in-residence at Indiana State University. In 1968 he was made poetry editor of *World Order*, the official literary organ of the Bahá'i religion in the United States. In 1969 he was awarded the Detroit Mayor's Bronze Medal for distinguished achievement by a native scholar. In the same year he became Bingham Professor at the University of Louisville and visiting poet at the University of Washington, and had an offer of a permanent post at the University of Louisville. All of this gave him the leverage that helped him get, in 1969, a post at the University of Michigan, where he remained until his death.[118]

The Successful Seventies

During this period Hayden published three volumes of poems. *Words in the Mourning Time* (1970) is a cathartic work, his poetic response to the Fisk confrontation with the black militants, an affirmation of his humanism, and the rejection of what he sees as evil.[119] It is not too difficult to see what his "abstractions" are and who the evil doers, in his title poem:[120]

> We must not be frightened nor cajoled
> into accepting evil as deliverance from evil.
> We must go on struggling to be human,
> though monsters of abstraction
> police and threaten us.
>
> (Stanza 9, lines 10–14)

Having achieved his catharsis, he followed it, two years later with *The Night-blooming Cereus* (1972). This is a slender volume of eight new poems, but it is nonetheless his second pivotal work, both in terms of subject matter and style. In this work, Hayden turns almost exclusive attention to the problem of reality, vis-à-vis appearance, and the meaning of art and life. In the prologue to the volume, in lines that are reminiscent of Plato's Parable of the Cave, Hayden announces his interest in the philosophic significance of his past:

> But I can see none of it clearly, for
> it all takes place in semi-dark.
> A scene one might recall
> falling asleep.

In the closing poem, "Traveling through Fog,"[121] he pointedly makes clear his assessment of the past in an allusion to the Platonic idea of the unsubstantiality of the world:

> Looking back, we cannot see,
> except for its blurring lights
> like underwater stars and moons,
> our starting-place.
> Behind us, beyond us now

is phantom territory, a world
abstract as memories of earth
the traveling dead take home.
Between obscuring cloud
and cloud, the cloudy dark
ensphering us seems all we can
be certain of. Is Plato's Cave.

Except for one literary allusion to Watts, linked with Hiroshima
and My Lai, in "The Peacock Room,"[122] Hayden does not treat in *The
Night-blooming Cereus* the Afro-American themes which had been,
until 1972, his *forte*. Obviously, the slender book is the product of the
poet grown, as he put it, old, and trying to see the meaning of his life
clearly.

In 1973 Hayden discussed the volume on which he was then still
at work.[123] He had already decided that he would call the work *Angle
of Ascent*, and he had a good idea of what poems he would include,
but he complained that notwithstanding his past poetic accomplishments he was having difficulty obtaining a publisher.

He commented on a poem he called "Ancestors." He described it
as a composite based on stories his mother told him about his grandfather and other men in her family. He observed that this source was
one on which he expected to continue drawing. As the poem finally
appeared in *Angle of Ascent* (1975), the draft copy that he gave me was
greatly expanded and was re-titled "Beginnings."[124]

Earlier, he discussed "For a Young Artist," another poem which
appears in the title section.[125] He wrote it, he said, in tribute to a
young Chilean artist, Gabriel Garcìa Màrquez, whose work he found
interesting. At the time he had been discussing his use of surrealism
which, he said, helped him in the development of fresh and effective
images. He said he was also impressed with José Donoso's *The
Obscene Bird of Night*. Both poems are important; "Beginnings"
reveals Hayden's deep concern with his family roots and his need to
establish his identity. "To a Young Artist" proclaims his most defini-
tive and conclusive thoughts about the role of the artist, and it reveals
the extent to which Hayden was influenced by the South American
writers.

The volume was published almost simultaneously with Hayden's election for "distinguished poetic achievement" as the 1975

Fellow of the Academy of American Poets. Noting this accomplish-
ment in his review of the book, Michael S. Harper observes that it
was a long time coming. He then devotes his attention, almost
exclusively, to the poetry that he sees as best capturing "the Afro-
American tradition of the black hero."[126] He praises Hayden as a
master conversationalist and handler of idiom and characterizes him
as a "poet of perfect pitch." His overall assessment of the new volume
supports the validity of the distinguished award.

In 1978 Hayden published both paperback and hardcover issues
of *American Journal*. The limited, elegantly executed volume of
thirteen poems affirms Hayden's commitment to Afro-American
history subject matter, makes good his promise to mine his memories of the Detroit ghetto and people, where and with whom he spent
very nearly the first three decades of his life, and continues his
penchant for the romantic, the exotic.

By the end of 1979, Hayden had completed a new volume that he
said would include the *American Journal* collection as well as new
poems. Also, he said it would be published by Liveright in 1980. It is a
volume that raises Hayden's productivity for the decade of the seventies to four volumes, an output that he had not heretofore obtained.
This volume, destined to be his last, was published posthumously in
1982.

Indeed, the decade of the seventies proved to be the most reward-
ing of Hayden's career, not only artistically but professionally and
financially. In 1975 he accepted a second opportunity to serve as
poetry consultant at the Library of Congress. He was offered the post
earlier but, he said, was discouraged from accepting it by his department chairman. He was appointed for the 1976–77 term. It was an
appointment that virtually made him poet laureate of the United
States. He was reappointed to serve the 1977–78 term, also an unprecedented honor for an Afro-American. He had "a role in the community [there]," William Meredith wrote, "that may have brought
his public usefulness to its greatest fulfillment,"[127] and it was an
appointment he filled with "distinction and graciousness" and to
which he brought "dignity . . . understanding, rapport with community and nation seldom found in such offices," wrote Arthur P.
Davis.[128] Hayden himself said he was in the effort to give unknown
writers, black as well as white, needed exposure.[129]

Concurrent with his association with the Library of Congress, academia showered him with its highest recognition. Three colleges and Brown University conferred on him the honorary doctor of humane letters degree. He was honored by the National Institute of Arts and Letters and the Michigan Foundation for the Arts. Unlike the prophet without honor in his own home, Hayden was accorded a certain amount of honor by the city of Detroit.[130]

Numerous readings at art centers, colleges, and universities throughout the nation, most of which Hayden gave during the 1970s, served to widen and deepen his influence. That he planned to continue these endeavors was made evident by his acceptance of the invitation to read at Fordham University on April 15, 1980. On another level, the many anthologies, including *Literature in America*, which bear the imprint of his editorship make evident the strength of his insight and guidance relative to American and Afro-American literature.[131]

These attainments, unfortunately, were accompanied by the poet's failing health. In 1977, Hayden said he had had a nervous breakdown. In 1978 he was anticipating, with some misgivings, an operation for cataracts and was involved in an automobile collision in which he suffered various contusions. In February 1979, very distraught, he revealed that he had cancer. Later that month, he said, eschewing chemotherapy, he would "undergo" holistic medicine. The university gave him the services of a part-time secretary, and he said on April 7, 1979, that he was "putting his papers and affairs in order."[132] However, later that year he wrote and mentioned his Fordham University reading.[133] By February 1980, "suffering from influenza, he was too ill to atend a testimonial that was held in his honor at the University of Michigan." One day later, February 25, he died.[134]

Before his death Robert Hayden submitted to his publisher what he knew would be his last volume of poetry. The book, *American Journal*, suggests the poet's "transcendence" into that mythical star-like state that he poeticized in "Stars," a state from which he will be lighting the way for those not yet so advanced.[135]

CHAPTER 2

The Apprenticeship:
Heart-Shape in the Dust (1940)

Critical notice of *Heart-Shape in the Dust,* at the time of its appearance, did not exceed a few paragraphs in primarily non-literary magazines, and none of the reviewers came to grips with Hayden's concerns in any but vague and unsupported terms. "A new and vigorous talent . . . promising . . . only other challengers Sterling Brown and Langston Hughes," wrote William Harrison in his favorable *Opportunity* review.[1] He notes the enthusiastic reception that a London audience gave to a reading of "Gabriel," one of Hayden's first Afro-American history poems, but he leaves the reader to speculate whether the response was to the work or the oral interpretation. He lists three poems he considers "best" and praises Hayden's command of moods, language, and originality of expression.

James W. Ivy's short, generally unenthusiastic review in *Crisis* credits Hayden with having lyrical ability and a sensitivity to the wrongs done his race, but he attacks many of the poems as banal and lacking in real poetic fire.[2] He considers "Autumnal" best, calls five other poems noteworthy, and concludes that Hayden is a poet worth watching. Both reviews are characterized by reservations, but both recognize some potential.

Recent criticism of *Heart-Shape in the Dust* is limited to the generally superficial remarks of anthology introductions, which place the work in the lyric tradition and mention the author as a proletarian writer of the thirties.[3] The volume is out of print now, and Hayden did not include any of the poems in subsequent collections, not even in his *Selected Poems.*

Heart-Shape in the Dust contains forty-six poems; eleven are unrevised reprints from his 1938 prize-winning Hopwood Collection, which had also been published in various magazines.[4] While the volume is an apprentice's experimentation with modes and idioms, is often stylistically derivative, and makes use of topical Marxist themes, it points, in its feeling for Afro-American history, its feeling for subjects that are not cast in terms of race, and in its sense of the general literary tradition, toward the central qualities of his mature work.

While the major thematic concern in *Heart-Shape in the Dust* is the social condition of blacks during the Great Depression, Hayden's interest in Afro-American history surfaces in several places. One can see how these two themes interact and are unified by comparing statements in poems which deal with the purpose of the black poet. In "To a Young Negro Poet" (p. 14), which uses the simple images and declarative sentences characteristic of his early style, he says:

> Make me a song, O dark singer,
> Brimming with the laughter of honest men
> And the beauty and laughter of valiant women;
> A song with the heart-beat
> Of inarticulate millions in it.

Those "inarticulate millions" are, of course, America's neglected, scorned, and undereducated blacks. And in "Dedication" (p. 15), he says that to be that "heart-beat" the poet must

> Clasp their hands, O poet, touch their hands
>   and know the ultimate meaning of your own.
> Pray that a new prayer shall be given unto them
>   and a new fulfillment; let their prayers
> Lie like a lover on your heart. Wrestle with them
>   as with angels and learn their gathering strength.

The sensual imagery ("clasp," "touch," "Lie like a lover on your heart," and "wrestle") exhorts the poet to intimate knowledge of the race based on emotional involvement with its people. The role of the black poet, however, extends beyond that of song maker and spokesman for "inarticulate millions." In "What Is Precious Is Never to Forget" (p. 52), the poet becomes the keeper of racial history—a history which must be understood if there is to be strength to bear the present and hope for the future—and his role is to speak *to* those millions:

> This is the spirit's true armament,
> Heart's true program of defence—

> That we remember the traveled roads of our history,
> That in the stream of heroic yesterdays
> We find those spas which shall renew our strength.

He remembers those "traveled roads" in "Gabriel" (pp. 23–24). It is the only poem in *Heart-Shape in the Dust* on a specific black historical subject, but it is the first of several poems Hayden was to write about major black cultural heroes, such as Cinquez, Harriet Tubman, Nat Turner, Frederick Douglass, and Malcolm X.[5]

The poem treats the last minutes of Gabriel Prosser, a slave who was hanged in 1800 for leading an uprising in Virginia.[6] It is a dialogue, in ballad form, between the speaker of the poem and the hero, who is about to be executed, but the applications to the time Hayden wrote the piece are obvious. The speaker asks Gabriel to reveal the future, and he foresees

> **a thousand,**
> **Thousand slaves**
> **Rising up**
> **From forgotten graves.**

In light of communist influence, it is not difficult to see those many slaves as spirits infusing their descendants with determination to strike a blow in the cause of freedom. Certainly these lines are revolutionary:

> **The blow I struck**
> **Was not in vain,**
> **The blow I struck**
> **Shall be struck again.**

Whether or not Hayden's treatment of his topic was indeed a response to the party line, the ballad meets certain requirements of a communist strategy which held that American blacks constitute a separate nation, complete with cultural heroes.

Hayden's early social concerns, in any case, are focused primarily on the spectre of lynching, which is either the subject or the subject of key allusions in over one-fourth of the poems in the book. In all of this group he treats lynching in symbolic relationship to God, man, and government. He probes the consciousness of those who often had the closest tie to the victim: the women, whether black or white.

For example, in "BROWN GIRL'S SACRAMENT," part 1 of "Religioso" (pp. 39–40), he evokes the bereavement of the lynching victim's beloved, and in part 2 he treats the grief of the victim's mother. In the girl's vision, her lover's death blends with the crucifixion of Christ, and the mother's lament evokes the image of Mary mourning for the crucified Jesus. The crucifixion motif, popular with members of the Wright generation and, still earlier, with Countee Cullen and Langston Hughes, suggests the inhumanity of the act of lynching and the universality of the suffering of women.

Two poems treat the white woman as the real or alleged victim of rape, a crime for which, in southern custom, the penalty was lynching. In "Southern Moonlight" (p. 16), Hayden examines the strength of sexual desire in an interracial relationship by showing the inadequacy of social taboos as a restraint on the human will. Indeed, it is the white lover who sings in incantation to the moon:

> That none may see—
> Oh, moon, moon, hide your light—
> That he is black
> And I
>
>   am white.

The second poem, "Diana" (p. 43), exposes the danger inherent in such an interracial relationship. When Diana is discovered with her black lover, she screams in panic, thus insuring his ritualistic death, for the "keepers of the white rose" must

> Expunge with fire
> the tainting hands
> of the black man-beast,

the sexual eyes
of the satyr.

She, too, however, is a victim, for she is the real creature of desire. In the first place, she is driven by the lure of the black-stud myth to deliberately seduce her lover while she bathes "naked / amid [the] oleanders" (lines 6–7). Again, she exercises the queen-like privileges of her "whiter womanhood." It is a role Hayden makes clear in the subtitle to the poem: "An exercise in southern mythology." It is a mythology kept operative by the "lords of purity"—a phrase that evokes what W. J. Cash calls Southern New Chivalry.[7] As a violated woman, as well as a racial symbol, she must be avenged. The interpretation of her scream as the anguish of the rape victim rather than as a reaction to the horror of discovery, and the ugly myths about the black man—he is "man-beast," a "satyr" with "sexual eyes"—set the ritual in operation for the "keepers of the white rose" who "Flay, rend, burn." What makes her a victim, of course, is that, seduced by myth to work seduction, her position and her fears compel her to act out her role as victim, thus violating humanity as she herself was not, indeed, violated.

While a poem like "Diana," which is a humanistic consideration of moral relationships, may well stir moral indignation, "Speech" (p. 27) treats lynching in terms of the labor movement. Here the poet sees it as a tool for stirring up racial animosity among the proletariat. He indicts as one and the same "the hand / Holding the blowtorch / To the dark anguish-twisted body" and "the hand / Giving the high-sign / To fire on the white pickets" (lines 5–8). In this context lynching is a means of preventing the workers of the world from uniting; the old ritual provides a convenient pretext for the modern entrepreneur.

Whatever the specific cause of a lynching, the practice becomes for Hayden a symbol of the situation of blacks in America. On one level there is the simple, stark horror. In part 7 of "These Are My People" (pp. 56–63), in lines that recall the chanting of the witches in *Macbeth*—perhaps to emphasize the ritualistic motivation of the lynch mob—he creates a vivid picture of violence and madness:

**Fire and rope
and stone and goad,**

a black body dragged
down a southern road.
Moon and stars
in the southern skies,
and the light gouged out
of the black boy's eyes.
The wind dream-talking
on a southern hill,
and the lynch-lust voices
crying: kill kill kill.

(P. 61)

In part 8 he treats the Scottsboro Case, which leads to the view of martyrdom as America's macabre reward for the labors of black people:

O black man ploughing
the American earth,
gathering a harvest
of blood and dearth.

(P. 62)

In "Coleman," subtitled "Negro veteran murdered by the Black Legion" (p. 45), Hayden condemns America for accommodating such "tolerated weeds of murder" (line 11). The poem, which is based on a real crime,[8] sees lynching as a ritual aimed at genocide—if not physical, then certainly spiritual. The lynching, Hayden asserts, is a symbolic act whereby "Through one they strike at the heart of our world" (line 10).

In "The Negro to America" (p. 26), he epitomizes the paradox, or contradiction, of the black experience in a democracy by pointing to lynching as the negation of the fundamental right to due process of law:

You are not free
So long as there's
A mortgage on
My liberty;
So long as I die
On the Klansman's tree,

You are not
Democracy.

Lynching, which went on well into the twentieth century, was primarily a southern phenomenon; yet it was foremost in the minds of the Afro-American masses everywhere.

During the Depression, which is the period Hayden treats in *Heart-Shape in the Dust,* the self-consciousness was also shaped and defined by the economic landscape, in which, as Seymour Gross says, the black man was "the most dislocated and deprived figure."[9] "Sunflowers: Beaubien Street" (p. 12) is perhaps Hayden's most successful depiction of the black slum-dweller's ability to overcome his degradation and allay what he suffered from dislocation and deprivation. The Beaubien Street setting is biographically authentic, for the street was actually a part of his old neighborhood, where sunflowers seemed to grow anywhere with little or no care.[10] Hayden develops them into a major symbol which represents the black people who lived there.

Dual themes operate throughout this important poem. One is revealed in the Afro-Americans' sense of displacement from, and longing for, the South—their "cruel, sweet" memories of the South they loved, yet prayed to escape; the other is displayed in images of the despair and poverty they experienced in the North, yet tried to allay by planting sunflowers.

1 The Negroes here, dark votaries of the sun,
2 Have planted sunflowers round door and wall,
3 Hot-smelling, vivid as an August noon.
4 Thickets of yellow fire, they hold in thrall
5 The cruel, sweet remembrance of Down Home.

6 **O sun-whirled, tropic tambourines**
7 **That play sad juba songs in dooryard loam,**
8 **Recalling chain-gang heat and shimmering pines;**
9 **O sunward cry of dark ones mute within**
10 **The crumbling shacks: bright image of their will**
11 **To reach through prayer, through long belief the sun**
12 **Fixed in heavens like Ezekiel's Wheel.**

13 Here phonographs of poverty repeat
14 An endless blues-chorale of torsioning despair—

15 And yet these dark ones find mere living sweet
16 And set this solid brightness on the bitter air.

In the first stanza the sun is a vital force in the lives of the "dark votaries." They cultivate the sunflower which both evokes the "cruel, sweet" remembrance of "Down Home" and protects them from the pain of remembering. The smell, heat, and color of the South are evoked in the synaesthetic imagery of lines 3 and 4, especially in the words "Hot-smelling" and "yellow fire."

Stanza 2 develops specific dimensions of the tension involved in the oxymoron, "cruel, sweet remembrance." In lines 6 and 7 the "sweet" memory of the South they knew flows into the older memory of Africa. From this perspective, "juba" is particularly evocative since it is both the name of a river in Africa and a dance popular with the slaves. On the other hand, the "cruel" is defined in evocation of "chain-gang" labor that is not eased by climatic conditions and, perhaps, the equally oppressive turpentine camps typical of certain sections in the South, where it becomes so hot the pines seem to shimmer in the sun. The sunflower image functions as a symbol of the "bright image of their will," a will that undergirds the transplanted African's hard-won Christian faith. Indeed, in lines that reveal a poignant element of the black man's acculturation in America, visual and spiritual values of the sunflower–sun symbol join with "Ezekiel's Wheel," a symbol of God's message of hope to Ezekiel and his people, a symbol that transcends place.

The last stanza shifts the focus from the South back to Beaubien Street. In contrast to the domesticity, warmth, and hope which dominates the sunflower imagery of the first stanzas, that of the third stanza is steeped in the atmosphere of the blues. Through alliteration, consonance, assonance, and onomatopoeia, Hayden makes effective use of verse texture to support the sense that the stanza conveys. The alliterative consonants and the assonant vowels together with the onomatopoeic "blues-chorale" and "torsioning despair" serve to evoke the sometimes harsh, choked-up frustration and wailing despair that characterize the blues. The blues ambience achieved here speaks of the unremitting personal agony in the slum dwellers' collective lives. They have not, in arriving at Beaubien Street, reached the "sun." It is only their hope, symbolized by the sunflowers, that enables them to endure—and even find "living sweet." To borrow Ralph Ellison's phrase, the poem owes its success to its realization of "both the agony of life and the possibility of conquering it through sheer toughness of [the] spirit."[11]

The Beaubien Street lyric is Hayden's first published poem that utilizes the sunflower image, which was to grow in importance as a symbol of the Afro-American lower classes with whom he became preoccupied. Also, the poem is one of two in the *Heart-Shape* volume that initiates a sharp imagistic pattern and is hence a departure from the direct narration characteristic of the other poems in the book.

The "dislocation" and "deprivation" theme is the subject of other poems in the volume—poems which seem to be the target of Harrison's gentle criticism that the book has "faint echoes of past and contemporary masters."[12] In "Shine, Mister?" (p. 42) and in "Bacchanale" (p. 44), the "faint echo" seems to emanate from the poetry of Langston Hughes. Failing to find work, the character in "Shine, Mister?" shines shoes, sings the "no-job blues," and schemes to leave town. The unemployed worker in "Bacchanale" drinks gin because the "factory closed this mawnin" and he "drawed that last full pay." Both men are reminiscent of Hughes's singer in "Evening Air Blues," who comes "No'th to find work, but who [chaws] de mornin air" for breakfast and decides to "do a little dancin / Just to drive [his] blues away."[13] In both of the Hayden poems, the diction is closer to Hughes's model than to the more naturalistic diction he developed later, for example, in "The Dream."[14] In his later work, he adopts an idiom that suggests the flavor of southern speech in general, rather than a too literal imitation of black speech. This contrast of Hayden's blues lyrics to those of Hughes, however, should not be stressed too greatly. Lacking Hughes's ability to orchestrate authentically the musicality and the mood of the blues, Hayden fails to exhibit Hughes's virtuosity, which is the point that justifies the Harrison criticism. At least in his early work, he takes too many liberties with the form.

As we have seen, Hayden exhibits a great sensitivity to the oppression of his people and their struggle to overcome it. It is not surprising, therefore, to find in *Heart-Shape in the Dust* two poems which clearly express a suicidal view of things, and perhaps even a death wish. In "Monody" (p. 33), a rhymed lyric of two quatrains, the speaker expresses his despair over continuing what he feels to be a hopeless struggle:

Better the heart should yield and fall, have done
With these ignoble battles never to be won;
Better the heart should be at rest that goes
In bannered march around unyielding Jerichos.

The "unyielding Jerichos" are, of course, those of the familiar Afro-American spiritual, "Joshua Fit de Battle of Jericho."[15] Popular with the slaves because of the message of hope it carries, and feared by the masters because of its threat to them,[16] the spiritual is one in which slaves compared their predicament in America with that of the dispossessed Israelites. While the speaker in "Monody" is cognizant of the parallels between unemployed American blacks and the Israelites, he does not foresee crumbling walls and prefers death to empty dreams.

In "Sonnet to E." (p. 31), the second death-wish poem, the speaker is obsessed with the "starless times when [he] . . . longed to join the alien hosts of death."

1 Beloved, there have been starless times when I
2 Have longed to join the alien hosts of death,
3 Have named death father, friend, and victory
4 More sweet than any triumph of the breath.
5 In hours extreme with weeping and despair
6 That turned my valor's blunted sword to rust
7 And tore the pennons of my strength from air
8 To lie in crumpled heart-shape in the dust—
9 Oh, in such hours death has seemed a kind
10 And balsam-handed lord . . . But not again,
11 By any gentle mask death has designed,
12 Shall I be fooled; I see his cunning plain,
13 Since love with generous wisdom tutors me
14 To see what hitherto I could not see.

The speaker is apparently overwhelmed by the same spirit of hopelessness which overcame him in "Monody," and the military imagery of lines 6 and 7 suggests that he is here engaged in similar battles.

The "crumpled heart-shape in the dust" is an allusion to the fourth stanza of Elinor Wylie's poem "Hospes Comesque Coparis" (Guest and Companion of [my] Body).[17] The fourth stanza of the Wylie poem states her aspirations before her death, namely, to be remembered by a flowering of creativity. Hayden's use of the word "crumpled" before the quotation, however, serves as an ironic implication of the speaker's emasculation. Likewise, the lexical ambiguity of the word "pennons," line 7, which may mean either *flags* or *wings*, adds to the reader's perception of his incapacity. If the word means *pinion*, it suggests that the speaker has been stopped in flight like a bird with a broken wing, that he has fallen to earth "crumpled." On the other hand, if the word means *flag* or *banner*, given the military allusions in the poem, it may mean his courage has been so subdued he feels his fight useless and prefers the sweetness of death to the ignominy of defeat. While the speaker repents his suicidal thought in lines 9 and 10, he immediately recalls his objection to it in lines 10 and 12.

Lines 13 and 14 assert the poet's resolve to achieve a broader understanding of those forces—forces that had caused him to take a militant stance and had so "blunted [his] valor" that he fell "crumpled," and momentarily regarded death as a release. Clearly, it is "E." (his beloved Erma) who brings about his rejection of death and his broader understanding.

One may read the sonnet as a love poem, structured along the lines of Shakespeare's "When in disgrace with fortune and men's eyes," where the thought of the "dear friend" dispels gloom. It is a typical Elizabethan device to speak of vast important things then shift the focus so that the beloved object stands out against them and reduces them to relative insignificance. In this poem, despite the noble battle itself and despite the speaker's reaction to apparent defeat, the beloved is finally seen as more important than all of it. Thus the death wish serves, ultimately, in her praise.

Heart-Shape in the Dust is by no means restricted to racial themes and subjects. While the fact of Hayden's racial identity and the fancies of Communist party strategy combined to infuse his art with an unmistakable ethnic flavor, at the same time his concerns were broadly humanistic and cosmopolitan, and these too found expression in his early work.

From 1933 onward, Hitler's assumption of power, the rise of Japanese militarism, and Mussolini's successful African campaign struck reflective men with apprehension. Year by year the brutal drama moved from one scene to another—Manchuria, Ethiopia, Spain, Shanghai, Austria, Czechoslovakia. The importance of these events soon became obvious in American letters. According to Robert Spiller, such world catastrophes changed the national attitude from isolationism to internationalism,[18] and Hayden's views coincided with this attitude.

It was the Spanish Civil War that captured the tardy interest of "reflective men," who should have been alerted by the earlier Italian invasion of Ethiopia.[19] According to Jerre Mangione, prominent members of the Federal Writers Project adopted the cause of the Loyalists against Franco, with strong participation provided by members in the New York, California, and Chicago Projects.[20] About this period Hayden met Langston Hughes, who was covering the activities of Afro-American volunteers in the International Brigades in Spain as a war correspondent for the Baltimore *Afro-American*.[21] This milieu of political concern, together with his longstanding interest in the Spanish language and culture, aroused the spirit of internationalism in Robert Hayden.

The philosophic focus of Hayden's World War II poems derives from the grim irony apparent in news headlines which juxtapose the season of rebirth with sterility and death. The first poem, entitled "Words This Spring" (p. 17), uses such a headline as its epigraph: "It is believed that the war will really get under way with a big offensive in the spring." Imagery in the first stanza evokes the human suffering which modern warfare imposes on its victims:

> The metal rumor of the skies
> Signals a fatal spring,
> Sets streamlined terrors burgeoning.
> Spring's schedules bring
> No pastoral silences, no wreathing cries
> Of birds—but steel and dum-dum agonies.

In the second stanza, however, the allusion to Robert Herrick's "Corinna's Going A-Maying" introduces an ironic *carpe diem* theme. The allusion, of course, is meant to be grotesque in that it further points up the subversion of the natural order:

> And when a-maying fair Corinna goes,
> She picks her way among the dead—
> Finds instead

Of posies in the grass, a stark death's head.
She wears a gas-mask, fair Corinna does,
And thinks of spring's first air-raid while
    seeking spring's first rose.

"The Mountains" (p. 25), too, is concerned with man and nature, but the emphasis is shifted away from the irony involved in the death-dealing confrontations of a military spring. Whereas in "Words This Spring" Hayden stresses the disruption of nature by uncontrollable forces entirely of man's making, in "The Mountains" he depicts nature as itself an uncontrollable force over which man establishes at best an uncertain dominion. Thus, even in the midst of his preoccupation with very real concerns, both domestic and international, Hayden can, even at this early stage in his poetic development, give artistic attention to questions which affect man in a generic sense and are philosophical and timeless, rather than merely topical, and couched in the language and allusion of the general poetic tradition rather than the black and Marxist tradition many were trying to create.

There were mountains in that place:
They hemmed us round,
A dusk-green storm,
Motionless, without sound.

At night we felt
The blacked-out ranges near—
A wingéd shadow, vast,
Upon the atomosphere.

Once in the imminent dark
We heard the crash of ledges
And knew time danced
Upon the mountains' edges.

The mountain mornings
Arched over us,
Intense, bronze-green,
And perilous;

And we were drowned
And sucked down under
Unfalling waves
Of rock-leashed thunder.

These impressions emanate from a speaker who is accompanied in the mountains by a silent companion for an evening, night, and morning. The poem merits discussion because it evinces both a knowledge of and an ironic stance toward certain Romantic conventions—a stance that characterizes much of his later work. The choice of language clearly suggests that nature is an intimidating force, divided from men.

In stanza 1 the pair are imprisoned—"hemmed in"—by the power that is represented by the mountains. In stanza 2 they feel the mountains as a dominating "winged shadow." They experience a threatening darkness, listen to the "crash of ledges," and realize their own frailty and transience in stanza 3. The coming of daylight in stanza 4 serves only to clarify and delineate more sharply that which they sensed the night before—that is, they are "arched over," not just "hemmed . . . round." In the last stanza they are symbolically "drowned / And sucked down under" (lines 17–18), entombed, overcome by their fear of the natural world whose forces are beyond their control.

The poem recalls both Wordsworth's "The Simplon Pass" and Shelley's "Mont Blanc." The central point in each poem is man in relation to nature—man's response to natural objects, mountains. However confusedly and imitatively, according to F. R. Leavis, who compared "Mont Blanc" with "The Simplon Pass,"[22] in reference to the mountain's awesome contrasts, Shelley makes the point that "the everlasting universe of things / Flows through the mind" (lines 1–2). Extending the metaphor, he raises the issue of power as manifested by the Arve River, fed by Mont Blanc, and makes the point that nature's indiscriminate power can be harnessed by the enlightened human will for constructive human ends. In "The Simplon Pass," Wordsworth details dreadful contrasts—"the tumult" and "peace," "darkness" and "light"—that he encounters in the mountain pass. Unlike Shelley in "Mont Blanc," Hayden does not attempt to show the ascendancy of man's mind in its power to control the forces of nature. Nor does he make the attempt to show, as Wordsworth does, that his speaker's sense of the "perilous," of being "sucked down under," his dread of the "blackness of night," the "brightness of day" are, as Wordsworth puts it, "workings of one mind"—"features of the same face" (lines 16–17).[23] However, in conveying nature's intimidating force and its essential separateness from man, Hayden's stand is ironic and twentieth-century.

While *Heart-Shape in the Dust* is not a great work, and while its major concerns are topical and heavily influenced by the racial, social, political, and international currents of the day, it does reveal Robert Hayden as a poet determined to draw on those sources relevant to his artistic vision, whatever they might be. It is the work of a man passionately involved in the history and fate not only of his own people, but of all people. The new symbols, such as the sunflower, stir and challenge his poetic imagination throughout. "Sunflowers: Beaubien Street" and "Gabriel" are especially significant in this connection. He is willing to make his point in the dialect of the Afro-American, but even at this early stage, he is clearly aiming at an art free of the topical concerns in current fashion or his own ethnic identity. Thus he is not totally controlled by the Marxist world view and obviously sees art itself as very important. Those "echoes" that Harrison hears contain the voices of Shakespeare, Shelley, and Keats, as well as Hughes. While they are obviously, and often blatantly, imitative, they hint at Hayden's eventual synthesis of his own concerns with the poetic tradition.

CHAPTER 3

The Exploratory Works:
The Lion and the Archer (1948)
and *Figure of Time* (1955)

The Lion and the Archer (1948)

If one accepts Auden's dictum that a fondness for words is the mark of poetic talent,[1] then *The Lion and the Archer* amply demonstrates that Hayden was indeed talented. The volume also demonstrates his ability to capture exactly the characteristic features of the region he was writing about. His empathy for foreign nationals remained active, and his powers of song show themselves to advantage in the poems about the Afro-American. The overall merit of the volume outweighs the occasional insecure control of metaphor, the strained language in "Invisible Circus," or the slip of scholarship in "Eine Kleine Nachtmusik"—something uncharacteristic of Hayden as his research for "A Ballad of Remembrance" and "The Lion" clearly shows.

The Lion and the Archer is a brochure of twelve lyrics, privately printed in an elegant format. Six of the poems are Hayden's; the others are by Myron O'Higgins, with whom Hayden also co-authored "Counterpoise 3." The jacket was designed by William Demby. Commenting on the collaborative nature of the work, Hayden said that he was fascinated by O'Higgins's sophistication, which was garnered, in part, from the worlds of theater and the fine arts. Demby was a student in Hayden's creative writing class, a veteran of World War II whose cultural perspectives had been enlarged by his tour of duty in Europe. In Demby Hayden found a kindred soul, one whom he welcomed into his home for many delightful afternoons of creative dancing, with Mrs. Hayden at the piano.[2]

The immediate critical responses to the brochure were few, but consistently favorable. Selden Rodman, for instance, noted that the work might possibly become the "entering wedge in the emancipation of Negro poetry in America," and that behind the work was "the whole weight of modern poetry at the service of a tragic human situation."[3]

Two years later, Margaret Walker recognized Hayden's poems in *The Lion and the Archer* as evidence of a decided growth in stature. She pointed to his increased sense of "choric movement" and his understanding of oppressed peoples as demonstration of his "due maturity and power." She further recognized him as one of a group of poets of the late forties who was moving toward more intellectual themes of psychological implication. However, she mistakenly grouped him with various artists who had become concerned with internationalism in the late forties—that is, poets who grew less preoccupied with the elementary theme of race *qua* race, and more with race as a complex point of departure toward "a global point of view," a view which she refers to as "the main emphasis of the volume."[4] In fact such a point of view is in evidence in *Heart-Shape in the Dust* as we have seen. *The Lion and the Archer* continues to develop themes of "global" responsibility.

Later criticism of the brochure is represented by that of Sterling Brown, who, in a short survey of black artists since the Harlem Renaissance, mentions Hayden only briefly as a poet of the densely symbolic.[5]

Symbolic Hayden certainly was, but symbolism is the métier of the poet, the transmuter and universalizer of experience, and in this Hayden stood in the tradition of Yeats. His topics and concerns, however, were his own. Slender though the volume is, *The Lion and the Archer* is thematically varied. It treats such subjects as the poetic imagination, the poet's black southern heritage, the dislocation and deprivation of blacks in the ghetto, and the situation of international man. Perhaps—as Seldon Rodman concludes in his early review, after offering what he considers a representative group of quotations from the booklet—whatever the individual theme, the focus of the work is on the "tragic human situation."

Stylistically this slight brochure reveals the extent to which Hayden took to heart Auden's principle that a problem in poetry should be treated like a problem in algebra, being essentially a search for fresh ways of handling subject matter.[6] The search took him through the territory of the Baroque poets and led him to examine the products of surrealistic thinking—films, painting, and prose.[7] While he was at Fisk, he met the European film producer Maya Daren, who visited the campus and demonstrated the underground films in which she used surrealistic techniques. He was also introduced to Romare Bearden, an Afro-American surrealistic artist whose paintings hang in the Museum of Modern Art. With such motivation he began to read in the surrealist area.[8] All the while he continued to read Yeats, or so a poem like "The Lion" would indicate.

"Magnolias in Snow,"[9] a four-stanza lyric, treats the true relationship between North and South, symbolized by the association of snow and magnolias. As the poem begins, the speaker, a Northerner, finds himself curiously disoriented in a snow-covered South. Only magnolia trees and the "hue" of speech give away the latitude. The snow "alters," "elaborates," "confuses," and "deceives." These qualities of ambiguity and obscurity are fraught with an ominous potential that may lure the speaker into a flagrant error, because he does not know what "error" might mean. The "summer-green" of the magnolias and "the certain hue of speech" keep him from making the geographical "error"; and his correct perception of his location keeps him from "error" in its secondary, or social, meaning.

Stanzas 2 and 3 develop the contrast between North and South. Stanza 2 pictures the North as a place of security and friendship, while stanza 3 characterizes the South as a place where one must create alternatives for the comforts defined in lines 9 and 10. Here, as the speaker sees it, one lacks freedom, and the human desire for friendship and security can be fraught with potential danger. If the antecedent of "things" (line 14) is "home and friends" (line 8), their significance becomes clear when understood in the context of the segregated South; it was not a place where one might walk freely with friends, especially if they were of another race. To do so was to court overt reprisal from the whites and censure from a tremulous black community.

In the final stanza the speaker issues a plea for sanity and change. As the landscape can accept, as "a baroque / surprise," the "ornaments of snow," no matter how "startling," so can it accept the human changes. Perhaps society can find the change, like the "dazzle clustered trees," beautiful.

The use of the word "baroque" in line 17 indicates the mode he is attempting. The poem demonstrates some of the devices Barbara K. Lewalski and Andrew J. Sabol attribute to the baroque school: paradox developed by central metaphor, nonmimetic use of external nature, an occasional catechresis (lines 9–10), as well as rich provocative imagery.[10] However, if one follows F. J. Warnke's formula, a recombination of qualities from nature that are frankly artifacts is not developed in the poem. Both the phantasmagoric, or dream-like, sequences of images and the amorous or religious theme of transcendence are lacking in "Magnolias in Snow."[11]

The "Magnolias" lyric marks a renewal of the interest in the South that Hayden showed in "Sunflowers: Beaubien Street." But his actual experiences in the area, his first-hand knowledge of the people and the land, gained after that earlier effort, give his delineation of the southern milieu an increased intensity and immediacy.

"A Ballad of Remembrance" (poem 2) is another examination of the South, both old and new, in terms of black-white relations (see Appendix A). It is perhaps his most brilliant. While it is true that "Ballad" makes no concession to the reader who may be ignorant of the niceties of slavery, the life-style of plantation aristocracy, and certain cultural practices in New Orleans, Richard Barksdale's charge that the poem is unnecessarily erudite is overstated. The examples Barksdale cites, such as "contrived ghosts / who rap to the metronome clack of lavalieres" and the "sallow vendeuse / of prepared tarnishes and jokes of nacre and ormolu," are not necessarily more intellectual than poetic.[12] These images effectively and accurately depict the French ambience and the plantation milieu of antebellum New Orleans and help develop the intricate pattern of audio and visual imagery which contributes to the central metaphor of the poem.

"Ballad" can perhaps best be understood within its surrealistic mode, which by definition stresses the multi-dimensional and the subconscious. The poem uncovers a nightmare world, where past and present, appearance and reality, merge in a shrill and terrifying carnival of death and corruption.

The poem derives its dramatic force from the kaleidoscopic

impressions of a series of three experiences that occur to the speaker in New Orleans. He finds himself caught up in the swirl of Mardi Gras festivities; he is subjected to an incident of racial discrimination; and, finally, he transcends the destructive potential of the traumatic experience through friendship with a kindred soul, the late Mark Van Doren.

Throughout the poem, the New Orleans setting is dominant. It is the bastion of slavery and the repository of slavery's relics. The first stanza focuses on the speaker's impressions of the city, certain participants in a parade, and the symbolic significance of both.

The color imagery with which the poem begins suggest the various hues of the Afro-American participants in the festival. It recalls the liberties that slave masters took with their female chattels and the New Orleans Cordon Bleu, which was a showcase for young quadroon girls groomed from early childhood to serve the sexual appetite of wealthy white planters.[13] The imagery, "Quadroon mermaids, Afro angels, saints / blackgilt," suggests the darker-complexioned sisters who served as mere field hands. Perhaps "blackgilt" is a reference to the grease paint some of the participants wore which, by exaggerating blackness, contributed to a sort of minstrel humor.[14] The images "fans of corrosion" and "tight streets" suggest the parade route and its psychological atmosphere. These images are based on the actual topographical layout of the streets—streets which were, in reality, roped off with canvas-covered steel wire to contain the flow of people and to seal off the homes behind the cable, a precaution which in effect secured a closed white society. The "switch blades of that air" is a psychological image intended to depict the sudden and lethal physical danger to which the participants are subject.[15]

The second stanza introduces the "zulu king" and the "gunmetal priestess." The Zulu king is a black-faced minstrel figure who dominates the parade.[16] His very name embodies the sardonic humor that is based on his function in the parade, the abject debasement of the heroic prestige of his heritage. As a willing clown he represents the "accommodationist" type, a ludicrously caricatured personage who portrays the grotesque through a combination of the ridiculous and the terrifying.[17] Operating as the Zulu king's foil is the "gunmetal priestess."[18] She seems to symbolize the city of New Orleans. Her name and title suggest that she is the leader of a pagan cult—undemocratic, hard, and unyielding—an inhumane power supported by firearms. Together, she and the Zulu king operate to keep the past alive, she in her whine for "blood," and he in his cry to "shadow" the past.

In stanza 3, the gunmetal priestess assumes another mask (the poem does not make clear whether this is indeed another mask or a different mummer, but this question does not significantly affect the interpretation) as the "sallow vendeuse." Her description reinforces the imagery of decay and deterioration. No doubt the poet takes as his reference point the items she hawks during the carnival, the trinkets and souvenirs; but he weaves a pattern of baroque imagery that indicts the embalmed, worthless, contrived, and mechanical quality of the New Orleans he saw.

The focus then swings from the spectrum of the city back to an image of the parade at a point where "masked Negroes" ride a "threat of river." The speaker becomes one of the dancers; he is caught up in the "dance of love and hate among joys [and] rejections" which defines the city. The imagery in lines 16 through 20 achieves the hallucinatory dimension of the nightmare, and the poet speaks to the reality that underlies appearances in the carnival and the city.

The fifth stanza further indicates the triple-leveled tension operating in the poem. In response to "love and hate among joys, rejections," the Zulu king affirms his enthronement by muttering "Accommodate." The mermaids, Afro angels, and saints chime "Love." Wearing a "spiked bellcollar," the badge of the recaptured runaway slave, the gunmetal priestess shrieks "Hate."

The speaker is not included in "those others" who are scattered by the gunmetal priestess's lethal power characterized by the bird of prey, firearms, and gunfire images in stanza 6. Still caught up in the "dance," however, he finds himself among "metaphorical doors, decors of illusion," one of which leads him to another experience: a confrontation with surrealistic "coffeecups floating poised hysterias" against which the somewhat Juvenalian satire of the stanza is directed. The gunmetal priestess—she who shrieked "Hate"—is now among those coffeecups and a waitress who will panic at the sight of the black speaker and his white colleague and refuse to serve them coffee.[19] The "mazurka dolls" offer "death's-heads of peppermint roses," a symbolic death.

Stanza 8 develops the speaker's recoil and prepares for the dedication. Out of the nightmare world of the festival and the irrationality of the "poised hysterias" of the restaurant, the speaker emerges, through communion with one who is "richly human," into the world of rational man. He is "released" from both his ambivalent participation in the debasing dance and the imposition of the "minotaurs of edict." As the beasts "dwindle feckless, foolish," he gains a solid sense of his own humanity, his own rationality.

The final stanza contains Hayden's dedication and tribute. In the *Lion and the Archer* version it reads "for Bernice and Grady, for George and Oscar, . . . but also, Mark Van Doren." The "you" of a later version is here diffused in the collective body of names, but as if the significance of the experiences out of which the poem came took some time to settle in, this line was emended for future publications.

The poem lends itself to interpretation as both a baroque and surrealistic lyric. Operating in favor of the former are the rich patterns of imagery. The color gradations of red and yellow and the auditory imagery that evokes the dry sound of distant gunfire develop the themes of moral corruption and decay, power and death. The sensuous peculiarities of the imagery are reworked into a nonrepresentational succession of shifting, dream-like visions. With respect to its central metaphor, the poem uses "the world as theater theme." It is a baroque particularity, Warnke says, that goes beyond the recognized similarity of the theater to the world to rest on the premise that the world *is* theater, and therefore illusion.[20] Thus, the illusionary Mardi Gras carnival Hayden treats is the real New Orleans world; the actors play themselves. He is concerned with mingling the levels of appearance with those of reality, the Mardi Gras with life. Hence, the speaker's choice to become one of the dancers convinces the reader that the dance is authentic and affirms the identification of stage (carnival) as life or world.

While the baroque hero is passive rather than active, and his triumph resides in making himself a sacrifice, Hayden's speaker makes a moral commitment to the death of the "minotaurs of edict"—the whole spectrum of New Orleans Jim Crow. His existential decision to make himself available to the experience of "coffeecups floating poised hysterias" and to wrench himself away from "the hoodoo of that dance" in order to identify with rational man removes him from consideration as Warnke's baroque hero.

As a surrealistic poem, "Remembrance" makes use of a nightmare-like sense of disconnected experience. Stark, discordant images—"angels," "saints," and "switchblades"—surface randomly from the depths of the subconscious, and the "crises of consciousness" that the poem provokes in the reader parallels the aim of surrealism. It falls short, however, of full commitment to this mode. Insofar as it develops sequentially in time, it is not a spontaneous dredging of the subconscious, though the imagery gives it that appearance. In contrast to the surrealistic strategy it indubitably carries a moral,[21] for it promotes, quite openly, the redemptive qualities of love and celebrates the power of thinking man.

"A Ballad of Remembrance" is in a technical sense—with its careful shifts of rhythm, its original, provocative imagery, and modulations of tone—the best poem in *The Lion and the Archer*. It is a subtle, highly controlled, yet impassioned treatment of the historical and moral nature of black-white relationships in the segregated South—a way of life the poem emphatically condemns and rejects. It is also, and perhaps most importantly, a statement of faith that rational communication can transcend situational vulgarity.

If the Afro-American experience, under the horrors of slavery and, later, under the exigencies of the segregated South, produced the accommodationist clown, it was also responsible for producing the folk artists who objectified and thereby made these situations bearable. Such a one was Bessie Smith, blues singer nonpareil, to whom Hayden pays his memorable tribute in poem 3, "Homage to the Empress of the Blues" (see Appendix A).[22]

The singer is an enchantress who reigns by merit of the charisma of her singing. The poem takes the reader into the heady, throbbing excitement of the great blues singer's performance. She appears in "yards of pearls," "ostrich feathers," and "beaded satin." "Flashed her golden teeth" (a dazzling cosmetic affectation of her day), "shone that smile," describes her stage sophistication and presence. She is so brightly scintillating, both as a personality and in attire, that she "puts the lights to shame," and she is as captivating as "a favorite scenic view." It is her singing, however, that draws her audience. She does not disappoint it. In her magnificent voice the folk artist sings of disappointments in love, physical hardships, fears of economic misfortune, and other trials and tribulations familiar to her people.

She appeals to those who suffer the kind of poverty in "Sunflowers: Beaubien Street." Hayden says the lyric speaks of the kind of desperation slum dwellers suffer living on the brink of catastrophe.

Under the menace of white authority, or exposure to winter, they can be cruel and violent toward one another.[23] She has no solutions to offer her audience, but her ability to objectify its sufferings in song results in catharsis.

Hayden develops the poem by focusing on stark patches where plaster has fallen away to show the exposed laths and other patches covered with pages cut from magazines with particularly attractive pictures. The practice is a common makeshift of the poor and serves the dual purpose of barring drafts and giving the occupant something pleasant to look at and dream of. The "alarming fists of snow," a Dali-like image, at once defines the harsh northern winter and the white harbinger—most often a law-officer—of statistical misfortune.

While the plight of the poor and dispossessed and the relationship of race to one's situation and outlook are deeply felt themes, Hayden continues to reveal, in *The Lion and the Archer*, the larger, humanistic interests that take him out of the category of an ethnic poet. In poem 4, "Eine Kleine Nachtmusik" (see Appendix A), he takes up again, as in the *Heart-Shape in the Dust* "Words This Spring" poems, his internationalist concerns by making a telling comment on the human suffering caused by war. He takes his title from Mozart's serenade in four movements, but does so with an ironic twist on Mozart's work. Mozart's serenade epitomizes gaiety, whereas Hayden's poem evokes a melancholy mood based on the destruction and human degradation wreaked by Nazi Germany in Europe.

Stanza 1 of Part 1 develops the general setting of horror and human suffering caused by the war in Europe. Surrealistic imagery sets the tone: "the siren cries that ran like mad and naked screaming women / with hair ablaze all over Europe" (lines 1–2). The scene shifts perspective from the whole of Europe to the nearly-destroyed Alt Wein, a famous amusement park in Vienna. Here, in the war's destructive aftermath, "the mended ferris wheel turns to a tune again / in nevermore Alt Wein," (lines 7–8). The elegant men and women who once, in better times, took rides on the Ferris wheel are now ghosts: "poltergeists in imperials and eau de cologne" (lines 8–9).

Part 2 concentrates on the individual and introduces Anton, the student, who "reads and hears / the clawfoot sarabande, the knucklebone passacaglia coming close" (lines 12–15). The diction, which denotes ordinarily slow music, is given here, through the use of

Hayden's modifiers, a funereal connotation. Anton, blue from the cold, puts on his "ancestral blue" and makes a failing effort to ward off freezing by the husbanded warmth from a "burntdown candle," while he "reads rereads the dimming lines" (lines 19–20).

In Part 3 the scene shifts back to Alt Wein where now, instead of the elegant figures of the past who once took rides on the Ferris wheel to "tunes," whores and their soldier escorts ride in an atmosphere of degradation epitomized by the popular ("neo") music:

22 Now as the ferris wheel revolves to extrovert neomusic
23 and soldiers pay with cigarettes and candybars
24 for rides for rides with famished girls whose colloquies
25 with death have taught them how to play at being whores:

Stanza 2 of Part 3 ends with a return to the picture Anton makes. The ending causes the reader to "think of Anton, Anton brittle, Anton crystalline" (line 29). Conditioned by previous use of "poltergeists," "burntdown candle," "dimming lines," "ancestral blue," together with the imagery which points to Anton's frail condition, the reader thinks of his imminent demise, which seems to be intended as a symbol of the intellectual and spiritual demise of Europe. For both Anton and Europe, it has been a night music—not of gaiety, but of death.

The poem is distinguished by an assiduous choice of vocabulary in keeping with its continental subject matter—the German "hexentanz" and "poltergeists," the Spanish "sarabande," the Italian "passacaglia," and the Austrian "Alt Wein."

One element in the poem seems questionable. If "Alt Wein" is the central image here, as it seems to be, it is not clearly present at all times. Rather, the poet diffuses the strength of the image between Vienna, world-famous center of music, and Vienna, the center of a world-famous amusement park. The poet himself clears up one error in judgment—that is, his mistake in allowing the ferris wheel to operate in the Austrian winter. In the 1962 version of the poem, republished in *A Ballad of Remembrance,* the time becomes appropriately "spring." One might call the poem to account on another score: although it offers an unqualified picture of Vienna's suffering under German occupation, and by extension the human suffering caused by the war, it does not take into account Austria's historic sympathy for Germany or its role as fellow traveler under the *An-schluss* policy from 1938 to 1945. Hence the poem seems to negate Lionel Trilling's view that the artwork partakes of history as it records historic fact.[24] Despite the unusual slip in scholarship, however, and despite the fact that Hayden did not choose to include it in his *Selected Poems,* according to the poet himself the poem won enthusiastic acceptance in Europe, and it remains a sophisticated and potent comment on the effects of warfare.

The remaining poems in the brochure treat the role of the poetic imagination and what the creative process meant to the poet. "Invisible Circus," (poem 5) is about a boy and a giraffe:

> Peacock's feather of a boy,
> piebald giraffe (obscurantist creature)
> on which he displays himself
>   with sprigged-with-sorrow joy:
>
> Oh they could show us jingling marvels
> but pelting us with subtleties
> make us create our own
>   comiques and flying devils:
>
> From their gemglitter stance we must infer
> the clocked and tilting frivols
> of Maximo the Merry
>   on his filament floor.
>
> Reefer whimsey of a conniving
> beast; nocturnal oddment of
> a boy—so nothing but
>   themselves: jewel in setting,
>
> Eye in socket. Yet a part
> of the living statuary
>   of the three-ring heart.

The boy is established as an ambivalent figure, as in "sprigged-with-sorrow joy," and the giraffe, by direct statement is an "obscurantist creature." The poem is not so much, of course, about a boy-giraffe act as it is about a poem—perhaps this one. Even more, it is about the relationship between the poem and its readers—"us." The boy-giraffe pair make demands upon us; while they are able to "show us jingling marvels," they make us "create our own / comiques and flying devils." (One might assume whatever marvels one wishes—perhaps sewing-circle didacticism decked out in rhyme and meter.) It is well to remember that this circus is invisible and that seeing the invisible requires an act of the imagination. The poet gives us an image of their "gemglitter stance" but admonishes that the reader "must infer." Inference is an activity; thus both poet and reader must be actively involved in the poem. Interestingly enough, though the poem is made through the activity of the reader making inferences about the given images, stanza four affirms the essential reality of the subject of the poem and by inference disclaims the right of the reader to interpret without sticking to the poem itself; the boy-giraffe act is "nothing but / themselves." They are artistic images, placed by the poet like "jewel in setting," but they are also "part / of the living statuary / of the three-ring heart." They have a tri-level reality—in the poet's experience, in that experience transformed into art, and through the medium of the poem, in the experience of the reader. They are—the boy, the giraffe, and their setting, the poem—"statuary," like Keats' "Urn"; but if they are cold stone in all three rings, it is finally the "heart" that encompasses them.

The importance of "The Lion" (poem 6) lies beyond its literal meaning—an archer's encounter with a lion:

>   I aimed, the archer said,
>   but did not have the heart
>   to kill that vernal beast,
>   and set a trap instead,
>   so cunningly rigged, so clever,
> and took him alive, the very emperor of anger:

>   The emperor of anger,
>   whom you see sleeping there
>   in the gilt and vermillion cage,
>   for whose exacting sake
>   I carry a whip, I wear
> this multifigured coat, this parakeet panache.

>   With flourishing panache
>   I bow to the applause

and open danger's door
while brasses breathe their Ahs
    and set the mood for courage
that is lionlike; with a crack of my whip I enter the
        cage:

I see when I enter the cage
a beast of Revelation,
    a captive prophet-king
in byzantine disguise;
    my soul in exultation
Holy Holy cries, as he leaps through turning fire:

As he leaps through circles of fire,
gold shadow of my will,
    dire beauty that creates
and tethers my desire,
    my soul, the archer said,
exults and Holy cries. And Holy cries, the archer said.

In the opening stanza, the archer meets the lion but refuses to kill "that vernal beast" apparently because the animal is too young. Instead, he takes the lion alive. In stanza 2, the lion is in a cage, and the archer is now a lion-trainer in a circus, carrying a whip for the lion's "exacting sake," and wearing a "parakeet panache." In stanza 3, responsive to the expectations of the audience and the encouragement of the brass band, the lion-trainer, thinking he is becoming more lion-like in courage himself, enters the cage. Stanzas 4 and 5 evoke the trainer's psychological response to his task once he enters the cage—the acknowledgment of his part in an apocalyptic-like creative act. He exults in his mastery of the beast and experiences an almost religious reverence for the lion's performance.

The allegorical import of this poem becomes clearer to the reader who understands that Leo the lion is actually Hayden's zodiacal sign and the major allusion in the volume's title. If the extended metaphor involved here is to be equated with Hayden himself, it may be that he is seeing himself allegorically in the process of creation. The archer would then be a concrete image for the artist who discovers the enormous complexity of experience represented by the lion. It is on the strength of his artistic discipline ("the whip") and self-confidence in his artistic discipline (his "parakeet panache") that he is enabled to attempt the awesome task of creating order from disorder.[25]

There is a certain ambivalence toward that order that ought to be pointed out. If the taming of the lion, and his eventual performance, is symbolic of the creation and the poem, then imposed order is both satisfying and not satisfying. Experience (the lion) in its raw state is, after all, "a beast of Revelation / a captive prophet-king." Something is taken away from it by its "gilt and vermillion cage." Similarly, Yeats's speaker in "Sailing to Byzantium" must give up the world of "fish, flesh, and fowl," to hear the bird upon its golden bough. Interestingly enough the lion mechanically leaping "through circles of fire," becoming a "god shadow" of the poet's "will," is described earlier as a creature in "byzantine disguise." In the pun on "Holy" in the last line, one finds the same ambivalent attitude one finds in the Yeats poem. That the wild lion has become a "shadow" of the archer's "will" is a "beauty," if "dire," "that creates / and tethers [his] desire," and it evokes the cry of "Holy." However, even if the whole process began out of the best motive (he "did not have the heart / to kill"), the circus setting of that noble beast captured and trained evokes a "Holy" cry which is *wholly* a cry.

The poems of *The Lion and the Archer* were written during a period in which Hayden personally suffered incidents of racial discrimination not only by whites but also by black status-quo advocates. These poems show Hayden as an individual who is concerned with the question of race and moral justice; they demonstrate his proximity to the people of his race and the knowledge of its oppression, historical and contemporary. They also demonstrate, however, that if Hayden is obsessed, it is with the poetic art; if he is committed, fundamentally it is to the universal experience of people.

Figure of Time

Figure of Time (1955) is the third volume in the *Counterpoise* series. It, too, was privately printed by the black Hemphill Press of Nashville, Tennessee. The booklet includes eleven new poems and three reprints of previously published lyrics.[26] The jacket was illustrated by a colleague, Aaron Douglas, artist-in-residence at Fisk University. Readers of the slender volume were limited mostly to the small cadre of students and colleagues interested in poetry and the fine arts who had gathered around Hayden at Fisk since 1946. The volume gained little literary attention—many of Hayden's anthologizers do not make any mention of it.

The dominant theme of the work is the suffering of the victims of various forms of oppression and the international and historical prospect of man's inhumanity to man, especially, but again, not exclusively, the black man. The spectrum of his concern embraces contemporary black-white relations, the Fascist "final solution" to the problem of European Jewry, the Spanish Conquest of American Indians, the apartheid practices of South Africa, the suffering of the Korean people, and the plight of the slum-dweller.

Through his sunflower image, Hayden still portrays man's ability to endure, even to maintain gaiety against "time's uncontrollable rages." However, seven years of worship and experience as a Bahá'í have drawn him to the mysticism of Bahá'u'lláh, whose martyrdom he has come to see as a symbol of the suffering of mankind,[27] a mysticism that motivates his prayerful supplication that man recognize the healing power of love. Hayden's literary treatment of the Bahá'í faith indicates the finality of his break with the American communism he had mildly espoused in his first volume and demonstrates the importance of cultural assimilationism as a motivating force in his life and work. In becoming a Bahá'í, he had moved from the vision of a world brotherhood based on politics to that of a brotherhood of religious assimilationism. His new faith may also be partly responsible for his present stance of non-involvement in black nationalist political issues, for whereas activism is mandatory in revolutionary communism, Baháism is deeply committed to passivism.

It is in this volume, too, that Hayden begins to evince a sustained concern with teleological questions and metaphysical answers. Heretofore, for instance, when he made use of Christian elements, he did so in order to establish a pathos that would elicit the reader's empathy. His work used certain elements of Christianity for melodramatic ends and according to the revolutionary strategy developed by the Communist party. Now, in such a poem as "In Light half nightmare, half vision" (p. 13), his attitude is clearly both religious and universal.

Indicative of his perception of the nature of suffering is the geographical spectrum crowded into this short poem, including, as it does, Germany, South Africa, Korea, and America. The catalog of individual agonies is linked to the martyrdom of Bahá'u'lláh—a martyrdom through which Hayden, perhaps, came to see suffering as the one single experience that can come to all humans rather than being limited to specific geographical, national, or racial groups.[28]

Though Hayden is by no means limited to themes with specific racial connotations, because of feelings on the subject that are his as a birthright, as it were, it is hardly surprising that many of his poems deal with the Afro-American, and most of those with the various forms his suffering has taken. In light of his educational background and his conversion to the Bahá'í faith, his racially linked poems become symbolic and universal.

"Figure" (p. 12) is a realistic, almost prosaic, delineation of the specific kinds of fetters used to secure a black victim before he is emasculated and murdered. Hayden compels the reader to see the victim through objective, photographic images, picturing the angle in which the "quelled head" hangs; the way the clothesline "nooses / both wrists, forcing his arms in an arrowing angle / out behind him," (lines 7–9); "His jeans . . . torn at the groin" (lines 11–12). From a somewhat matter-of-fact documentation of one black man's personal agony, however, the poem proceeds to consider the universal significance of violence and hatred. This lynching, any lynching, is a crime against all humanity; the South, where the action of the poem takes place, becomes, in figurative terms, the world where such crimes are committed daily. The particular victim becomes a "metaphor of a place, a time." If to geometrize "our time" means to put it into perspective as an intersection of the lines and angles of all time, then he is a symbol of suffering itself—the injustice, the violence, the hatred of the ages seen through a particular time ("ours") and place (the South).

"Locus" (p. 4) takes the South as a particular place and Afro-American slavery as a specific topic, but it, too, develops allusions that reach beyond the geographical location.[29] The poem presents seven indictments, each one of which satisfies the given condition: "Here the past, adored and forgiven" (line 30). One of the most incriminating of the indictments ironically exposes the latent, explo-

sive danger that characterized the South Hayden knew—a danger
that is nurtured by "memorial sentinels and backward-looking
hate":

5   Here violent metamorphosis
         a look, a word, a gesture
     may engender, with every blossom fanged and deadly
         and memorial sentinels,
     their sabres drawn, storming fire-wood shacks,
10   apartheid streets. Here raw-red earth and cotton-
         fields like palimpsests
     new-scrawled with old embittering texts;
         rock-hoisted hills where sachems
     counseled or defied, where scouts gazed down
15   upon the glittering death-march of De Soto.

The "violent metamorphoses" indictment may be seen as a
further development of Hayden's "switchblades of [the] air" imagery
in "A Ballad of Remembrance," and his "what egregious error" line of
"Magnolias in Snow"; it explains the historical reasons that engendered white hatred of black people—the "memorial sentinels" persona and the "palimpsest" cotton-fields are allusions to the Civil War
and the use to which the slave was put. Hayden censures the socioeconomic results of hatred and the cultivation of the past—"fire-
wood shacks" and "apartheid streets"—and argues that the South's
heritage of hatred for and oppression of the black man is the same as
South Africa's apartheid policy.

Another indictment underlines Hayden's deepening historical
perspective on the South as a place where an exploited population can
be traced back as far as the Spanish conquest of the Indians. The
phrase "death-march of De Soto" evokes the history of exploitation
and genocide perpetrated on the Indian and serves to link the black
and the American Indian as common victims of Europeans.

The setting of " 'Summertime and the Living . . .' " (pp. 2–3) is a
black ghetto presumably in Detroit, Michigan.[30] Its theme is the
oppression of the Afro-American, and its point of view is that of a
child. In the McCluskey interview, Hayden says that during the
fifties he felt he had developed sufficient "psychic distance and

craftsmanship" to do a series of poems about his childhood. Though his first volume included "childhood" poems, Hayden expressed reservations about them because of their apprentice nature.[31]

The poem is a study of the quality of the black man's life, its violence, ugliness, and spiritual beauty. The title is taken from George Gershwin's musical adaptation of Du Bose Hayward's *Porgy* (1925), a musical about a black ghetto in Charleston. The poem is developed from the point of view of a boy. It is his agony and alienation that dominate the work's eight stanzas from first to last (see Appendix A).

The reader is informed of the stultifying strictures slum penury exerts on the boy's sensibility. It is an existence lacking in the beauty symbolized by the roses for which he longs. Instead of roses, sunflowers abound—unordered, uncared-for, and like himself accidental and "vivid."

The lack of beauty symbolized by the missing roses is reflected in "the quarrels and shattered glass" which define the boy's real world. In order to cope with the real world, he attempts to redefine his existence by creating a fantasy world:

> There circus-poster horses curveted
> in trees-of-heaven above
> the quarrels and shattered glass
> and he was daredevil rider of them all.

The older people's fractious existence, however, overpowers the boy's deepening longing for the roses:

> No roses there in summer—oh never roses
> except when people died—
> and no vacations for
> his elders so harshened after each unrelenting day
>
> That they were shouting-angry.

The speaker's memory of the rich and positive elements of his ghetto childhood evoke the "mosaic eyes" of the grown people, and the sight of "Jack Johnson in his limousine," which encourages their dreams of a millennium for black people—"Ethiopia spreading gorgeous wings" (line 32).

On another level, " 'Summertime and the Living . . .' " has additional importance in that it reveals the unforgettable trauma of Hayden's childhood, the insecurity of his family life, and the tension-filled circumstances of his adoption. It also shows the state of his artistic consciousness even as a boy. It reveals his longing for roses, for instance, which might have been a symbolic longing for a beauty and order that he could in a sense control. Meanwhile, of course, he was storing in his consciousness for future reference impressions of sunflowers, circus posters, quarrels, shattered glass, and funeral parlor fans—a multiplicity of elements that provide the environmental basis of " 'Summertime and the Living. . . .' " and other ghetto verses.

The other memory poems included in the volume are "Incense of a Lucky Virgin" (p. 9) and "The burly fading one" (p. 8). "Lucky Virgin" was discussed in chapter 1. The second lyric adds to Hayden's picture of the black man as developed in his poetry.

> The burly fading one beside the engine
> holding a trainman's lantern in his hand
> is Uncle Jed. Bullyboy he is
> of wintered recollections now.
>
> Coal miner, stevedore and railroad man,
> oh how he brawls and loves from Texas clear
> through Illinois, a Bible over his headlong
> heart and no liquor on his breath.
>
> And when he dies, dies not in his own
> well-mastered bed but in the waters of
> the Johnstown flood in wild attempt,
> so sibling innuendoes all aver,
>
> To save the jolly girl
> his wife for months had hopelessly wished dead.

The poem is a brief character sketch of a picaresque hero. The speaker muses over the hero's "wintered recollections" about his travels and various occupations and the double tragedy in the circumstance of his death. Aside from the slice-of-life vignette involved, what Hayden accomplishes here is the evocation of a patriarch-centered family, the patriarch being a virile, hard-working, and courageous black male.[32]

" 'Lear is Gay' " (p. 19) provides another dimension of Hayden's Yeatsean influence.[33] This lyric is a tribute to a certain kind of aged person—that gallant, courageous individual who bears with happily excited yet detached gaiety "time's uncontrollable rages":

> That gaiety, oh
> that gaiety I love
> has white hair
> or thinner or none;
> has limbs askew
> often as not;
> has dimmer sight.
>
> Can manage, can,
> in rags, fevers,
> in decrepitude.
> Is not silenced by
> sweet pious rage
> against time's
> uncontrollable rages.
>
> Can smile and oh
> can laugh sometimes
> at time
> and all we fear from it.

The title derives from Yeats's "Lapis Lazuli."[34] It is taken from the second stanza, which develops the idea that the artist can cope with the transcience of his existence by not succumbing to self-pity and that, in his gay awareness of ineluctable defeat, tragedy is wrought to its uttermost. Hayden also echoes an idea which Yeats reiterates in many of his poems—that man dreads death:

> All perform their tragic play,
> There struts Hamlet, there is Lear,
> That's Ophelia, that Cordelia;
> Yet they, should the last scene be there,
> The great stage curtain about to drop,

If worthy their prominent part in the play,
Do not break up their lines to weep.
They know that Hamlet and Lear are gay;
Gaiety transfiguring all that dread.

("Lapis Lazuli")

One must watch one life succeed another, youth succeed age, with detachment, like the three old men in Yeats's poems "The Three Hermits" and "The Old Men Admiring Themselves in the Water." Only through such an ability can comfort be found for the tragedy of age and death:

All things fall and are built again,
And those that build them again are gay.

("Lapis Lazuli")

As Yeats expands upon this idea in *On the Boiler,* "The arts are the bridal chambers of joy. No tragedy is legitimate unless it leads some great character to his final joy."[35] In a world where "things fall apart; the center cannot hold,"[36] two things alone have value: art and those men and women who shape lives or deeds into beauty. The poet's job is the celebration in poetic forms of such persons and things.

" 'Lear is Gay' " is dedicated to Betsy Graves Reyneau, a contemporary American painter who was for a number of years a personal friend of Hayden. Hence, in his tribute to Reyneau he announces that he, too, in his turn, is celebrating in his practice of art the artist who has achieved her kind of lapis lazuli.

On another level, Hayden's tribute to a woman artist (one who had a special role in leading him to important visual art experiences, thereby enlarging his artistic consciousness) is one that recalls Yeats's tribute to his subject in "Upon a Dying Lady," especially Parts 1, 5, and 6.[37] The qualities that Hayden praises in Reyneau—a knowing kind of gaiety, the lack of "sweet pious rage / against time's uncontrollable rages," laughter in the face of time's inexorable toll— are precisely the qualities that Yeats attributes to the subject of his poem. Yeats establishes in Part 1 that "with eyes . . . laughter lit" she keeps her "distinguished grace," and in Part 5, "She has not grown uncivil / And called the pleasures evil." In Part 6, he states that her soul has flown to "the predestined dancing-place," where she comes face to face with "Achilles, Timor, Babar, Barhaim, all / Who have lived in joy and laughed into the face of Death."

If the echoes in his handling of language do not make the influence of Yeats on Hayden's poetic output clear, his indirect tribute to Yeats in " 'Lear is Gay' " ought to, for that tribute consists in the acceptance of Yeats's philosophic ideas on the poet in relation to his art and posterity. One might suspect, too, that those uncontrollable rages of time refer to the social and psychological problems both Hayden and Yeats faced. Hayden accepts the "way" the Irish poet handled the Irish question of nationalism, and probably he accepted the crucial corollary to the achievement of that way. In the case of Yeats it was a clinging to the legendary and folk Ireland as the source of his imagery; similarly, Hayden calls upon the Afro-American folk experience. Again, as Yeats was inspired to create an Irish national literature for the purpose of liberating the Irish people, Hayden creates an Afro-American literature. During his Writers Project years, influenced by encouragement from spokesmen of American Marxist communism, Hayden wrote poetry based on the Afro-American's history and socioeconomic plight. However, unlike Yeats's original strong commitment to Irish nationalism, which he later modified, if Hayden's stance served Marxist nationalist strategy for blacks, it did so inadvertently. His primary concern from his earliest poetry was to correct distortions in Afro-American history.

The intention in pointing out these similarities is not to suggest that Hayden was a slavish follower of Yeats, nor that he was overmuch concerned with borrowing his art from a white or European literary tradition, to the exclusion of his own black literary sources. It is rather to suggest that the Yeatsean influence is real and important. Hayden, like Yeats, drew freely on the rest of the literary world, of which Yeats is a significant part. In doing so, Hayden denied that racial background places any restrictions whatsoever on the range of the artistic imagination or limits the production of art.

Figure of Time was Hayden's last contribution in the *Counterpoise* series. In a sense its publication marked the demise of that special cadre of talented and productive young writers at Fisk who had lionized him for a decade. If *Figure* signaled the end of an era, so did it affirm Hayden's progress toward mastery of his art. " 'Summertime and the living . . .' " reveals his attainment of high lyrical powers; "Incense of the Lucky Virgin" continues his interest in what he said are "baroque" characters and situations; " 'Lear is Gay' " is his first poetic declaration of his indebtedness to Yeats; and "The Prophet" announces his commitment to Baháism. Also to be noted, in sharp contrast to *The Lion and the Archer* (1948), *Figure* is distinguished by word economy, greater lucidity, and lack of heavy symbolism.

CHAPTER 4

A Ballad of Remembrance (1962)

Between 1941 and 1962, a volume of Hayden's collected poems did not exist, and it was not until 1966 that an American house accepted such a work. However, *A Ballad of Remembrance*, a collection of Hayden's most representative pieces since *Heart-Shape in the Dust*, was published in Europe in 1962 by Paul Breman, who became acquainted with Hayden's works through Rosey E. Pool, who, like Breman, was an expatriate of Holland living in London.

The result of Breman's editing was a substantial compilation of thirty-five poems. Three of them are revised reprints from *The Lion and the Archer*, and ten are revised reprints from *Figure of Time*. At least eight of the remaining pieces are revised versions of poems that first appeared in various periodicals (see Appendix C). Thus, about fourteen of the poems in *A Ballad of Remembrance* are new.

The book received favorable, if limited, reviews. Arna Bontemps noted that the "special quality of [his] meticulous art is his synthesis of old and new elements." Hayden, he said, had proved his craftsmanship and in "Homage to the Empress of the Blues" found a middle passage through the dilemma of utilizing folk sources on the one hand and meeting the requirements of New Criticism on the other.[1] Ralph Mills examined the book's strengths and weaknesses, citing "Tour 5" as particularly demonstrative of its "quiet understatement" and "dispassionate observation." He noted Hayden's ability to achieve special effects, including musical ones, especially in "O Daedalus, Fly Away Home." However, Mills felt that these effects were more advantageously used in "Middle Passage," which he felt demonstrated Hayden's capacity for capturing the subtleties of human motives in dramatic fashion.[2]

Four years after *A Ballad of Remembrance* was published, Hayden was awarded the *Grand Prix de la Poésie* for it. Rosey E. Pool, in her press release announcing the award, characterized Hayden as "a remarkable craftsman . . . a striking singer . . . who gives glory and dignity to America through his attachment to the past, present and future of his race."[3] Certainly the international award was the most impressive evidence of the work's reception. His competitors were the Caribbean poet-playwright Derek Walcott and Christopher Okebo, a Nigerian. The international, interracial panel of judges included Langston Hughes, Katherine Dunham, Gerald Moore, and Abiolo Wole. Alioune Diop, president of the First International Festival of Negro Arts, presided; and Léopold Sédar Senghor, president of Senegal and a famous poet in his own right, announced the award and later presented it to Hayden in New York City.[4]

Because almost half the volume consists of revisions of poems in the two brochures that preceded it, the work necessarily repeats certain themes; however, the Afro-American cultural hero theme, introduced by "Gabriel" in *Heart-Shape in the Dust*, comes to full flower. Afro-American history was an element in the 1948 and 1955 brochures, but it is the basis for major thematic development in *A Ballad of Remembrance*. The second main emphasis in *A Ballad of Remembrance* is memory poems about his childhood and ghetto life. There are twelve of these in all, four of which are revised reprints. Another major subject is Mexico. During his sojourn there, when he wrote the poems for *Figure of Time*, Hayden kept a notebook in which he entered his observations and experiences.[5] Later, upon his return to Fisk and between 1956 and 1961, he used his notebook to develop the book's seven poems about Mexico. It is the Afro-American history poems, however, that are responsible for the acclaim the volume won.

He was inspired to write his historical poems by a challenge Stephen Vincent Benét issued in *John Brown's Body* (1928). Dissatisfied with his treatment of the Afro-American in his poem, Benét wrote:

O black-skinned epic, epic with the black spear,
I cannot sing you, having too white a heart,

And yet, some day, a poet will rise to sing you
And sing you with such truth and mellowness.[6]

In response to Benét's challenge, Hayden undertook to write *The Black Spear*, which was to be a volume of Afro-American history poems.[7] "The Negro people's struggle for liberation and their participation in the anti-slavery movement and the Civil War" was its intended theme. He did not complete the project, but he included one of the best poems from it, "O Daedalus, Fly Away Home," in *A Ballad of Remembrance*.

Taken together, these poems provide a fictionalized chronicle of the Afro-American and his acculturation to America. In "Middle Passage" he treats the origin of the slave trade in Africa as it relates to the development of the new ethnic group—the Afro-American. In "O Daedalus, Fly Away Home" he treats the Afro-American's wish-fulfillment mechanism that reflects his discontent with America and his desire to return to Africa. In "The Ballad of Nat Turner" he shows a Messianic figure being thrust up from the agonies of a people that had been uprooted in the early 1600s from their native land, held in bondage in their new home, become an American sub-society, and, if Anthony Wallace's revitalization movements theory is applicable, by the mid-1800s were experiencing the early stages of a revitalization period.[8] In "Frederick Douglass," he treats the Afro-American intellectual activist who fights for his people's freedom. Thus Hayden develops the history of the Afro-American's transition from tribal man to slave, to rebel and soldier, to statesman.

"Middle Passage" tries to achieve a two-fold purpose.[9] Hayden says that he wanted to fulfill Benet's prophecy and to write a poem that would give the lie to bigots who had distorted the Afro-American's history.[10] Though it was inspired by epic intentions and contains elements of the epic, it is not quite that. The traditional epic depicts the values and patterns of the life of an entire people or culture through the experience of a hero who represents in himself certain ideals of that culture. "Middle Passage" attempts through a hero to present the values, both positive and negative, of the slavery era and the Afro-American's historic condition, depicting his dislodgment and displacement from his mother country to an alien land.

The hero of the poem is Cinquez, the captive prince who inspired and carried out the *Amistad* mutiny. This figure, however, blends with the poet-observer, who enunciates "the deep dark immortal human wish / the timeless will to be free" (lines 172–73).

Another epic element in "Middle Passage" is the device of cataloging—the listing of the ships and the listing of the African tribes, all historically authenticated by Hayden's research.[11] It begins *in medias res* with the depiction of ships under full sail carrying slaves in mid-Atlantic. Its tone is dignified. The ending is not without a note of triumph, though this term does not adequately describe the mystical exaltation of the concluding stanzas.

Yet, the poem is not an epic. It is too short. Moreover, it is more lyrical than narrative; whenever a narrative section appears, it is telescoped or fragmented. The issue of religion is handled with great irony and for the purpose of condemnation. Intervention of the gods is lacking. The intervention of John Quincy Adams is the nearest approximation to this convention. And the hero does not engage in monologues; his words as well as his deeds are presented from the reportorial consciousness of the poet-observer.

The poem is set in the classic framework of a journey—one that begins when the African principals leave their villages. The exodus is engineered as much by the African kings who sell their captives to satisfy their greed for "luxuries" as it is by the Spanish greed for gold. The first lap of the journey is to the "factories"—places where the captives are sorted out, processed, and subdued for their coming enslavement. The second lap, the horrific "Middle Passage," is the journey across the Atlantic Ocean to America and slavery. The third lap, only alluded to in the poem, is the journey from the barracoons in America to the plantations.

Part 1 begins with a chilling description of the inhumane treatment slavers gave the Africans aboard various slave ships. Moving from the general to the particular, part 2 presents the reminiscences of a corrupt old slave-trader who is stopped from plying his trade only by the physical toll the tropics take on him—"fevers melting down [his] bones." Ironically his greed for gold is shown as being of a piece with that of the African kings' greed for luxuries. Part 3, the climactic section of the poem, is the poetic recreation of the *Amistad* mutiny, which occurred in 1839 and became a cause célèbre.[12]

The personae are the omniscient poet-observer, the African tribal chiefs and their subjects, the heroic Cinquez, the Spanish captain of the *Amistad*, common seamen, Celestino the mulatto, and the silent voice of John Quincy Adams, who argues the case for Cinquez and his people and who, in fact, argued the case for the *Amistad* rebels.

It is a tribute to Hayden's poetic genius that in the poem, otherwise so brilliantly and uniquely his own, he stands in debt to two poets who demonstrated conflicting views of America. Evident in "Middle Passage" are the techniques T. S. Eliot used in "The Wasteland" and the influence of Hart Crane's vision of crucifixion and resurrection, horror and squalor out of which radiates hope and light. As Crane, in "The Bridge," attempted to forge the American identity, Hayden likewise forges in "Middle Passage" the American identity of the Afro-American.

In part 1, Hayden introduces the technique of fragmentation which Eliot used with striking effect in "The Wasteland." It is a device that lends itself to a vivid portrayal of the disintegration of a society—in "Middle Passage," the historic disintegration of African society. Accordingly, the development of part 1 includes sequential presentation, without transition, of names of ships, a section of a ship's log, a sailor's prayer, a portion of a sailor's letter, and a legal deposition. The Eliot-like motifs that achieve unity are the refrain "Jesus Savior Pilot Me" (a hymn line which creates an ironic commentary), the biblically derived names of ships, and the poet-observer's chorus-like voice.

From a vantage point that spans time and place, the poet condemns the horrors of the Middle Passage, describing it as a "voyage through death" (lines 3–7). He condemns American greed—that of the New England shipping interests as well as that of the southern plantation owners:

> Standing to America, bringing home
> black gold, black ivory, black seed.

> *Deep in the festering hold thy father lies*
> *of his bones New England pews are made,*
> *those are altar lights that were his eyes.*
>
> (Lines 15–19)

The "altar lights" motif establishes an ironic relationship with Shakespeare's theme of death and resurrection in *The Tempest*. The allusion is to Ariel's speech to Ferdinand that falsely reports the death of Ferdinand's father. Hayden explains that his intention was based on his feeling that there was some connection between the sea change Shakespeare describes and "the change from human beings into things—objects, suffered by the enslaved Africans—the idea that slavery was a kind of death."[13]

Hayden's immediate purpose in using the allusion, according to Charles Davis, is to mock "a less than spiritual transformation."[14] While reminding the reader of a supposed death by drowning, which in reality led to a regeneration through sea change, Ariel's song also portrays a metamorphosis from blindness to new vision. (The sailor writes that "Opthalmia has struck the Captain as well as the Africans aboard the ship.") The line "those are altar lights that were his eyes" may be seen as a scathing indictment of a Christian people with eyes blind to the enslavement of their fellowman. It is a blindness that prevails in the poem until John Quincy Adams, as the champion of human rights, speaks "with so much passion of the right of chattel slaves" (lines 164–65) and their will to be free. When the justice he represents proves not to be blind, it opens the way for the African "to life upon these shores."

According to Elizabeth Drew, Eliot uses the Shakespeare line "Those are pearls that were his eyes" as the central symbol for the whole of Western tradition, which, as he saw it, was lifeless as a pearl. Eliot also used the symbol to suggest metamorphosis from blindness to vision. Drew further notes that Eliot's purpose in making the allusion was to symbolize the transmutation of life into art—a creative act the poet must find, not only through suffering but *in* suffering.[15] Whether in response to the Eliot model or not, Hayden develops this dimension of the metaphor in the sailor's letter:

> "8 bells. I cannot sleep, for I am sick
> with fear, but writing eases fear a little
> since still my eyes can see these words take shape
> upon the page & so I write, as one
> would turn to exorcism.
>
> (Lines 26–30)

The passage speaks of the transformation from blindness to vision that can be effected through the arts.

The blindness theme is continued in another variation of *The Tempest* motif which appears in part 3:

Deep in the festering hold thy father lies,
the corpse of mercy rots with him,
rats eat love's rotten gelid eyes.

(Lines 108–110)

In this passage the poet also decries the rotting bodies of his ancestors interred in the holds of slave ships. The contrast of "rotten" with what ought to be living thoughts—"mercy" and "love"—is reminiscent of yet another precedent set by Eliot in "The Wasteland," especially in "Burial of the Dead."

Further reminiscent of "The Wasteland" is the use of several voices, some of them ghostly, including those of the poet-observer, of the praying sailor, of the old slaver, and of the attorneys who speak for the Spanish deponents. As in "The Wasteland," though to a lesser extent, Hayden shuffles history, past and present, in his depiction of the African's "coming to life upon these shores."

Hart Crane's epic "The Bridge" also influenced the shaping of "Middle Passage." After announcing his vision of hope, which he contrasted to Eliot's negations,[16] Crane attempted to create, through the use of history and folklore and of his key bridge symbol, the American identity, achievement, and future hopes. It is, certainly, a subject matter for a myth that could support an American epic. This is a vision similar to that of Hayden's poem—a vision that creates an Afro-American identity around the central metaphor of the "Middle Passage" and a vision that carries, indeed, a constructive note of hope.

At the time he composed "Middle Passage," Hayden was a young man with certain identifiable ideas about Afro-American history, justice, and social change. He was, however, a poet who was making a search in himself for a new iconography that would inform his poetry along with the beliefs he had accepted. He was tossed up to rhetorical heights by his reckless faith in his poetic genius and scholarship; yet he was brought to a more even keel somewhat later by his stern sense of self-discipline and self-criticism. The true extent of these flights of optimism and the degree of his self-discipline and self-criticism cannot be known. Hayden said that the working sheets of "Middle Passage" are long since lost.[17] Nonetheless, there are four published versions of the poem: version A, in *Phylon* (1941); version B, in *Cross Section* (1945); version C, in *A Ballad of Remembrance* (1962); and version D, in *Selected Poems* (1966).

The painstaking revisions of "Middle Passage" from 1945 to 1966 produced a poem that won the acclaim of eminent critics and fellow-poets. A passage from the letter that Allen Tate wrote to him about the poem will indicate the measure of that approval: "I am especially moved by 'Middle Passage,' a beautifully written poem. The power is in the restraint and the purity of diction."[18] More important is the fact that the poem was produced by a black poet speaking of black history and heritage in the most sophisticated traditions of twentieth-century western poetry.

In "The Ballad of Nat Turner" Hayden turns to the second stage of Afro-American acculturation in America.[19] Turner is a black cultural hero who, having been a part of the mass movement of Africans to America, suffers the stress of enslavement and consequent acculturation and is in revolt. He was the slave of a Virginia planter, Benjamin Turner. The ballad recreates the ecstatic vision which led to a Messianic mission and resulted in a revolt of some Virginia slaves.[20] The poem falls into two distinct but related parts, with each part developing a particular set of circumstances. Dialogue in the poem is indirect; the tragic situation that the content treats is not presented with the simplicity of his earlier "Gabriel." Rather, the style is richly allusive and symbolic, and the tone is religious, ecstatic, and visionary.

The first section of the poem, stanzas 1 through 5, delineates the conditions of stress in the slave sub-society to which Turner reacts:

> Then fled the mellows, the wicked juba
>   and wandered wandered far
> from curfew joys in the Dismal's night.
>   Fool of St. Elmo's fire.
>
> In scarey night I wandered, praying,
>   Lord God my harshener,
> speak to me now or let me die;
>   speak, Lord, to this mourner.
>
> And came at length to livid trees
>   where Ibo warriors

hung shadowless, turning in wind
    that moaned like Africa,

their belltongue bodies dead, their eyes
    alive with the anger deep
In my own heart.

The imagery in stanza 1 evokes the ideal pastoral setting—"mellows" and "curfew joys." The hero, however, has come to see it as deceptive. He perceives that the toned-down quality of this environment hides the harshness of a "wicked juba," an evil dance which casts a spell, or St. Elmo's fire, which can mislead ships at sea. From this reality he flees to the night of Dismal (Swamp).[21] But he flees in vain, for once in Dismal he is confronted with the apparitions of Ibo warriors "turning in wind / that moaned like Africa." What he sees is his suffering Mother Africa contemplating her emasculated sons brought to a cultural death in America that is as final as that of the dead, hanged and swollen-tongued. He calls on his newly adopted Christian God.

God answers in the second half of the ballad, stanzas 6 through 17. The answer is a revelation given through an apocalyptic vision. Unlike Bahá'u'lláh in the Garden of Ridwan, who prayed surrounded by benevolent presences in the midnight air, Turner prays in Dismal, where he is surrounded by hostile, evil presences.

And wild things gasped and scuffled in
    the seething night; shapes
of evil writhed upon the air,
    I reeled with fear, I prayed.

In this vision the spiritual presences are like those in Hawthorne's "Young Goodman Brown." He is transported by his fervor and is shown an awesome revelation. Though the description of what he sees is couched in mystical language, it demonstrates that Hayden was continuing to forge the specialized language of religious transport which he began in his Bahá'i poems:

Sudden brightness clove the preying
    darkness, brightness that was
itself a golden darkness, brightness
    so bright that it was darkness.

When the personae in the vision appear, Turner sees that they are "angels at war / with one another" and that they are engaged in "holy battle." His description of this battle faintly recalls the war imagery used in the battle scene in Book VI and the expulsion scene in Book I of *Paradise Lost*. The Miltonic echoes seem evident in stanza 10, in which occurs such imagery as "The shock of wing on wing and sword / on sword," and in stanzas 12 and 13:

> I saw oh many of
> those mighty beings waver,
>
> waver and fall, go streaking down
>   into swamp water, and the water
> hissed and steamed and bubbled and locked
>   shuddering shuddering over

Nonetheless Turner's description of the holy war and his response to it bears the unmistakable imprint of Hayden's signature in its reflection of his early religious beliefs. This may be seen in the allusions to fundamentalist religion. An example occurs in Turner's emotional response to the vision he beholds

> the fearful splendor of that warring.
>   Hide me, I cried to rock and bramble.
> Hide me, the rock, the bramble cried.
>   How tell you of that holy battle?

Lines 2 and 3 of this stanza echo the Afro-American spiritual, "There's No Hiding Place Down Here," which was probably based on Amos 2:10–22, a passage that gives the prophet's description of judgment day. A second example occurs in stanza 11:

> for the wheel in a turning wheel which is time
>   in eternity had ceased
> its whirling, and owl and moccasin,
>   panther and nameless beast

The allusion in lines 1 and 3 is to an Afro-American spiritual that owes its primary source to Ezekiel 1:15–21, "Vision of the Wheels." Once again, as he does in "Sunflowers: Beaubien Street," Hayden makes symbolic use of one of the most striking of all of Israel's prophets. A man of God, a visionary, and iconoclast, and a prophet of hope, he ministered to the Israelites for at least twenty-two years, during the Babylonian captivity when they were becoming forcibly acculturated to an urban and alien way of life. Ezekiel's message was one of warning, to bring Judah to repentance and true faith in God, and also one of comfort and hope for the future, especially in his promises for the restoration of Israel. Moreover, his teachings promoted the idea of individual responsibility and divine retribution. The wheel allusion, then, refers to Ezekiel's inaugural vision in which he is called to be a prophet of God. Ezekiel is shown the omniscience of God—the chariot wheel-within-a-wheel that transports God from Jerusalem to Babylonia. And Ezekiel is commissioned to speak to the rebellious nation, summoning them to hear the word of God.[22] Turner, himself a zealot, a mystic, an avid reader of the Bible, and a leader of the slaves about him,[23] could have seen the similarities between his situation and that of Ezekiel. Certainly it seems to be the rationale which informs Hayden's design in the poem.

Another dimension of the poem which bears Hayden's distinctive signature is his portrayal of local color. It is the particular cachet of the southern swamp that he evokes in the poem. In stanza 11, lines 3 and 4, the creatures he names are precisely the inhabitants of such places: "owl and moccasin, / panther and nameless beast." In stanza 13, his references to swamp water and his description of its activity further and accurately develop the verisimilitude of the region.

Stanzas 14 and 15 recreate the birth of Turner's messianic mission at the moment it is revealed that, like his own, the conqueror's faces are black:

> and I
>
> beheld the conqueror faces and, lo,
>   they were like mine, I saw
> they were like mine and in joy and terror
>   wept, praising praising Jehovah.

The last two stanzas develop Turner's resolution of his problem and further describe his religious experience as a crucible in which he knows a death and a rebirth:

Oh praised my honer, harshener
    till a sleep came over me,
a sleep heavy as death. And when
    I awoke at last newborn

and purified, I rose and prayed
    and returned after a time
to the blazing fields, to the humbleness.
    And bided my time.

The closing work in *A Ballad of Remembrance* is "Frederick Douglass."[24] It is also the final Afro-American history poem in the book. It may be considered thematically in terms of the Afro-American's search for freedom and dignity; structurally, as a Hopkinsean sonnet.

The sonnet is a tribute to the Afro-American writer-orator, abolitionist, reformer, who rose against formidable odds to become a leader in the service of mankind. He spent the first twenty-one years of his life as a slave, separated from his parents. He was taught how to read by his owner's wife and then forbidden by her to do so. He was threatened with emasculation by a slave-breaker. When he was twenty-one years of age, he escaped from slavery; and, within the subsequent four years, he had become an internationally known abolitionist, writer, and reformer. By the time he was forty-six years of age, he had become a confidant of President Abraham Lincoln.[25]

The subject matter of the sonnet is confined to a definition of the significance of freedom, a definition of the inherent qualities of man's need to be free, and a tribute to Douglass that recognizes these qualities in him:

1 When it is finally ours, this freedom, this liberty, this
   beautiful
2 and terrible thing, needful to man as air,
3 usable as earth; when it belongs at last to our children,
4 when it is truly instinct, brainmatter, diastole, systole,
5 reflex action; when it is finally won; when it is more
6 than the gaudy mumbo jumbo of politicians:
7 this man, this Douglass, this former slave, this Negro
8 beaten to his knees, exiled, visioning a world
9 where none is lonely, none hunted, alien,

10 this man, superb in love and logic, this man
11 shall be remembered. Oh, not with statues' rhetoric,
12 not with legends and poems and wreaths of bronze alone,
13 but with the lives grown out of his life, the lives
14 fleshing his dream of the beautiful needful thing.

Lines 1 to 3 show elements of the natural environment indispensable to human existence on this planet, each of which is equated with freedom, to show how utterly essential freedom is to man. Lines 4 and 5 show man's absolute dependence on freedom in the same sense as man's existence is dependent on certain biological components of his body's characteristics and functions. Freedom is more, he goes on to say, than the "gaudy mumbo jumbo" of "politicians"—a satirical image which evokes not only the ambiguity of the politicians but the deviousness (as the poet sees it) of the lawmaker. Lines 7 through 11 recall Whitman's use of incremental repetition to support his presentation of an idea. Hayden begins by speaking of his subject first as a man, then as a person identified by name, then as a "former slave," then as a representative of a "race," yet endowed with the persisting vision of a world in which such disabilities may have become only memories of a painful past. To this capacity for envisioning a better future, he adds Douglass's further positive attributes—"logic" and "love." In line 8 the dominant features of his subject's life are telescoped, with "lonely," "hunted," "alien" as the key words. From line 10 to the end of the poem, while paying tribute to the part played by imaginative artists in perpetuating the memory of Douglass, Hayden shows that the actual persistence of Douglass's example and influence transcends the rhetoric expressed in statues, or even presumably in the Emancipation Proclamation itself. The grandest testimony of all to the greatness of Douglass is eloquent, Hayden says, in the "lives"—Afro-American lives certainly, but also the lives of all[26] the beaten yet hopeful persons before and after Douglass—of those who had embodied, or were to embody, the great reformer's "dream of the beautiful needful thing."

The poem provides an impressive example of how sound can support sense. This feature of the lyric is of crucial importance in promoting the achievement of "inscape" and "instress," which he was committed to do in taking Hopkins's sonnets as his model. Vocabulary creates images which combine with rhythm and sound to capture the unique totality of the subject, thus achieving Hopkins's "inscape" or vividness. Likewise, as his choice of specific words promotes "thisness," or the essence of the person and the idea of the preciousness of freedom in the poem, Hayden achieves Hopkins's "instress."

Hayden's choice of words in respect to their brevity and relative simplicity is not without significance here. Of the 103 words, 85 are one-syllable words, 26 are two-syllable words, and only one is a four-syllable word. Such choices make for directness and force. In several instances, the sound is an almost exact parallel to the sense, even in syllable count and manner of articulation: "diastole," "systole," "reflex," and "mumbo jumbo" may serve as examples. "Mumbo jumbo" serves also, because of its African origin, to help Hayden develop a special Afro-American flavor in this poem. Hayden's word usage is conducive to the richly subtle alliterative slant characteristic of this poem. He also has selected words which contribute to the sprung rhythm effect for which he was indebted to Hopkins (see line 5 for example).

Although Hayden has said that he wrote the poem when he was reading Hopkins, it is an interesting probability that he may have got his syncopated effect in this and other poems from Afro-American jazz. Line 3 of the sonnet provides a good example of Hayden's metrics; the line opens with a dactyl and is followed by an iambic, a trochaic, two more iambics, and a foot with two unstressed syllables followed by a stressed syllable and another unstressed syallable. This irregular line with its interposed downbeats is one of syncopation much like that of jazz.

The entire sonnet is made up of only two sentences. In the first, the thought is asserted; in the second, it is developed. Lines 1 through 11 (center) contain a periodic sentence made up of a series of conditional dependent clauses followed by an independent clause that drives home the point—"this man shall be remembered." Lines 11 through 14 contain an antithesis made up of two negative statements in which the clause "this man shall be remembered" is understood. The major divisions of thoughts are so interwoven that the sonnet structure becomes subordinate to meaning rather than vice-versa. Hayden uses run-on lines to emphasize his views. Similarly, in the first part the order of the sentence structure with three semicolons is used to contain his major points, only to release them at once with greater force. A similar structure is used in the second part, this time with a series set off by commas. Hopkins's "Duns Scotus's Oxford" provides an interesting structural parallel to this lyric.

Closely related to his Afro-American history poems but actually an Afro-American folk theme poem is "O Daedalus, Fly Away Home." It is the sole reprint from Hayden's prize-winning Hopwood Collection, and it is the poem that finally rewarded Hayden's efforts to have his work appear in *Poetry*.[27] The poem is a skillful blend of Afro-American folk and classical subject matter. An epigraph in-cluded in the first two versions of the poem indicates that it is based on the "Legend of the Flying African," which Hughes and Bontemps state is a part of the folklore of the Georgia Sea Island blacks.[28] This dramatic poem of six stanzas develops the speaker's invitation to a girl to dance with him:

1 Drifting night in the Georgia pines,
2 coonskin drum and jubilee banjo.
3   Pretty Malinda, dance with me.

4 Night is juba, night is conjo.
5   Pretty Malinda, dance with me.

6 Night is an African juju man
7 weaving a wish and a weariness together
8   to make two wings

9 *O fly away home fly away.*

10 Do you remember Africa?

Enchanted by the night, the music, and the girl, the speaker reflects on his slave heritage and his African roots. He recalls that his "gran" was one of those slaves who escaped slavery by flying back to Africa:

11 My gran, he flew back to Africa,
12 just spread his arms and
13 flew away home.

The classical Daedalus image compliments the "flying gran" image. The images together symbolize the blend of Western civilization with that of Africa, which the Afro-American actually represents.

African words and the names of African religious figures create a diction that promotes the voodoo theme so important in the lyric. The voodoo theme in "A Ballad of Remembrance" was a negative force that drew the observer into the charade of the Mardi Gras dance; in "Incense of a Lucky Virgin" it was treated as an unsuccessful potion that failed to bring her man home to a deserted mother. It is also used in "Witch Doctor"—a long character sketch included in *A Ballad of Remembrance* in which Hayden examines a modern avatar of a witch doctor who practices a mixture of voodooism and quasi-religious fundamentalism.[29] In "O Daedalus, Fly Away Home," however, voodooism is pictured as a positive force that effects escape from a dehumanizing plight. In the original legend, according to Bontemps, on a certain plantation there was an old man to whom the slaves turned for help when their suffering became unbearable. He would whisper a magic formula to them that was inaudible to others, whereupon he transformed them into winged creatures who flew back to Africa.[30] Thus the poem demonstrates the truth of Ralph Ellison's perceptive critique that Afro-Americans in their folklore "[back] away from the chaos of experience and from ourselves," in order to "depict the humor as well as the horror of our living."[31]

Hayden's use of literary voodooism draws from the well of folklore that is an integral part of the Afro-American literary tradition. In this respect he joins a series of Afro-American writers from Paul Laurence Dunbar to Jean Toomer to Ralph Ellison. Hayden, furthermore, could not have been unmindful of the example set by W. B. Yeats in his artistic use of Irish folklore.[32]

Notable among the memory poems of Hayden's childhood are those about his adoptive father who died in 1938.[33] As early as his first volume Hayden had answered his need to make a statement of filial love for him. In "Obituary," the most outstanding of a group of three in *Heart-Shape in the Dust*, he eulogized his adoptive father as a devoutly religious patriarch. In "This Grief," he expressed faith that his sorrow would pass and leave him "Unbowed, unbroken / scarred and wise," (lines 7–8).[34] In "Rosemary"—a title reminiscent of its symbolic use with Shakespeare—for the first time Hayden expresses the thought that he did not appreciate his father while he was alive.[35]

He never lived for us
Until he died;
We never knew him
Till he moved
Beyond the need
Of our too laggard knowing.

It remained, however, for "Those Winter Sundays" to capture the
essence of Hayden's particular regret: "time lost is spent."[36] In its
surface meaning the lyric is about a working father who rises earlier
than the other members of his family each day, including Sundays, to
make the house warm.

Sundays too my father got up early
and put his clothes on in the blueblack cold,
then with cracked hands that ached
from labor in the weekday weather made
banked fires blaze. No one ever thanked him.

I'd wake and hear the cold splintering, breaking,
and smell the iron and velvet bloom of heat.
When the rooms were warm, he'd call,
and slowly I would rise and dress, fearing

the chronic angers of that house, speaking
indifferently to him, who'd driven out
the cold and polished my
good shoes as well. What did I know,
what did I know of love's austere and lonely offices?

In one of his favorite ironic uses of romantic conventions—that
of drawing an analogy between external nature and human actions—
Hayden poses the "blueblack cold" of predawn Sunday mornings in a
reflection of wintry family relationships that are lacking in the
warmth engendered by love and mutual consideration. The phrase
"chronic angers of that house" suggests the corrosiveness of the
actual relationship. The image evokes a milieu of long-standing,
deeply rooted resentments that resist all efforts to be eradicated.
Confronted with this prospect, the boy is reduced to indifference or,

in another view, the need to resort to an adolescent ploy of seeming unconcern. One is reminded of the "quarrels and shattered glass" and of "elders" who "after each unrelenting day" were "shouting angry," a situation from which the same boy escaped in his fantasy world as a daredevil rider on "circus-poster horses."

Another poem, "The Whipping," gives the reader a further clue as to the nature of the relationship between the boy and certain adults.[37] It is a lyric about a woman who exhausts herself by whipping a boy to achieve her personal catharsis. Developed from the point of view of the poet-observer, the spectacle recalls Hayden's own childhood experience. What he remembers is not the humiliation of having his head caught between the woman's knees while she applied blows to his posterior, but:

> the fear
> worse than blows that cruel
>
> words could bring, the face that I
> no longer knew or loved. . . .

Noting that among the elements of ghetto life is the inhabitants' "cruelty to one another," Hayden states that this "is a sad poem, one that I had to write, almost as an act of expiation."[38]

The third subject group in *A Ballad of Remembrance* is "An Inference of Mexico," a suite of seven poems.[39] It was a great distance that Hayden had to go in order to create his Mexican poems, but only in terms of miles. He already had the interest and the language preparation. Also, his longstanding friendship with Langston Hughes, who had spent some time in Mexico with his father, may very well have had some influence on developing his interest in the Spanish-speaking country. Hughes, together with Arna Bontemps, sponsored Hayden for a Ford Foundation Fellowship in Creative Writing that provided his sojourn in Mexico from 1954 to 1955.

The dominant theme in Hayden's Mexican poems seems to be the reality which lies behind Mexico's appearance. The worst dimension of what he perceives to be Mexico's reality is the stultifying condition of poverty there that either shrouds the victims with apathy or reduces them to a demeaning scramble for subsistence. He reveals these perceptions in what he sees as Mexico's toleration of public begging and prostitution, its preoccupation with death, and its acceptance of poverty as a way of life for many of its citizens.

In contrast to this reality, Hayden ironically poses Mexico's awesome natural beauty—the beauty that the rich *turista* comes to see and enjoy. With the eyes of a painter, in "Veracruz" (poem 2), he sees the ricocheting brilliance of sun on water—the "arabesque ornately green" waves. In "Sub specie aeternitatis" (poem 5), he is struck by the sight of Mexico's "firegreen mountain" and "gothic rocks."

Beyond both the concrete reality of social wrongs and the local color that excites the tourist, Hayden perceives the ancient heritage of the land—a heritage that begins with the brilliant civilization of the ancient Aztecs and their too-exacting gods, of which he writes in "Idol" (poem 3, p. 50) and that includes the Aztec's conquest by the Spanish, who came with the sword in one hand and the Bible in the other to erect the fort and the convent, both of which, in their turn, were to fall.[40] The present point in this continuum is, of course, the plight of the Mexican poor.

These themes find their most successful symbiosis, perhaps, in "Veracruz," which demonstrates a cinematic development. Divided into two parts, it has Hayden's artistry with words, which he uses as a painter uses his brush, to achieve a Gauguin-like impression of the scene he surveys. The personae include several peons and the omniscient poet-observer:

> A shawled brown woman
> squinting against
> the ricocheting brilliance
> of sun and water
> shades her eyes and gazes
> toward the fort,
> fossil of Spanish power
> looming in the harbor.

In stanza 2, standing now at the site of the "fossil of Spanish power," the observer defines the shoreward view:

> the shore
> seen across marbling waves

is arabesque ornately green
that hides the inward-falling slum,
the stains and dirty tools of struggle;

The beauty of the shoreline, of course, represents an appearance which hides a harsh reality.

Hayden is more specific in his characterization of the "dirty tools of struggle" in both "Market" (poem 6, pp. 53–54) and "Day of the Dead" (poem 1, p. 46). For example, the Indian boys who fish and idle in "Veracruz" are, possibly, the same "ragged boys" who "lift sweets" during the week that he writes of in "Market"; they steal in the same market where the "barefoot cripple," crying "Por caridad, por caridad,"

foraging crawls
among rinds, orts,
chewed butts, trampled
peony droppings—
his hunger litany
and suppliant before
altars of mamey,
pineapple, mango.

In stanza 3 of "Veracruz," from the vantage point of the "pharos," the observer shifts his attention to the sea which he pronounces the sole reality:

Here only the sea is real—
the barbarous multifoliate sea
with its rustlings of leaves,
fire, garments, wind;
its clashing of phantasmal jewels,
its lunar thunder,
animal and human sighing.

The imagery in the stanza, echoing the harshness of the "bickering spray" and "ricocheting" imagery of stanza 1, evokes a reality that is brutal—memories of the Spanish galleons that came with gunpower, some of which sank, but a sufficient number of which remained to take away the riches.

Stanza 4 centers on the poet-observer. Is he overwhelmed by the reality of this ancient heritage of suffering as he was overwhelmed by the Afro-American's plight in "Sonnet To E."? Or is it that this reality serves only to intensify his own sense of inadequacies? In either event, as he does in "Sonnet to E.," and "Monody," again he clearly expresses a death wish:

> Leap now
> and cease from error.
> Escape. Or shoreward turn,
> accepting all—
> the losses and farewells,
> the long warfare with self,
> with God.

If the poet does, after all, propose a voluntary death for the Mexican peon in "Veracruz," he is not so puzzlingly oblique in showing the prospect of their involuntary death in "Day of the Dead." Here, the advent of death looms so significantly in the peon's life that a special day is set aside in observation of it. Death can be, he says, as commonplace for them as is the candy, the "marzipan skulls," that the children play with, and it can be as certain as is the kwashikoor, so endemic with the Mexican poor, which is as fatal as "almond sweetness"—a lethal potion of cyanide.

On the other hand, it could be the "error" of the peon's spiritual death and degradation through male and female prostitution that overwhelms the poet-observer in "Day of the Dead":

> In flowered shirt, androgynous,
> the young man under palmleaf knives of sunlight
> invites, awaits, obliquely smiles.
>
> > Such pretty girls, señor,
> > but if instead—

Here, Hayden demonstrates discerning realism and perceptiveness in his treatment of the morally stultifying tentacles that, in his view, have sprung from the peon's economic plight. This dimension of his literary concern, first focused on ghetto blacks, then, successfully, on poor whites, Jews, and European war victims, firmly emphasizes, in *A Ballad of Remembrance,* his thematic stance on the oppressed of all nations. It is a stance that indicts the oppressors and it is one from which Hayden does not waver in his subsequent volumes.

CHAPTER 5

Selected Poems (1966)

Twenty-six years after the American publication of *Heart-Shape in the Dust*, Hayden found an American publisher for *Selected Poems*, a compilation of forty-one pieces. Reviews of the volume were, with few exceptions, favorable. David Galler, however, criticized Hayden for being "saddled with both sentimentality [and] super erudition." Hayden, he said, "oscillat[ed] from semi-dialect and corrupted ballads to Poundian notation." He also accused him of "high eclecticism on the theological plane" and with not being satisfied with the example of Jesus as a white man would be. Galler's most cutting criticism, however, was in the form of an ambiguous compliment: although Hayden is as gifted a poet as we have, his problem is not one of talent but of frame of reference. Citing what he felt to be the finest verse in the book, the ironic speech in "Middle Passage" spoken by the Spanish sailor who witnessed the *Amistad* mutiny, he criticized Hayden's use of his "best" irony to depict the Spanish cause. He concluded his review by stating that Hayden had "not chosen his *forte;* it had chosen him."[1]

On the other hand, Robert Moore Allen wrote in the *Tennessean* that Hayden's "poetic talent is of the first order, and his poems reveal the hands of a skilled craftsman." He added that Hayden "had reached a profound understanding of his experience first as a human being and then as a human being involved in a particular situation . . . that of the Negro in the United States today." Whereas Galler stated, rather obscurely, that Hayden was mistakenly at his best when he portrayed the Spanish cause, Allen lauded Hayden's ability to portray

the Mexican peon's oppression and suffering, especially in "Market."
He joined other critics in pointing to "Those Winter Sundays" and
"The Whipping" as the superior poems in the volume.[2]

Gwendolyn Brooks, writing before her conversion in 1967 to the
black nationalist position, distinguished Hayden from the poet who,
"gasping in the field, writes right then, his wounds like faucets above
his page." She saw Hayden, rather, as one who "finds life always
interesting, sometimes appalling, but consistently amenable to a
clarifying enchantment via the power of Art." She cited "The Whipping" as an example of "life not lost in the refining process" and
"Middle Passage" as being powerful.[3]

Others who praised Hayden included book editor Herbert A.
Kinney, Cynthia Sinderis, and Allen Tate. Kinney proclaimed Hayden to be the "foremost Negro poet in the United States today," and
Cynthia Sinderis, unlike Galler, found Hayden's blues poetry and
ballads impressive.[4] Both she and Kinney were impressed with Hayden's use of his talent for artistic rather than propagandistic purposes.
Allen Tate wrote that he "greatly admired" Selected Poems as a book
done in Hayden's maturity when he would not, therefore, have to live
down his youthful poetic mistakes. "There are," he said, "many fine
short, or shorter poems" in the volume, and he cited "Middle Passage" as the piece that moved him most.[5]

Selected Poems demonstrates the maturation of Hayden's craftsmanship. In a sense, as Hayden stated, it is the volume that marks the
beginning of his career as a poet.[6] Presenting as it does so much
revised material from A Ballad of Remembrance, the Selected Poems
necessarily repeats the themes of the earlier volume. The measure of
Hayden's philosophic growth and thematic range during the 1960s,
therefore, rests significantly on A Ballad of Remembrance, from
which twenty-seven of the pieces in Selected Poems are revised
reprints. Of the remaining poems, five were published previously
while nine are new.[7] His habit of constant revision, however, demonstrates the growth and perfecting of his craftsmanship.

The nine poems that were not included in A Ballad of Remembrance make up part 1 of Selected Poems. Three other poems not
published in A Ballad of Remembrance appear in other parts of the
volume. The eight poems which will be discussed in this section
were chosen from these poems, and they represent Hayden's development from 1962 to 1966. However, it should be acknowledged that

Hayden's growth is also indicated by his careful but non-thematic and minor editing of all the selections carried over from *A Ballad of Remembrance* and included in *Selected Poems*. The most representative of these poems were discussed in the preceding chapter. Because Hayden's editing was non-thematic, none of these poems will be discussed here. The burden of testimony for *Selected Poems* will rest on the eight poems referred to above.

These "new" poems may be categorized thematically in three areas: man in relation to man, man in relation to nature, and man in relation to himself.

The first of these thematic concerns may be seen in "The Rabbi," a poem about man's sense of alienation from other men.[8] This nostalgic poem recreates Hayden's sense of exclusion from the religious rituals of his Jewish playmates, David, Hirschel, and Eva. The reader will be poignantly reminded that these are the real-life children whom Hayden elegizes as Nazi victims in "From the Corpsewood Piles, from the Ashes" (p. 60), a new version of "In light half nightmare, half vision" from *A Ballad of Remembrance.*

The man-in-relation-to-man theme continues in two poems about black-white relations in the South. One of them is biographical in origin. As mentioned in chapter 1, Hayden was inspired to write "The Ballad of Sue Ellen Westerfield" both by accounts of her past told him by his adoptive mother, who is named in the title, and memories of his natural mother.[9] The ballad gains a special significance in that it is Hayden's sole contribution to the "tragic mulatto" theme. It is of further interest because it does not portray the conventional resolution to that theme, for the virtually white lover does not reject Sue Ellen once he finds out the reality beneath her appearance.

The poem narrates the tale of a beautiful mulatto riverboat chambermaid and her white lover. The first stanza brings alive the spectre of so-called miscegenation that hung over the South; Sue Ellen is the child of a "white man who had wept and set her black mother free." Hardened in perilous river towns until "after the Surrender," she became a maid on "Floating Palaces" (lines 5–6). Stanza 2, developed in flashback, now that she is an old woman who can never forget him, describes her "lover with blue eyes" and the courtship which caused her to "[curse] the circumstances" (line 22). Stanza 3 describes the horror-filled night when the riverboat caught fire, her lover rescued her, and they decided to flee in "the wild and secret dark" (line 40). The denouement, given in stanza 4, develops the idea of the lovers' precarious existence as fugitives from society and Sue Ellen's eventual rejection of her lover because "she could not forfeit what she was" (line 46). The Sue Ellen ballad speaks, as no other poem in Hayden's canon, of the human dilemma of a reality so poignantly but irremediably contrasted with an appearance that even the powers of love cannot solve it.

"Night, Death, Mississippi" also is concerned with interracial male-female relations.[10] Unlike the Sue Ellen poem, however, here the most rigid of the racial taboos has been broken—that is, the black man/white woman taboo. "Night, Death, Mississippi" is about the penalty imposed on the black man for breaking this taboo as well as the moral and psychological involvement of the victim's executioners. Hayden chooses to avoid the graphic treatment of the lynching victim that he gave in "Figure"; instead he frames the grisly episode in the imaginings and the physical and psychological responses of an old white man. The cry of a "screech owl" interwoven with what might be the victim's outcries introduces the problem of reality vis-à-vis appearance that is not resolved until the last stanza, when "Boy," whom the old man awaits, returns home from the lynching and "Maw" matter-of-factly says to the children:

> You kids fetch Paw
> some water now so's he
> can wash that blood
> off him.

What motivates Paw and his clan is indicated in Hayden's oblique but telling allusion to William Faulkner's "The Bear." However, whereas Old Ben is such an admired and loved symbol of the wilderness, of freedom and courage, and of the fruitful earth that Sam Fathers and the McCaslins sham-hunt him for years and destroy him only when he turns on the exploiters of the earth, Hayden's hunters kill their prey out of vengeance and the grisly thrill of blood-letting:

> Christ, it was better
> than hunting bear
> which don't know why
> you want him dead.

The old man, reminiscing about past lynchings that he has been a party to, recalls with pleasure an occasion when they "unbucked . . . one"—a graphic description of the physical emasculation of the victim—and plans a macabre celebration:

> Have us a bottle,
> Boy and me—
> he's earned him a bottle—
> when he gets home.

The poem is Hayden's most devastating attack on lynching as what was, even in the sixties, an integral part of southern society.[11] The poem reveals how the neo-chivalric elements in southern society and the deep-seated theoretical and pragmatic aspects of lynching have become pervasive—a way of life—at the level of the common redneck who participates in a treasured spectacle that relieves the monotony of his dull and empty life.

"Runagate Runagate," as well as its companion Afro-American history poems (new versions of selections from *A Ballad of Remembrance*), develops the man-in-relation-to-man (through black in relation to white) theme. In it, Hayden treats the exploits of the celebrated black revolutionist Harriet Tubman, who freed many slaves. The poem was first published in 1949 but did not at that time really satisfy Hayden, who revised it for the *Selected Poems*.[12]

"Runagate Runagate," an archaic expression for a runaway slave, opens with especially keen heights of dramatic tension that bring alive the sense of dangerous enterprise and desperate, breathless, and uneven flight that the runaway slaves must have experienced:

> Runs falls rises stumbles on from darkness into darkness
> and the darkness thicketed with shapes of terror
> and the hunters pursuing and the hounds pursuing
> and the night cold and the night long and the river
> to cross and the jack-muh-lanterns beckoning beckoning
> and blackness ahead and when shall I reach that somewhere
> morning and keep on going and never turn back and keep on
>   going
>
>   Runagate
>   Runagate
>   Runagate

Verbs in the present tense, lack of punctuation, use of various feet from the prevailing trochaics in line 1, extra syllables in line 4, help evoke the sense of dramatic tension and create reader involvement in the situation. Throughout the remainder of parts 1 and 2 of the poem, changes in cadence, the techniques of fragmentation that he used so effectly in "Middle Passage"—lines from hymns, spirituals, anti-slavery songs, wanted posters, voices of the slaves and of Harriet Tubman—and typographical spacing that helps carry the sense of the passages while further demonstrating Hayden's debt to T. S. Eliot, reveal that the poem does, indeed, belong to the same creative period as "Middle Passage." "Runagate Runagate" however, must surely have been intended as a companion piece to "The Ballad of Nat Turner," for it treats the part of the female revolutionist in the anti-slavery war that blacks raised in their own fight to be free.

Hayden's revisions of "Runagate" for the 1966 version are characteristic: rearrangement of passages for better order, cadence, and emphasis; a stripping away of rhetoric to develop sharper images. These changes, slight in part 1, are marked in part 2, where he shifts the emphasis from a rhetorical and laudatory description of Harriet Tubman to a few lines that show her in action and vividly evoke her presence.

On the other hand, in "Kid," a poem on the Mexican theme, Hayden achieves a new emphasis.[13] Here he makes his most telling criticism of the great disparity he sees in Mexico between the peon and the rich—that is, the rich American visitor. The poem develops further the idea in his earlier poem "Market" of the Mexican boys who steal sweets. Here their misery and poverty are contrasted with silly "gringos in dollar bills / [who] deplore and sip."

Two of the new poems treat man in relation to nature. In the highly dramatic "Electrical Storm," the subject is his and his wife's narrow escape from fallen high voltage wires in the aftermath of a storm.[14] He uses the incident to ponder the effect of a storm on common folk whose superstitions and faith in God see them safely through it and his own intellectual distance from these beliefs, which he once held. Was it, he wonders, chance or God's design that caused a neighbor to caution them about the fallen wire and so prevent their death? The other poem, "Full Moon," is a reflective piece about man's exploration of the moon.[15] Although it was composed before the first landing, Hayden realized that the conquest of the moon was inevitable. The speaker takes a romantic view and sees the conquest as a violation of ancient concepts, folk beliefs, and his own childhood ideas. Its exploration takes some of the mystical aura from Christ in Gethsemane and Bahá'u'lláh on the exile's path.

"Approximations" is another of the memory poems, and through Hayden's personal bereavement develops the theme of man in relationship to himself.[16] By 1960, both his natural parents and his adoptive parents were dead.[17] By shifting the scene from one place to the other and the perspective from one time to another, the poem develops the disorderly rush of impressions attendant upon grief. The reader is with the mourner in the falling snow at the grave site, with him while he fumbles in the dark getting ready to make the sorrowful trip, and again at the grave site where he recalls their ghetto Beaubien Street past:

> Not sunflowers, not
> roses, but rocks in patterned
> sand grow here. And bloom.

The final haiku stanza delineates the railroad depot where both mail bags and coffins are waiting in approximation to each other, each to be taken to its final destiny.

The subject matter of "The Diver," the poem which opens *Selected Poems*, is obliquely private.[18] Literally, it is about a deep-sea diver who descends to the ruins of a ship long lost at sea, where he almost succumbs to "rapture of the deep"—nitrogen deficiency intoxication—which might have made him unable to resurface. The poem is notable for Hayden's characteristically accurate evocation of atmosphere and occupational flavor.[19] Thus, the diver "sank through easeful azure . . . swiftly descended . . . tree-falling . . . weightless . . . plunged." Enchanted by what he sees in the ship, he lingers almost fatally. Brought to realize his danger, he "in languid / frenzy strove . . . began the measured rise." The sea atmosphere is described with scientific accuracy: "azure, a canyon of cold / nightgreen emptiness . . . infra- / space," "darkness . . . iron cold . . . fogs of water." Then there is the "dead ship," a carcass, her metal obscured by moss of bryozoans. In the ship are "flower creatures . . . voracious life," lively blue-and-yellow angel fish, snappers, gold groupers, bubbling manfish. The great ballroom, which now contains "dancing gilded chairs," "[swirling] garments," and "drunken shoes," seems to be filled with "hidden ones" perhaps dancing to the music of the "drowned instruments" that were buoyant. The scene is illuminated by the flashlight. Finally, in a passage that recalls Frost's spectator in the snowy woods, the "respirator's brittle belling" alerts the diver to resurface.

A second group of images creates another level of meaning: the rejection of pleasure that is based on the senses. But first the principle of sensual pleasures is clearly established. Both the poem's title and content carry an allusion to "Deep Sea Diver," an erotic Afro-American blues which extols the prowess of a virile black lover. Moreover, notwithstanding Maurice O'Sullivan's objections,[20] the poem's central metaphor—diving into the sea—is a Freudian symbol for the sexual act, the sea being a female symbol and the poem itself typographically suggesting a phallic symbol. Beyond these, there are certain ambiguities of diction: "explored her . . . I entered . . . feeling . . . probing . . . buoyancy . . . I yearned . . . I craved . . . yield . . . have done with self . . . I began the measured rise." Later these sensual allusions become identified with, and perhaps dissolved in, "those hidden / ones" whom the speaker—like the speaker in Keats's "Ode to a Nightingale," who is "half in love with easeful death"—wishes to join. Thus death becomes a half-wish and is seen as beautiful and attractive. In it the speaker begins to see a sensuousness beyond mere sensual pleasure.

There are a number of parallels between "The Diver" and the Keats poem, some of them imagistic and others thematic. The parallels in imagery are probably due to Hayden's longstanding admiration for Keats; the similarities in theme are probably due to similar emotional outlooks.

Like Keats's speaker in "Ode to a Nightingale," Hayden's diver flees "the numbing kisses that [he] craved." Keats's listener suffers from a "drowsy numbness"; Hayden's diver "sank through easeful / azure" (which in addition to recalling Keats's "easeful death" line in "Ode to a Nightingale," recalls his "azure-lidded sleep" line in "The Eve of St. Agnes"). The diver's experience as he "sank into canyon of cold / nightgreen emptiness" where hidden ones gestured and whispered to him is not unlike that of the speaker in "Ode to a Nightingale" in which he "Lethewards had sunk," then heard the bird singing among "shadows numberless." Furthermore, Hayden's "nightgreen emptiness" and "darkness" that is illuminated only by his flashlight's beam recalls Keats's

> But here is no light,
> Save what from heaven is with the breezes blown
> Through verdurous glooms and winding mossy ways.[21]

Just as the diver who has "yearned to find those hidden ones" wants to "yield . . . have done with self and / every dinning complexity" (lines 50–53), so does the speaker in "Ode to a Nightingale" want to

> leave the world unseen,
> And with thee fade away among the forest dim:

> Fade far away, dissolve and quite forget
> What thou amongst the leaves hast never known,
> The weariness, the fever, and the fret
> Here, where men sit and hear each other groan;

Hayden's diver seeks to escape "every dinning complexity" in a "nightgreen" sea; Keats's speaker seeks to escape the "fret," etc., in a "beechen green" forest. Both places epitomize nature; both are sides of the same coin. Hayden's sea teems with exotic and gorgeous marine life, including "moss of bryozoans" which cover the ship. Keats's forest is replete with luxuriant flora and "winding mossy ways." As the diver "fled the numbing kisses," likewise, the speaker in "Ode to a Nightingale" withdraws from a "drowsy numbness." Furthermore, the agent that perhaps saved the diver's life—the "respirator's brittle / belling"—seems to echo the agent that alerts the speaker in Keats's poem—"the very word . . . like a bell" that "tolls [him] back from thee to [his] sole self!"

Beyond these imagistic tracings, there are deeper similarities. According to Earl R. Wasserman in *The Finer Tone*,[22] Keats outlined in "Endymion" a "pleasure thermometer" as a series of increasing intensities that result in one's becoming selflessly assimilated into essence. As the experience becomes more exquisite, one is more free of the physical self and the phenomenal world and at last lives in essence. As one retreats from passionate selflessness, the two elements separate out of their organic union into strong emotion and loss of self. And if these two are evaluated, not as they carry one toward the dynamic stasis of heaven but as they appear within the framework of merely mortal experience, the powerful emotion becomes only painfully exquisite sensation, and the selflessness—the wrong kind—becomes a drowsy numbness, a slipping Lethewards, such as takes place in "Ode to a Nightingale," rather than the spiritual elevation Porphyro and Madeline achieve in "The Eve of St. Agnes." In this view, then, what Hayden seems to be describing in "The Diver" is a situation the protagonist faces that would gratify the senses at the expense of elevating the spirit. As Keats's speaker turns away from the symbolic bird of song to return to the affairs of men, likewise Hayden turns away from his unseen musicians to resurface and rejoin the affairs of men—his own kind—for, as he says in "The Ballad of Sue Ellen Westerfield," "[he] could not forfeit what he was."

But what is the specific cause of the death wish expressed in "The Diver?" In three earlier poems Hayden has had a speaker contemplate the benefits of suicide, twice in *Heart-Shape in the Dust*, in "Monody" and in "Sonnet to E." In both of these instances the death wish seems to have come when his speaker wearied over, but continued in, the cause of the black struggle.

Again he considered the death wish in "Veracruz." This time the wish "stemming from ambiguous causes" seems to be prompted by the hopelessness of the Mexican peon that surrounded him—or the sense of his speaker's *"long warfare with self, / with God."* Hayden states that he was motivated to write "The Diver" by a "sense of his own inadequacies." Adding to his publicized statement that the poem is a private one, he states that it has a very personal meaning— one that comes of a period of despondency during which he hit new lows, but from which he managed to rise.[23]

What Hayden deletes from his 1960 Notebook version of the poem should supply some insight as to the origin of the poem, if not its final version.[24] He takes out:

> I swam to her,
> anxious, elated,
> feeling more
> keenly now
> the iron cold,
> the hammering thrust
> and heavy tension of the heavy depths

"Narrow passageway" and "frenzied languor / interlocked me" are also phrases in the Notebook draft.

The sensual quality of the experience carries over into the 1966 version, but clearly it is subdued, less specific. Less specific also is the nature of the ship, traditionally a female symbol. In the 1960 draft it is "ghostly white." It is in this draft, also, that the diver leaves the ship with a particular destination and purpose:

> began the ascent
> the tortuous climb
> back to troubled
> light and my own
> kind again.

Is it, indeed, the question of an intimate alignment with a person of another color,[25] or the fact that he was caught up, as ever he was, in what he said was his "condition"—his being "bisexual"—that the poet equates with death? If so, Hayden is careful in his portrayal of death as the consequence of the experience he describes; he develops the picture of ruin, decay, darkness, cold, a cancelling-out of identity, numbness. Is the poet saying that such an alignment which would gratify the senses at the expense of himself as thinking man, an alignment with a person who seems to be identified as white, would be tantamount to the death of his true self and his higher achievement as a singer of the black experience? If so, by the time of the 1966 version in *Selected Poems* Hayden saw fit to generalize the experience, to emphasize the small bell that reminded him of the world above. His diver

> strove, as
> one freezing fights off
> sleep desiring sleep:
> strove against the
> cancelling arms that
> suddenly surrounded
> me, fled the numbing
> kisses that I craved.

If, then, there is either a racial problem or the vicissitudes he said he suffered in his sexual identity buried in the origins of "The Diver,"

Hayden's artistic sense resolved it into human experience, colored with his own sense of hope. What the speaker will do when he surfaces is left to the imagination. It may be said, however, that unlike Keats's listener, he has struggled to get there. This essentially modern struggle is characteristic of Hayden's career.

Beginning in 1941, he became more concerned with the human predicament than with the question of race. He consciously created a distance between himself and his subject matter. His themes, although oriented to the racial question so dominant in the sixties and seventies, have essentially progressed from exposé in *Heart-Shape in the Dust* to consideration of the black experience as it applies to every man. The black experience which Hayden describes in *Selected Poems* is, therefore, often universal. The finest weapons in his arsenal are truth and love. Each of his key poems evinces a maturation of his craftsmanship and resounds with truth reinforced by a sense of passionate commitment and love engendered by his humanistic vision of man free of poverty and oppression.

Selected Poems marks a turning point in Hayden's career. Up until this point he was an experimenter and an apprentice. Though he had distinguished himself with Afro-American history poems and characterizations, and though he had revealed a fine sense of the past in relation to the present, his poetry was often flawed by unevenness, flamboyance, and virtuosity to excess. At times he lost himself in symbolism for its own sake. His production following *Selected Poems* shows signs of a different set of assumptions. This volume is characterized by a new economy and a surer command of the poetic device in service of the subject.

CHAPTER 6

Words in the Mourning Time (1970)

A year after his departure from Fisk University and the Deep South in 1969, Hayden completed *Words in the Mourning Time*. Chiding his "noisome detractors," in this volume he restates and reaffirms his values as a poet. The biographical significance of the book is revealed in his statement that it is a work of catharsis.[1] The creation of *Words* was probably inspired by the chafing experience at the Black Writers Conference at Fisk in 1966.

Despite the militancy of the times, it is, therefore, ironical that Hayden's new volume was favorably received by most black writers. Richard Barksdale, for example, observed that *Words in the Mourning Time* was a successful encounter with the black experience and a confirmation of Hayden's ability to sustain a high quality of writing over the years.[2] Julius Lester praised Hayden's ability to render images that give the reader a new experience of the world and to "choose words with the care of a sculptor chipping into marble." He cited "El-Hajj Malix El-Shabazz" as demonstrative of this artistry.[3]

White critics were likewise generally favorable. Fellow-poet Chad Walsh wrote that Hayden "is beginning to be recognized for what he is—the finest Negro poet living in America, and one of the handful of top American poets of any skin." Walsh was especially impressed with several pieces in the volume, including the Malcolm X poem, which he judged to be one of the few successful elegies on recent assassination victims. Unlike other critics, Walsh felt that Hayden's Bahá'í note was unobtrusive, though the book ends with a strong declaration of faith. In closing, Walsh recommended that

Hayden be given a Pulitzer Prize or a National Book Award for the volume.[4]

The theme of *Words in the Mourning Time* is suggested by the title. A topical work, the collection deals with the decade of the sixties, characterized by racial unrest, disruptive political dissent, assassination of leaders, and the unpopular Vietnam War. The book is an affirmation of Hayden's belief that the solution to the ills that plague America lies in man's love for his fellow man. Based on his belief, he makes his most insistent avowal of Baháism as a precept of the corrective force of love.

It is "mourning time," the key phrase in the title, that sets the dominant tone in the book. In the broader etymological sense of the phrase, and concerning the public subjects treated in certain of the poems, Hayden implores the reader to remember and mourn the decade of the sixties as symptomatic of manifest evils in the fabric of American society. More than that, he would have the reader channel his anxiety in correcting evils that resulted in assassination of the country's leaders and that might well have wrecked the ship of state. On the private level of his own psyche, and as he approaches the sunset of his own life, he mourns what he has begun to think of as his own sins.

The public domain is treated in the two poems that develop section 3 of the book. "El-Hajj Malix El-Shabazz (Malcolm X)" is an elegy to the assassinated controversial black leader, and "Words in the Mourning Time," the title poem, elegizes the Reverend Martin Luther King and Robert Kennedy, also assassinated. While the civil unrest and the Vietnam War are subject matter in these two poems, their major significance lies in the fact that they carry Hayden's most severe indictment of America's social oppression as well as his most emphatically stated solution to these problems.

If the fact that the Malcolm X assassination predated the respective assassinations of King and Kennedy thus dictated Hayden's placement of the poem first in this section, so might we speculate that Hayden saw the Malcolm X killing as a forerunner of the others. The elegy is a four-part treatment of the fallen black leader, as he lived in Detroit; as he awakened to see himself and fumbled to attain a viable identity; as he was a Black Muslim leader; and as he developed fatal differences with other leaders in a sect which is an off-shoot of the orthodox Islam faith, became converted to the latter, and died a martyr. The elegy demonstrates Hayden's craftsmanship in evoking, objectifying, and giving new significance to Malcolm X's life and his meaning for America.[5]

Part 1 both introduces the effective compression that character-izes the poem and develops a severe indictment of the iron circum-stances that characterized Malcolm X's early years:

> The icy evil that struck his father down
> and ravished his mother into madness
> trapped him in violence of a punished self
> struggling to break free.
>
> As Home Boy, as Dee-troit Red,
> he fled his name, became the quarry of
> his own obsessed pursuit.
>
> He conked his hair and Lindy-hopped,
> zoot-suited jiver, swinging those chicks
> in the hot rose and reefer glow.
>
> His injured childhood bullied him.
> He skirmished in the Upas trees
> and cannibal flowers of the American Dream—

The "icy evil" metaphor that serves to effect compression is sup-ported by an image cluster that includes the picture of the mother who was "ravished into madness," a "punished self," self as quarry from its "own obsessed pursuit," an "injured childhood" that the subject tried to escape by capitalizing on his charms with women and by taking drugs, an adult "bullied by his childhood" whose struggles amounted to mere skirmishing with the "enemy / powered against" him. The enemy is the perverted American Dream, which is equated with poisonous trees and flowers that devour. The language serves to ironically evoke the confines of the Afro-American ghetto life-style into which Malcolm X was locked as well as the American Dream he sought to find. That life-style is characterized by the black man who "conked [straightened] his hair" in the effort to define himself by the white man's image, a man who became a "jiver," a Don Juan type who exploited women, and a drug addict who sought escape by smoking "reefers" (marijuana). Thus, the metaphor evokes the oppression, persecution, and death suffered by Malcolm X's father, who was a Marcus Garvey activist in then-racist East Lansing, Michigan; it evokes the madness that befell the black leader's mother as a result of her failing struggles to cope with hunger, insecurity, and dashed hopes when her husband, the father of their seven children, was killed; and it evokes Malcolm X's own traumatic experiences with disruption of his family life, displacement in foster homes and reformatories, and struggles as a product of his background.[6]

Hayden develops part 2 through use of a central analogy that is based on a Dantean allusion in which Malcolm X, the ghetto con man of part 1, is now seen as " 'Satan' in the Hole" (line 20). Here, the poet characterizes the hero's life as being governed by the dark—that is, spiritual darkness—albeit a darkness that "would shift a little" so that, driven to realize the American Dream as he was, "he saw himself / floodlit and eloquent" (lines 18–19). The black leader's quest for a viable identity led him to become a Black Muslim—a commitment which attains for him mere partial vision: "adulterate attars [that] could not cleanse / him of odors of the pit" (lines 29–30).

Hayden's criticism of Black Muslim racist precepts about the nature of God and man is explicit. It is a criticism that Hayden continues in the "Yakub's white-faced treachery" (line 27) reference to the Black Muslim theological explanation of the origin and nature of the white race.[7] Hayden extends his criticism, moreover, to include fundamentalist Christianity—that is, Calvinism—which he unfavorably characterizes in his "hellward-thrusting hands of Calvin's Christ" (line 25), clearly an allusion to Jonathan Edwards's "Sinners in the Hands of an Angry God" sermon. The Dantean allusion and its logical extension in the Mather allusion is developed with such terms as "dark," "cold," "satanic," "The Hole," "black light," "hellward-dipping," "pit," effectively suggesting the depravity that marked the assassinated leader's early days.

The Arabic expression *"Asalam alaikum!"* begins part 3 of the elegy. It is an Islamic greeting, meaning "Peace be with you," which manifests Hayden's characteristic command of relevant ambience and establishes an ironic tone. On the one hand, the expression evokes the Near East flavor and setting of the orthodox religion. On the other hand, it sets up the contrast between the peaceful meaning of what is said and the almost warlike fervor of what was done—that is, Malcolm X's militant role and action as a Black Muslim minister who would rightly scourge his people from the "lush ice gardens of their servitude" (line 37), but who wrongheadedly scourged them into racial and political separation. Appropriately, this section ends with the second Melvillian allusion in the poem: Malcolm X rejects Captain Ahab of *Moby Dick* as a white man, but accepts Ahab's monomania:

> Rejecting Ahab, he was of Ahab's tribe.
> "Strike through the mask."
>
> (Line 40)

The relationship of the two is that Malcolm X, at the point of his Black Muslim ministry, and Captain Ahab both endeavored to solve the conundrum of the nature of evil but became a part of the evil they sought to define. In the "Strike through" admonition, Hayden decries Malcolm X's Black Muslim ministry as merely a mask that cloaks an evil it purports to correct.

The final section of this elegy treats the results of Malcolm X's Black Muslim involvement: his "Hejira" [Hejra] to Mecca and conversion to orthodox Islam, which successfully ended his search for a viable identity but also brought his "ironic trophies of his [Black Muslim] faith" . . . that is, the "karate killer / knifer, gunman" (lines 42–44). The death that they deal, however, is a martyr's death, one that comes from an ominous source: "the fruit of neo-Islam" (line 46)—militarily trained young male Black Muslims who reinforce internal discipline within the Black Muslim group, as well as provide security from outside forces.[8] In the hero's death Malcom X finds a viable identity—viable, certainly, to the extent that the new religious commitment affiliated him with a "raceless Allah" and assimilated him into a raceless world brotherhood[9] which, certainly the reader will recognize, are ideals that Hayden shares.

Concluding the delineation of Malcolm X's martyrdom is the Arabic expression, *"Labbayk! Labbayk!"* (line 41), chanted by pilgrims on their way to Mecca. According to Malcolm X, the expression means "Here I come, O Lord."[10] Given this interpretation, Hayden's use of the expression perhaps suggests the leader's spiritual ascendancy as an orthodox convert to Islam. The structural and connotative ambiguity of the Arabic language, however, gives credence to another interpretation: according to one authority, the Arabic expression means "For your father! For your father!"[11] If this interpretation is correct, the expression further develops Near East spirit as well as alludes to the convert's fulfillment of his deceased father's Garveyite mission. It may also be read as Hayden's allusion to Malcolm X's forerunners in his gallery of Afro-American heroes—Cinquez, Crispus Attucks, Gabriel Prosser, Nat Turner, and Frederick Douglass—who fought to make the black man free.

The *Words in the Mourning Time* version of "El-Hajj Malik El-Shabazz" is an emended version. The elegy was first published in *For Malcolm*.[12] In comparison with the *Words* version, it reveals that Hayden's emendations are characteristically not thematic, but are minor and serve primarily to refine meaning. For example, the earlier version A of lines 20–21 is

> yet how could he, "Satan" in The Hole
> guess what the waking dream prefigured

In the later version B, the semantically and accentually weak "prefigured" becomes the emphatic and accentuated "foretold." In a second instance of emendation, the interesting oxymoron "black light" in version A, "then black light of partial vision came" (line 22), becomes "false dawn" in version B. It is a choice that more concisely and precisely alludes to the mistaken and misleading precepts of Black Muslimism that Malcolm X had embraced. A third emendation occurs in line 25. In version A the line was characterized by placidity: "the hellward-dipping hands of Calvin's Christ—." The substitution of "thrusting" for "dipping" more appropriately evokes the dynamic force of Satan locked in his titanic struggle with God for the soul of man. Other very minor emendations occur in version B, where the decision has been made to begin stanzas with capital letters only at the beginning of sentences—a choice that more effectively underlines the areas of the elegy's organization of thought. The last emendation was made, perhaps, to achieve unity: the last two stanzas in version A become one stanza in version B.

Reviewers of *Words* noted that the Malcolm X elegy is one of the outstanding pieces in the book. An examination of the many elegies written in memory of the fallen black leader in *For Malcolm* will reveal that Hayden's poem is, indeed, superior. Fair characterizations for most of them would be philippic, rhetorical, one-dimensional, and even such a relatively superior poem as Conrad Kent Rivers's "If Blood is Black then Spirit Neglects my Unborn Son"[13] does not contain the rich allusion, symbolism, comprehensivity of Hayden's poem.

The fallen leader theme recurs in the title poem, albeit less effectively.[14] The sustained lyric of ten parts opens with a tribute to Martin Luther King and Robert Kennedy, the assassinated religious and political leaders:

> For King, for Robert Kennedy,
> destroyed by those they could not save,
> for King for Kennedy I mourn.
> And for America, self-destructive, self-betrayed.
>
> I grieve. Yet know the vanity
> of grief—through power of
> The Blessed Exile's
> transilluminating word
>
> aware of how these deaths, how all
> the agonies of our deathbed childbed age
> are process, major means whereby,
> oh dreadfully, our humanness must be achieved.

Although Hayden places King and Kennedy prominently in the opening stanza, this prominence is quickly dissipated in the second and third stanzas in what eventually becomes the second of the two dominant themes in the poem—that is, Baháism. The "Blessed Exile's / transilluminating word / . . . whereby, / . . . our humanness must be achieved" (lines 8, 11–12) is an allusion, of course, to the founder of the Bahá'i religion, Bahá'u'lláh, and to his precepts. What is thus far an expression of grief for the two fallen leaders and the bad times that had befallen America becomes now a consolation in which the poet submits gracefully to the tragedies and inevitability of death and declares his conviction that immortality and hope lies in Bahá'u'lláh's example.

The third theme is the poet's continuing preoccupation with man's ultimate fate—death—his own death. It is, moreover, the ameliorating force of the Bahá'i promise that social calamities, war, suffering, are the necessary crucibles in which the individual, the nation, is honed to attain a temporal millenium—"The Most Great Peace" as well as ultimate spiritual oneness with God.[15]

In part 2, keeping his strategy to juxtapose domestic unrest in America with the international conflict abroad, Hayden alludes to the Vietnam War. He develops a grim paradox that evokes the picture of a war that is fought to save and free the very people that it devastates and destroys with napalm. In part 3, the discordant note of the poet's voice rings out in prosodic, strident empathy and a graphic description of the key attendant to war—death, whom he personifies as a guest at his own table who leaves the grisly remnants of his trade.

In part 4, Hayden makes clear the specific war that the napalm reference foreshadows: "Vietnam bloodclotted name in my consciousness / recurring and recurring" (lines 21–22). Like a litany, Vietnam recurs throughout the section as Hayden establishes his sympathy for the Vietnamese people, their school children, and his former students who are sent to destroy them. Likewise, the poet's concern with his own mortality strikes again its insistent note "the obsessive thought many midnights / now of my own dying" (lines 23–24).

Turning to the domestic scene in part 5, Hayden develops a synecdoche that links the racial strife at home with the war abroad: "Our world— / this violent ghetto, slum / of the spirit raging against itself" (lines 34–36). Accordingly, in part 6, there is a powerful evocation of the conflict that hung so heavily over America in the sixties:

```
Lord Riot
        naked
            in flaming clothes
cannibal ruler
        of anger's
                carousals
        sing hey nonny no
terror
        his tribute
                shriek or bloody glass
his praise
        sing wrathful sing vengeful
            sing hey nonny no
```

gigantic
      and laughing
            sniper on tower
I hate
    I destroy
        I am   I am
      sing hey nonny no
      sing burn baby burn

Hayden's indictment is daring and unpopular, but it is not unexpected in its denunciation of both the rioters and the malice that set them on destructiveness. In support of this sense he shifts the rhythm of this section from that of old English song to that of the black militant's chant. Also in support of sense, he uses a Cummings-like typography which zigzags in a broken, unpunctuated arrangement. Cacaphony also contributes to sense and tension.

In part 7, Hayden offers a daring solution to the Vietnam War and the social unrest at home. Through the "voice in the wilderness," no doubt King's, Kennedy's, and his, as well as Bahá'u'lláh's voice, the poet issues a ringing call for universal love.

Again focusing on the American strife as it involves the Afro-American, in part 8, Hayden elaborates on "our deathbed child-bed age . . . whereby . . . our humanness must be achieved," lines of part 1:

Light and the
        distortions
              of light as
the flame-night
        dawns
            Zenith-time and the anger
unto death and the
        fire-focused
           image
of a man
      invisible man
         and black boy and native
son and the
      man who
         lives underground whose

```
      name nobody
              knows
                     harrowing havocking
      running through
                 holocaust
                          seeking the
      soul-country of his
                   meaning
```

Rich with literary allusions, the section reaffirms Hayden's commitment to the Yeatsean mandate to pay tribute to the artist as well as
his commitment to emulate the Yeatsean ability to universalize a
people's experience so that it can be interpreted as a judgment on the
condition of all men. It is to Ralph Ellison's *Invisible Man* (1952),
Richard Wright's *Black Boy* (1945), *Native Son* (1940), and "The Man
Who Lived Underground," and James Baldwin's *Nobody Knows My
Name* (1954) as they define the Afro-American's experience in America that Hayden refers.

Section 9, which may very well have concluded the elegy, is most
significant in its cautionary import and its ringing reaffirmation of
Hayden's love for his fellowman:

> We must not be frightened nor cajoled
> into accepting evil as deliverance from evil.
> We must go on struggling to be human,
> though monsters of abstraction
> police and threaten us.
>
> Reclaim now, now renew the vision of
> a human world where godliness
> is possible and man
> is neither gook nigger honkey wop nor kike
>
> but man
>
>   permitted to be man.

The cautionary serves Hayden's own experiences with the censure
black militants placed against him beginning in 1966 at Fisk Univer-

sity as much as it does the country's involvement in the domestic unrest of the period and the Vietnam War.

Part 10, the conclusion, is a Bahá'i hymn that Hayden first published in 1967 for the Bahá'i centennial held that year. The lyric contains praises of Bahá'u'lláh and his spiritual ascension and expressions of the poet's commitment to his doctrine. In tone, this section is devout and fraught with conviction, a conviction so deep that it leads the poet into the position of offering Bahá'u'lláh as the solution to all of the ills that he is concerned with in the poem, making it quite clear that it is through the lesson of Bahá'u'lláh's life that society may learn the difficult lesson of how to attain this love:

> I bear Him witness now:
> towards Him our history in its disastrous quest
> for meaning is impelled.

In section 1 of *Words*, Hayden is concerned with man as a victim of circumstances—a "psychic joke" over which he has no control ("Sphinx," line 15). Those circumstances may produce suffering of a nature that defines the human condition, but out of which can come something positive. He is concerned with the "conundrum" that defines his own psyche, with what he perceives as his own "inadequacies."

The deep plunge into his psyche that Hayden takes in the poems next to be discussed should be set in correct perspective. It would be a distortion to see his plunge as precipitate, rather than one that was a long time in the making. Accordingly, an examination of the available evidence reveals that during the late 1950s he wrote two poems that suggest, on a biographical level, his deviate sexual interest.[16] Then, in early 1962 he published an early version of "The Diver."[17] He maintained for years that it was a "private poem." However, at the end of 1963, in his Notebook he entered "The Diver" as number 5 in a list of poems under the title, "Poems Completed in 1963."[18] Three years later he chose this poem to open *Selected Poems* (1966). This version of "The Diver" and an early working draft were discussed in chapter 5 of this study in relation to their Freudian elements.

The Notebook reveals that Hayden was preoccupied with psyche in regard to his sexuality and attributed certain poems to this concern, as well as the other poems that were his reference points in the title, but were not named:

Poems from Dion by Glaukos of Myrina—
My first venture into frankly homoerotic poetry.
Nine or ten in what I think is suggestive of the
Greek mode. . . .

Esos poemas expresan una emoción intensa e
insoportable. Sin escribirlos creo no habria
podido eudurar los problemas y chascos de estas
semanas terribles.[19]

(*Translation*)
Those poems express an emotion that is intense
and unbearable. Without writing them, I believe
I would not have been able to endure the problems and disappointments of these terrible weeks.

The entry is notable for three reasons. It reveals that Hayden felt the need to rationalize his "condition." This he effectively does in his astute choice of ethos inherent in classic Greek concepts of love; in the "Greek mode" or way, homosexual love fulfills the highest de-sires in men. Second, it reveals something of the wracking trauma that Hayden suffered as a bisexual. Third, it indicates that almost two decades before his demise, he consciously began the process of objec-tifying his condition by writing "homoerotic" poems. It is not certain that the poems now to be discussed are included in Hayden's "Poems from Dion by Glaukos" group. He did not list them. Nonetheless, these poems, as well as the homoerotic poems he was to write, came out of the trauma he experienced, which became, from 1963 until his death, progressively harrowing.

In a forerunner of what flowers in *The Night-blooming Cereus* (1972), Hayden turns to classic Greek literature for the vehicle that carries his metaphor. Thus, in "The Sphinx,"[20] he uses the Greek mythological figure as a symbol for Fate and he ironically treats Fate's inexorable, inscrutable dictates. These are dictates, his speaker ob-serves, which man suffers, endures, and, perhaps, should not ques-tion because what can only be conjectural answers may be too un-bearable.

In the conclusion of this important poem, the Sphinx taunts her victim with his suffering and admonishes him:

(Consider anyway the view from
here.) In time,
        you will come to regard my questioning
with a certain pained

        amusement; in time, get so
you would hardly find
        it possible to live without
my joke and me.

The poem is obviously concerned with an aberration or condition that sets the speaker apart. It could be the poet's severe myopia that forced him to wear unsightly spectacles. He grew accustomed to his myopia, but he never accommodated to the ridicule insensitive persons thrust on him because he wore unusual eyeglasses. His disquietude still with him, he once said, "Would you believe they laughed at me? Mocked me?" However, Hayden did say the poem concerns the "psychological, . . . some inner conflict one may have which . . . makes him what he is." One may in time, he added, come to accept his condition as the definition of himself.[21]

The real clue to the "psychic joke" lies in its psychological and fixed quality. The speaker is held "captive" within "reach" of "blood-matted paws" (lines 5–7), in pain.[22] The pain is tied to a feline blood image connected with the speaker's thralldom to the ambiguously sexed Sphinx.[23] That the speaker's involvement is abiding is indicated by such time indicators as "hold," "endure," "shall not leave," "live with." All of this is Hayden's dramatization of what he called his "condition"—a condition, he said, that brought him only the pain of "disappointing choices" of *amoureux*. More than that, we may speculate, was the pain involved in his efforts to maintain the facade of his marriage in "tradition directed" societies—the black Baptist fundamentalist community in Detroit, where he spent almost three decades of his life, and the staid black bourgeois community at Fisk, where he served as English professor for almost two and a half decades. Above all, because he was so deeply religious, was the threat of censure, or worse, by the Bahá'ís, whom he served in an important position.

Continuing his concern to strike through the mask, to establish true identity, Hayden uses an Afro-American folk image and a setting reminiscent of the South in " 'Mystery Boy' Looks for Kin in Nashville."[24]

> Puzzle faces in the dying elms
> promise him treats if he will stay,
> Sometimes they hiss and spit at him
> like varmints caught
> in a thicket of butterflies.
>
> A black doll,
> one disremembered time,
> came floating down to him
> through mimosa's fancywork leaves and blooms
> to be his hidden bride.

The central "black doll" image suggests what the speaker's conundrum is, perhaps—what he wants to escape and who wants to keep him a prisoner. Reminiscent of Ralph Ellison's tenacious Sambo-doll image in *Invisible Man* (1952), it is also a favorite character type of the minstrel show. A black-faced Sambo (smeared with burnt cork or grease paint, whether black or white, into the grotesque semblance of the archnigger), the character is created to exorcise with high jinks and ritual jokes the threat of black rebellion and the white man's sense of guilt, which secretly demands it as penance or purge. The image of "mimosa's fancywork leaves and blooms" (line 9) suggests the relationship of the slave era to the black-doll stereotype. This image of trees so indigenous to the South evokes the tree-shaded lawns that marked the antebellum plantation where the black man was wedded to the Sambo alter ego. The "puzzle faces" of line 1 suggest the southern segregationist descendants of slave owners who deluded themselves that blacks were satisfied to maintain the status quo, while the phrases "promise him treats" and "hiss and spit" encompass decades of southern strategy designed to entice, delude, threaten, and intimidate the black man into assuming and keeping the Sambo personality. The former image ("promise him treats") with "Boy" serving as the antecedent of "him" evokes the traditional paternalistic dispensation of trivia to the adult black male, who was always assumed to be childish and never treated like a man.

In stanza 3 "the name he never can repeat" (line 15) may suggest Mystery Boy's motivation to "take off in spite of the angry trees." We may speculate that the referent for "name" is man, and what "Boy" seeks is his manhood in terms of absence of belittling stereotypes. However, in this view, in comparison with the striking evocation in stanzas 1 through 3, the concluding stanza tapers off on a negative note:

And when he gets to where the voices were—
Don't cry, his dollbaby wife implores;
I know where they are, don't cry.
We'll go and find them, we'll go
and ask them for your name again.

Crying and continuing his search outside of himself, "Boy" neither finds his manhood nor his negritude.

Yet, Hayden said " 'Mystery Boy' " is a "private poem." A search for identity and human dignity by the Afro-American would hardly be put in the "private" category. The poem, then, is perhaps more about a search for sexual identity than it is about a search for identity as a man regardless of race. The poem makes use of Freudian phallic symbols that are reminiscent of Whitman's Calumus tree symbols. One of these is the elm tree, a tree that is distinguished by serrated leaves, oblong fruit, emission of a fluid when tapped, and a trunk that can be used as a drain pipe. Sturdy and broad-spanned, it is a haven for both fowl and man. Another phallic symbol used in the poem is the mimosa. It is a tree noted for its mimicry of conscious life, its sensitivity and timidity. As a pair, the two trees may dramatize the poet and his choice of *amoureux;* he was a sensitive and timid man, his "comrades" by preference were "strong, *macho* men who could get things done."[25]

Hayden said the "black baby" in stanza 2 is "meant to be an alter-ego." If the above is true, we can be certain the "black baby" is an alter-ego of himself. It has been his "bride" for so long, its coming is "disremembered." Nonetheless, implicit in his diction, time has not spoiled it, nor has his reception for his "bride" become jaded. Thus, when they beckon, "now and then," the speaker, fully aware of what he is, but "never can repeat," takes off in frisson so intense his heartbeats thunder.

The denouement in the poem reveals the trauma this experience induced in the speaker. His guilt reduces him to tears. Whereupon his "dollbaby wife," perhaps a term for the ideal and traditional wife, implores him not to "cry." She assures him that she "knows" how they can regain his "name." If she is meant as a traditional wife, the "name" she knows about is, in the traditional sense, husband.

"Voices" and "puzzle faces" are given another form in "The Mirages."[26] A lyric of eight lines and a "personal poem," according to Hayden, it should be considered as complementary to "Mystery Boy." Ostensibly it is about a man in a desert who pursues "mirages" knowing "what they were." On a deeper level, the poem is about the desert places in a man's life and his search for links with his humanity. Knowing full the nature of reality, he yet finds solace in that which only appears to be real. Even this tenuous grip on his humanity lessens his loneliness and makes his life bearable. On another level, given the biographical facts of the poet-speaker's life, the sought-for "name" may refer to his familial identity rather than his sexual identity. In this case, the wife would also "know" that he could have his name legally changed from Robert Hayden, the name his foster parents gave him, to Asa Bundy Sheffey, the name his natural parents gave him. This he later attempted.

The guilt and trauma that are treated in " 'Mystery Boy' " burgeon into self-reprehension in "The Broken Dark."[27] It is a lyric poem about the hospitalization of the speaker, who shares a room with a dying man. In the relative inactivity of late night, the dying man's groans elicit the speaker's reflections on a "theorem yet to be proved" (line 24), his own death. It is a "theorem" to be deduced from a proposition defined by negative elements:

> Ah and my life
> in the shadow of God's laser light—
> shadow of deformed homunculus?
> A fool's errand given by fools.
> Son, go fetch a pint of pigeon's milk
> from the drugstore and be quick.

The quality and significance of his dying will prove or disprove, the speaker posits, a life that has been feckless and futile and, what is worse, the life of a man who is "deformed" and who carries the burden, as we have seen, of a "psychic joke" that renders him monstrous. Kept apart from his public life, his "iniquity" will be caught in "God's laser light."

The idea of the "deformed" or monstrous reappears in "Aunt Jemima of the Ocean Waves."[28] The central concern in the poem is protest against racial stereotypes—those directed especially against the black woman. However, in protesting the Aunt Jemima and black clown stereotypes, the speaker wonders about

> the logic that makes of them
> (and me) confederates
> of The Spider Girl, The Snake-skinned Man. . . .
>
> (Lines 6–8)

It is the refusal of the show's producer and the audience to accept the black entertainers except as one of a kind with the "Spider Girl" and the "Snake-skinned Man" that provokes the speaker's "wonder." Moreover, his wonderment is intensified by his realization that he, too, is regarded as a freak.

As the Zulu king and the Sambo stereotypes erroneously define the black man, so does the Aunt Jemima stereotype erroneously define the black woman, a characterization that reveals she is likewise an avatar of the black mammy stereotype—a symbol of the antebellum surrogate mother whom Stephen Vincent Benét so accurately described in *John Brown's Body*.[29] This character is the key persona in the poem in that she helps to develop the dramatic structure that rests on a dialogue that she holds with the speaker. She is the female half of an entertainment duo on Coney Island. After watching her and "Kokimo the Dixie Dancing Fool" do a "bally for the freak show," the speaker moves on to the beach, where he ponders their "psychic joke."

On the beach he encounters the unmasked Aunt Jemima. Without her kerchief and free of her clown role, she regales him with her life story because he reminds her so much of a former boyfriend. In an account that is reminiscent of Josephine Baker's life, she reveals that at the zenith of her career she, too, had danced before kings. Now suffering misfortunes that include loss of fame, fortune, and her lover, she has become "fake mammy to God's mistakes" (lines 57–58). These "mistakes" are, we have seen, "Spider Girl" and the

"Snake-skinned Man." Moreover, by extension, these "mistakes" also include the speaker, who, of course, is raceless in the poem and who believes he is their "confederate." Hence, we may well speculate on the nature of the speaker's aberration. Is this an aberration that defines him elsewhere in these poems as a "deformed homunculus"—deformed because he suffers a "psychic joke," a joke that we have learned he perceives his bisexuality to be? We can be certain that the decision to make the speaker a "confederate" of "Spider Girl" and the "Snake-skinned Man" is deliberate. The poem is a revised version of "from The Coney Island Suite," which first appeared in *Figure of Time* (p. 7). In the early version the question is asked:

> By what perverted logic they
> are made confederates of the Snake-skinned man,
> the boy with elephant face.

In "Aunt Jemima of the Ocean Waves" the speaker walks to the beach

> pondering the logic that makes of them
> (and me) confederates
> of The Spider Girl, The Snake-skinned Man. . . .

With "and that's the beauty part" (line 59), a distinctly Afro-American folk retort in recognition of exquisite irony, Aunt Jemima reevaluates her "fake mammy to God's mistakes" role. What she means is that just as she is not really a "mammy," likewise, her charges are not "God's mistakes." He does not make mistakes.

This evaluation should have quelled the private grief the poet mourned. To the extent that no further consideration of these concerns is included in the volume, it did. However, as the discussion in the last two chapters of this study reveals, Hayden's preoccupation with his sexuality was to become an insistent note in his later poems.

Although "The Dream"[30] is placed in section 1, its treatment of the Civil War justifies its consideration with section 2. Here, Hayden humanizes the titanic struggle that defined the Civil War by treating the deeds and hopes of particular individuals. He shows that in this war the Afro-American was both a symbol and a participant. He was not only the paramount cause of the war but was an active participant on the battlefields and on the home front.

The dramatic poem is developed from the point of view of both Sinda and Cal. Sinda remains on her master's plantation and awaits the victors, among whom she hopes will be Cal, a young slave who left the plantation to fight in the Union Army. Old, near death, she dreams of the conqueror's messianic coming and fiercely hopes to live long enough to greet them. She symbolizes the slaves who were too weak or old to join the ragtag multitudes who attached themselves to Union forces but gave those forces their deepest moral support. In dramatic contrast to Sinda is Cal, whose letter to her evokes his matter-of-fact determination and his courage as a noncitizen soldier in combat duty. The portrayal belies any negative images of the slave-soldiers' mettle on the battlefield. It suggests that these soldiers were brave—notwithstanding the discriminatory treatment that the Union Army gave its "contrybans" (contraband soldiers).

Such folk expressions as Cal's "jump over the broom stick" (get married) to some "ficety (vivacious) girl" achieve effective regional ambience, and the letter also captures the atmosphere of the Union Army on the march as in the flavor of uneducated language.

If T. H. Dickinson's qualifications for melodrama are applied to it, "The Dream" is not necessarily melodramatic.[31] The action in the poem is governed by old Sinda's strong emotional commitments: she fails to join the Union forces because of their "onery, funning, cussed commands" (lines 8–9); she clings to her dream to see the victors' triumphal return, and in her last efforts she struggles to reach the road where she thought she heard them marching. The memory of "Charlie sold to the rice fields . . . " (line 24) causes a strong emotional commitment to the fight for freedom. The development of the poem as well as Sinda's characterization is telescoped, of course, but it provides the reader enough clues to develop the picture of a character neither good nor bad who is simply motivated by her messianic vision of victory and freedom. The concrete images in the poem offset the fact that the action takes place on a plastic stage.

Prior to writing "The Dream," in his efforts to correct the "distortions of Afro-American history," Hayden had treated the slave activist and revolutionist in "Gabriel," "The Ballad of Nat Turner," and "Runagate, Runagate"; and he portrayed the African as an unwilling victim and an awesome foe in his fight to be free, the slave as an activist in the fight for his freedom, and the ex-slave statesman in

"Frederick Douglass." In this portrayal of the slave as a voluntary Union soldier and the slave who remained bound to the plantation where he served, he continued to round out his depiction of Afro-American history.

Section 2 of *Words* treats the country's historical involvement in war, preparation for war, and treatment of the victimized. This section opens with "Locus," which is discussed in detail in chapter 3.[32] "Locus" traces the history of victimization and violence in the South from the "death march of De Soto" through the era of slavery. This poem is followed by a lyric that serves to update the chronicle of wars that Hayden has treated through the Vietnam War. "On Lookout Mountain"[33] repeats the theme from the point of view of the speaker, whose omniscient perspective includes the idyllic site where his reveries occur, its Civil War past, and the war in Vietnam:

> I gaze through layered light,
> think of the death-for-foothold inching climb
> of Union soldiers struggling up
> the crackling mountainside.
>
> And here where Sunday alpinists
> pick views and souvenirs,
> here daring choices stained
> the clouds with dubious victory.
>
> A world away, yet nearer than our hope
> or our belief, the scions of that fighting climb
> endless hills of war, amid war's peaks
> and valleys broken, scattered fall.

Here, as in "Locus," Hayden reviews the legacy of the Civil War. His concern is with its "dubious victory." He deplores "Kilroy's cries" and the "scions of that war" who, yet, "climb endless hills of war" and "scattered fall."

His disapproval of war and its death and destruction shows again in "Zeus Over Redeye,"[34] which treats a tour of the Redstone Missile Arsenal. What the poet sees there elicits his warning that any victory that guided missiles can bring about will be a "headless armless Victory," a victory empty of purpose or function. We are led to see that a war with guided missiles will be no less devastating to man-kind than any of the other "endless hills of wars" that Hayden decries in "On Lookout Mountain." Moreover, going beyond the tangible, he probes the human psyche to reveal what is, perhaps, a disturbing truth. "Redstone," he says, is a "sacred phallic grove." If this is true, the horror is that man's indulgencies in war are innate and, therefore, inevitable.

In placing "Kodachromes of the Island"[35] in this section, Hayden seems to suggest that man's major concern should be not the pursuit of war but rather recognition of the abject poverty and oppression so many are condemned to suffer. In fact, he announces that to write poetry about the denial of humanity through oppression is his raison d'etre.

As in the Mexican poems of *A Ballad of Remembrance,* there is in "Kodachromes" the evocation of the abject poverty and squalor of the Mexican peons, the counterparts of his earlier children, who idled and fished on Sundays and stole sweets through the week. Against an ironic background of tropical beauty and splendor, some of them sing "for coins" (line 2) while others are engaged in meaner activities:

Black turkeys, children,
dogs, foraged and played
under drying fishnets.
(Lines 25–27)

One of the children, less fortunate than the others, is the counterpart of the beggar in "Market." The "Kodachrome" beggar "with finger-less hands" promises "Dios se lo pague" (lines 11–12)—"God (him-self) will repay you." Meanwhile, in indifferent acceptance of their fate:

On the landing, women
were cleaning a catch and
tossing the guts to

squealing piglets. A tawny
butterfly drunkenly circled
then lighted on the offal.
(Lines 19–24)

Contrasted with these scenes of human misery and squalor is the
extravagant natural beauty of the island that he evokes in the most
striking imagery—an island where

> Gold brooms had swept
> the mist away,
>
> (Lines 4–5)

Confronted with these contrasts, it is then the poet-speaker reaffirms
both his connection with Yeats and his own poetical stance:

> Alien, at home—as always
> everywhere—I roamed
> the cobbled island,
>
> and thought of Yeats,
> his passionate search for
> a theme. Sought mine.
>
> (Lines 31–36)

The one light moment in section 2 is found in "Unidentified
Flying Object."[36] A drunk and a maid are the personae in the poem.
Through the guise of his fabrications to save himself from being a
suspect upon the disappearance of the maid, his girlfriend, he describes her sudden departure. He said he had been sleeping off a drunk
when he awakened to discover an unidentified flying object had
landed near him. After hiding himself in the bushes, he observed a
hatch open and a ramp slide out of it. "Mattie Lee / came running
from her house" (lines 28–29) and "[scurried] up the ramp" (line 34),
he claimed. He did not call her back because of her laughter, he
explained.

Beyond the humorous charade that is Will's fabrication, the
poem also suggests the desperate impoverishment that characterizes
Mattie Lee's life. Hers is such a mean existence, her only hope lies in
the realization of her fantasy. And that fantasy, her "sunflower hat"
reminds us, is one that is made and limited by a deprived and ill-
prepared person. Someday, somehow, somewhere she will find a way
out. Her dreams have prepared her for even transport to another world
in a UFO. Hence, in her eagerness to get away, she is not appalled by

the strange craft; rather, she runs to it. She is so joyous to be free of the drudgery of her life and job, she is "transformed" with radiance. Including the ineffectual Will, who is given to drinking, she decides to leave all, to throw in her lot with the out-of-space visitor. It is so final, she leaves "without even a goodbye glance" (line 50).

In section 4, Hayden is concerned with the function of art, with the artist's ability to create his vision of reality, and with his conscious experience of the isolation of culture from the rest of society. In "Monet's 'Waterlilies,' " he commends the property of art to suggest "the aura of that world / each of us has lost"—to master what "was not, was, forever is" (lines 14–15, 12). In a revised version of "The Lion,"[38] a poem discussed in chapter 3, he praises the artist's ability to create "his vision of the real" (line 16). In "The Return,"[39] he gives tribute to a fellow artist, Boris Pasternak, who, like himself, was persecuted for his unpopular artistic stance, yet remained true to his vision of the real, albeit with graver consequences. The poem describes the isolated dacha to which Pasternak's fictional characters Dr. Zhivago and his lover fled. Zhivago's fears that "they would hunt us down tonight" (line 8) applied as much to Hayden's feelings at Fisk University that the black militants' activism of the sixties would be directed against him as it did to the Russian novelist's difficulties with his government.

Also included in this section is a revised version of a poem discussed earlier in chapter 3, " 'Lear is Gay.' "[40] The poem is a double tribute to artists who had special influence on Hayden's art and career. It is dedicated to Betsy Graves Reyneau, the late portrait artist, who was a friend and contributed to the development of Hayden's artistic tastes, and to W. B. Yeats, one of two poets who greatly influenced his poetic development.

"A Plague of Starlings" concludes *Words* with final reflections on the importance of art and the artist.[41] Notwithstanding adversity, Hayden's ideal artist will hold true to his vision. In this poem, implicit in both his concrete subject—the systematic slaughter of starlings that invaded Fisk's campus in the late 1960s—and his symbolism—the starlings represent his black militant persecutors at Fisk—Hayden offers America in its mourning time words that are far more shattering for Vietnam, for Kennedy and King than those in the title poem:

And if not careful
I shall tread
upon carcasses
carcasses when I
go mornings now
to lecture on
what Socrates,
the hemlock hour nigh,
told sorrowing
Phaedo and the rest
about the migratory
habits of the soul.

The allusion is, of course, to Socrates' belief that the soul is divine, immortal. Moreover, in this view, the soul is worth a lifetime of concern and tending so that a man's whole way of life should reflect this concern. Thus, Socrates justified his way of life. Hayden's choice to use the allusion suggests that likewise does he justify his own way of life—the way of the artist dedicated to his vision of the real. With this turn to classic Greek philosophy, our poet foreshadows the philosophic retrospection that colors his next volume, *The Night-blooming Cereus.*

CHAPTER 7

The Night-blooming Cereus (1972)

By 1972 Hayden had developed a sense of financial security and professional well-being. From his meager Fisk University salary of $3,000 he had progressed to the salary of a full professor at the University of Michigan, his alma mater. As an unknown poet he had had to publish his own volumes privately; now his career activities brought him an annual income of $10,000. Gentle and witty, he was in demand as visiting poet; he had won the esteem of such fellow poets as Karl Shapiro, Allen Tate, and Robert Heilman.[1] Further, at least one important black critic gave his stamp of approval to *Words in the Mourning Time*, thereby mitigating the sting of the black militants' attack on him in 1966.[2] With these assurances, at nearly sixty years of age, Hayden waxed introspective and philosophic— turning, he said, "to the problem of the meaning of life . . . art . . . what he was doing . . . the nature of reality."[3] *The Night-blooming Cereus* (1972) is clearly the product of his new outlook.

The volume, consisting of only eight poems, all previously published in little magazines, was first brought out in an edition of 150 signed copies by Hayden's old friend Paul Breman in London, England. Despite the sparse notice it received (there was little other than a brief piece in *Essence*[4]), the poems are pivotal thematically and, in their compression and lucidity, stylistically also.

Included in the London edition of *Cereus*, but deleted in *Angle of Ascent* (1975), is a significant proem that indicates the introspective and philosophic concerns of Hayden at fifty-nine years of age. Here he ponders the obscurity of life's meaning:

But I can see none of it clearly, for
it all takes place in semi-dark,
A scene one might recall falling asleep.

When the diligent researcher reads this opening note in juxtaposition
with "Traveling through Fog,"[5] the philosophical significance is further detailed and clarified:

Looking back, we cannot see,
except for its blurring lights
like underwater stars and moons,
our starting-place.
Behind us, beyond us now
is phantom territory, a world
abstract as memories of earth
the traveling dead take home.
Between obscuring cloud
and cloud, the cloudy dark
ensphering us seems all we can
be certain of. Is Plato's cave.

The "blurring lights" image, repeated in images of similar meaning
throughout the poem, alerts the reader to Plato's Parable of the Cave.[6]
    Inside the cave is the world of sensations, quarrelsome opinion,
ambiguity, change and becoming. Outside the cave is the intelligible
world of knowledge, truth, and permanent being. The philosopher
takes the journey upwards to enlightenment and escapes the cave, as
he must; but for society's sake, he is obligated to return to enlighten
his former fellow prisoners, who remain ensnared in misguided con-
ceptions, so that they too may make their escape.
    In "Traveling," Hayden deplores the inscrutability, the sphinx-
like enigma, that fogs the meaning of life from the "starting-place" to
the "phantom territory" that lies both "behind us" and "beyond us."
However, he limits his poem to Plato's cave *before* the enlightened
philosopher returned to it. Hence, "Traveling" reveals a world where
unremitting uncertainty, hopelessness, and ambiguity hold sway.
    This interpretation of the proem and "Traveling" is underscored
in "The Ballad of the True Beast," another poem included in the
London edition of *Cereus* but omitted in the *Angle of Ascent* collection.[7] Again, because the omitted poem further delineates Hayden's

philosophic concern about the nature of life's complexity—here, man in relation to man and man in relation to the unknown—it is relevant to take note of it.

"Ballad of the True Beast" is a narrative poem about a "Stranger" who tells villagers of a "lurking," "hiding" beast. Not unlike the denizens of Plato's cave, who come to accept shadows for the real thing, believing and relishing the worst, the villagers accept the tale and expand upon it and begin to imagine themselves a part of it. The speaker and his friend actually see the creature, but what they see is at once "beast-like" and "child-like"—both "vaguely charming" and "grotesque." Upon the encounter, after giving a "timid greeting," it "skedaddled." When the speaker and his friend report what they saw to the villagers, who react as their counterparts in Plato's cave reacted, they are met with derision, disbelief, and, indeed, threats. The denouement further treats the conflict of appearance versus reality and man's nature in dealing with it; "worse much worse" than the villager's attitude is that the friends begin to quarrel over what each thought he had seen and soon are "bosom enemies."

"Ballad of the True Beast" is placed, in the London edition, immediately before "Traveling through Fog." Thus placed, it leads directly to Hayden's allusion to Plato's parable in the "Traveling" poem. In this perspective, Hayden's stranger may be seen as a counterpart of Plato's philosopher, who, having made the journey to the outside world, with its experience and enlightenment, returns to the "cave"—his village. There, we are reminded, the ancient forerunner of Hayden's stranger, too, is met with ridicule and possible danger.

Yet, despite the lack of comforting insights in these poems, elsewhere and abundantly in the volume, the poet is indeed a returned philosopher, one with positive, optimistic values, who enlightens and assures the reader. He sings praises of hard-won truths including those that place the highest value on the arts, on the artist, on those who are able to endure through the "vengeful harmonies" of life, yet are able to see "the beauty part of it" and practice "gaiety despite all that dread." Indeed, it is precisely these themes and Hayden's artistic surety in handling them that make *Cereus* not only a pivotal work but one of his best.

In "Richard Hunt's 'Arachne,' " Hayden turns to Greek mythology. The title of the poem is a tribute to the Afro-American sculptor who created a metal sculpture of the mythological Greek maiden in metamorphosis.[8] While Hunt concretes the frozen moment of Arachne's change, Hayden alludes to the mythological context and imagines the psychological as well as the physiological moment of Arachne's transmigration:

> Human face becoming locked insect face
>   mouth of agony shaping a cry it cannot utter
>   eyes bulging brimming with the horrors
>   of her becoming
>
>   Dazed crazed
>   by godly vivisection husking her
>   gutting her
>   cutting hubris its fat and bones away
> In goggling terror fleeing powerless to flee
>   Arachne not yet arachnid and no longer woman
>   in the moment's centrifuge of dying
>   becoming

In line 8, the poet emphasizes the cause of her guilt—inordinate pride and disrespect for the gods. While stanza 1 emphasizes the physiological anguish of Arachne's metamorphosis, stanzas 2 and 3 describe the psychological trauma. The poem achieves meaning in the typography, which constantly reminds the reader of the hacking process referred to in line 8. The poem treats one of man's oldest truths: he who does not have reverence must suffer punishment.

In "The Night-blooming Cereus," Hayden dramatizes the fleeting minutes of an epiphyllum's annual blooming and is again concerned with transformation.[9] "Cereus" is Hayden's most deeply moving recognition of the creative life force. From the beginning the emphasis is on the cactus as it appears leading up to, and during, bloom. The point of view is that of the speaker-devotee. To convey this natural phenomena, which is seen as a miracle, the poem is developed in stanzaic descriptive sequence. It progresses like movie camera projections taken in manipulated time exposures from surrealistic perspective. The poem opens with the plant in "heavy bud." The cereus is next seen as a "neck-like tube / hooking down" (lines 5–6). Caught in air turbulence, the bud "swayed . . . moved." In stanza 5 the bud seems, grotesquely, to be an "eyeless bird head" ready to "squawk" (lines 15–16). It burgeons with "tribal sentience." Just short of the moment, "belling . . . tropic perfume," it signals. The speaker and his companion, who have been called from the vigil they have been keeping by what now seem to be "trivial tasks," hurriedly return to behold the "achieved flower." It is a short-lived moment, even as they stand in gratified awe: "the outer perianth recessing," the bloom is "already dying" (lines 54–55, 58).

Beyond recognition of the natural process, Hayden's speaker thinks of causes and meanings. The cereus at its zenith and in its decline is part of a "rigorous design" and is "energy" "focused" by a "will." Moreover, it is the same "will" that governed the rise and fall of the great Egyptian, Indian, and Mexican civilizations to which "Osiris, Krishna, Tezcatipoca" (lines 63–64) allude and which also revered the creative process.

The poem's interest arises from Hayden's insistence in recognizing both the spiritual and the physical. It presents the reaction of a sensitive, intelligent man whose roots in the human race are as ancient as the civilizations he cites. He is fascinated by observation of the natural process. The dramatic tension is high because we await the unfolding of the unknown, and because his vigil is idealistic, romantic, philosophic—his companion's, on the other hand, matter-of-fact, pragmatic. On the metaphorical level, the speaker's painstaking vigil and reward are symbolic of the metamorphosis that takes place when the developing poet reaches mastery of his art. It is an achievement, a moment of self-transcendence likewise worth waiting for.

The poem is artful in its tactics as well as in its strategy. For example, the names in the denouement are of fertility gods in widespread areas of the world. The lines are tied together with alliteration. In the fifth stanza are such pairings as "sometimes," "snake," "bird," "beak," "gape," grotesque." The paralleling of emotional response to the creation of beauty is an effective poetic convention. The poem brings together themes that had long been important with Hayden—reverence for life in all of its forms and the importance of beauty.

Whereas in "The Night-blooming Cereus" Hayden treats beauty in nature, in "The Peacock Room" he is concerned with beauty as it is represented in art.[10] The poem has an interesting history. It is dedicated to the memory of Betsy Graves Reyneau, the portrait artist who was responsible for introducing Hayden to the room, which had been installed in the Smithsonian Institution. Also a kindred soul who suffered from poor vision, she, too, actually lost her sight.[11]

The poem makes apparent Hayden's ability to see poetic parallels between his own life, life in general, and art. It comes much closer to Eliot's idea of the "objective correlative" than does "The Nightblooming Cereus." In his comments to John O'Brien, Hayden said, "I consider it one of my most important poems . . ." It was not easy, he said, to transcribe the feeling of sensuous enjoyment and sadness he felt during his visit to the room in the Smithsonian, and he admitted that the problem of organization gave him the greatest difficulty.[12]

The poem begins with a question:

> Ars Longa   Which is crueller
> Vita Brevis   life or art?

There is a seeming answer in subsequent references to taking "shelter" from life "briefly" in the Peacock Room, memories and all. In the second and third stanzas, however, after contrasting the outside world of "Hiroshima Watts My Lai" (line 13) with "the vision chambered in gold / and Spanish leather" (lines 15–16)—the "exotic," unreal world of the room, he finds much about the room that is very like the "outside" world of life. Though here life is ornamental, structured, the real history of the room—including the artists, the connoisseur, Betsy Reyneau—reminds the speaker of the severe "vengeful harmonies" of life in general.

The fourth stanza evinces a relationship between life, with its "terror," "malice," "claws," "cries," etc., and art, with the same things. In the fifth stanza the present reality of the room—the peacocks that "spread their tails concealing her" and the memory of a "beloved friend" (Betsy Reyneau)—becomes blended with the sensuousness of the room in its present appeal. Here is the vision of civil death, which evokes sadness, coupled with the vision of military death, which also evokes sadness. Both are outside the room, yet the artificial room calls them both to mind. The existential moment makes it clear that, despite history's scorning of "the vision chambered in gold / and Spanish leather, lyric space," there is a real connection between life and art that "rebukes, yet cannot give the lie / to what is havened here" (lines 17–18).

It is a long way from "fin de siècle" unreality to the outside "terror" and "malice" of the present—to the plaintive "No more. No more" of the present—and finally to serenity. But it was here, in this room, the poem lets the reader know, that the passage was achieved, and it also lets him know the way the vision of "Bodhisattva's ancient smile" is achieved: the birds (mere "birds" now and not peacocks) resume the pose of their plastic representation, but not before an act of the imagination on the part of the speaker has seen them "flutter down."

The Peacock Room, then, is just a room; but because of the art of their execution and the imagination of the perceiver of art, the peacocks fly—surrealistically, of course, but in the heart of the speaker of the poem, both realistically and comfortingly. "The Peacock Room," in its tightly focused rendering of vague emotions into concrete terms, is a superior poem.

Where the setting of "The Peacock Room" is exotic and "The Night-blooming Cereus" describes a wish of an exotic action, "The Performers" at first seems to be made up totally of the commonplace.[13] The speaker sits at his desk on the seventh floor watching "two minor Wallendas . . . washing the office windows." In fantasy, he is one of them "until straps break" and "iron paper apple of iron I fall" (lines 6–7). Thus, though the scene is part of the workaday world, in the imagination of the speaker it becomes exotic.

Actually, what is happening here is rather commonplace in itself. It is what makes an adventure movie successful: the audience for a while suspends its belief in the surroundings of the theater and becomes part of an action that builds toward a thrilling climax. Like the theater audience, which leaves safely after the show, the speaker of "The Performers," after falling like what is probably an accidentally kicked lunch box, finds himself "safely at my desk again" (line 9).

But there is a significant difference between the speaker and the moviegoer, for the speaker is not relying upon the imagination of scriptwriter, director, actors, etc., to create adventure for him. On the contrary, he has injected a sense of adventure into an action that could not be more ordinary and invests it with the death-defying suspense ("hairline walkers") of a circus act. The window washers and their utilitarian task are transformed, thus, into performers; the ordinary is delved for its human potential.

The final two-and-one-half lines might be read in two ways, and both hinge on one's interpretation of the "sir" in the final line. In thanking the speaker for his recognition of their "risky business," Hayden may be reinforcing the contrast between the vision of the speaker, who sees the job as a performance, and the commonplace vision of the workers, who see it as a normal activity. The thanks of the men is thus simply an acknowledgment (small talk, really) of the words of a superior. On the other hand, that "sir" may represent an honest recognition of what the speaker has seen with his imagination—the ability of man to choose his course, even along high ledges, and his skill to follow it. That self-determination and that skill might indeed make the commonplace special, romantic.

Two other poems complete this collection. In one of them, again Hayden is concerned with the prospect of the transcience of life. "Smelt Fishing,"[14] developed in three Haiku stanzas, gives the picture of fishermen at night on a frozen lake as melting snow falls. "Cries for help for light" interrupt the scene, and the speaker provacatively posits man's aquatic origins and wonders:

> Who is he night-
> waters entangle, reclaim?
> Blank fish-eyes.

There is a sense here of life's unity, its common origin, but clearly there is also a vision of its division: the "fevered" fishermen surround the lake while the smelt perform a natural function. Over the scene, however, blows the not-too-cold wind of death—common death. The fishermen, probably not aware that death is their purpose at the lake, are intent upon taking the fish. The victim, however, because of his sporting distance, re-joins the fish, even though the fish's element has "reclaimed" him. His eyes become blank, like those of a fish, but his eyes are blank with death, even as the real "blank fish-eyes" are engaged in the production of new life.

One cannot read this poem as a plea from an ecologist, or even as a moralistic warning about scorning lesser life forms. It is merely a fleeting glimpse of the human position in the heavy irony of life—so fleeting, in fact, that the speaker does absolutely nothing about saving the drowning fisherman. The poem, which is perfect as a haiku, in this sense, captures the instant of his wonder—a transient, ironic vision of life as one and many.

"Dance the Orange"[15] is also about the transcience of life. It is a tribute to Rainer Maria Rilke, the German poet whose surname appears under the title. The title itself is an excerpt from Rilke's "Sonnet 15."[16] More complex than it appears, it merits further discussion and is presented in full below:

> And dance this
> boneharp tree
>
> and dance this
> boneflower tree
>
> tree in the
> snowlight
>
> miming a dancer
> dancing a tree

The twenty-seven-syllable poem is developed in stark images. On the surface level is the picture of a leafless tree that looks like a creative dancer imitating a tree. Complementing the ambiguity of appearance is the duality in the contrast between the "snowlight" season, which suggests death, and the dancer, who, of course, symbolizes life. Beyond the obvious picture, however, the Rilkean allusions imply a deeper significance, both in terms of what the poem says and in reference to their relevance to Hayden's outlook.

In the Rilke sonnet the twice-repeated phrase "dance the orange" symbolizes the essence of a girl's state of being, her "freshness of life" and "openness toward the other wound–open half"—death.[17] The orange, tight with its sweet juices, symbolizes the girl, who epitomizes life, but just as the orange's quintessence is, of necessity, "already in flight" (line 1), so is the girl's life. According to Rilke's belief, her foreordained death is developed concurrently with and during the course of life, and, like the ripened orange, it, too, is a fruition after which there is no beyond.

Hayden's tree, a second Rilkean allusion, also carries provocative import. An important Rilkean symbol, the tree represents life that is capable of self-regeneration.[18] On the one hand "bone" and "snowlight" symbolize death. Hayden's "boneflower" and "boneharp" image clearly alludes to the duality of Rilke's life-in-death dynamic. On the other hand, "flower," like tree, symbolizes life at the highest peak. "Flower" in this sense, reinforced by "harp," most probably is a play on Rilke's frequently used lyre symbol. In Rilkean use, the Orpheus-Eurydice myth is the principle vehicle in *Sonnet to Orpheus.* Accordingly, he often uses the lyre image in allusion to Orpheus's mastery of death through his excellence in playing the harp. Thus Hayden's choice of "boneflower" and "boneharp" develops a life-death synthesis.

Yet another Rilkean allusion is at work in this tanka-like poem of Hayden's. Hayden's "dance" is a key symbol in Rilke's sonnets. Rilke used the dancer and the dance in literary reference to Vera Ouckama Knoop, a young girl who was extraordinarily gifted in the arts, especially in music and dancing, and whose untimely death inspired him to write *Sonnets to Orpheus.* In Rilke's use, the dancer epitomizes life and the dance indicates a totality of experience that includes his life-into-death synthesis.

Notwithstanding these tracings, "Dance the Orange" is decidedly Hayden's own. The poem is severely economical—an economy achieved through use of one-syllable words and kenning-like compounds. It is starkly imagistic, being just three words short of a true tanka, a form most unlike the sonnet, Rilke's chosen form.

Yet Hayden's choice to celebrate Rilke prompts one to consider the reason that possibly motivated him. Is his tribute in answer to Yeats's call to celebrate the artist once again, or is it that he, past his earlier courtship of death and now fearing it (as, essentially, as Rilke is purported to have feared it), seeks to conquer it, perhaps conquer it as both Yeats and Rilke did, through the arts? In its tribute to the dance and the dancer, the poem's link to Yeats may be more pronounced. The importance of both as Yeatsean themes and symbols is treated by Helen Hennessy Vendler.[19] She suggests that the dance and the dancer in book 3 of Yeats's *A Vision* symbolize the artistic process. The dancer belongs to the world of artistic creation and can be called an artist. The dance represents the created image. A double symbol, perhaps even a triple symbol, the dancer embodies "Muse, Artist and Art." Similarly, so may Hayden's dance and dancer in "Dance the Orange" be seen.

The Night-blooming Cereus illustrates the range of Hayden's meditations when at fifty-nine years of age he had returned to his intellectual home base, the University of Michigan, where twenty-three years earlier he had begun his intellectual odyssey. If it was a homecoming that offered him the welcome, heady stimulation of reaffiliation with a major university after his twenty-three-year hiatus, so was it a return to the fierce necessity of holding his own with brilliant competitors. Thus, it is important that *Cereus* shows him in decisive command of his art, able to make compellingly moving poetry about such favorite themes as reverence for nature and life, the nature of reality, the importance of art; and it is worth noting that never before has his social protest been as oblique as, yet more telling than, in "The Peacock Room."

The act of developing these reflective meditations actually served to reaffirm for the poet his creative powers. According to Hayden himself it was a reaffirmation that he sorely needed, having come, he believed, to a sere period in his creativity.[20] Moreover, the questioning, probing, and assessing, as well as honed craftsmanship evident in *Cereus* enabled him to ascertain the existence of a major creative fount from which he was to develop many of the new poems in *Angle of Ascent*.

CHAPTER 8

Angle of Ascent: New and Selected Poems (1975)

In 1973 Hayden was working on a new volume of poetry that he planned to title *Angle of Ascent.* He knew he would have to obtain a new publisher because his old publishers, Harcourt Brace Jovanovich, were scheduled to relocate in another state. He began what turned out to be the unpleasant task of finding a new publisher, only to be told repeatedly that publishing poetry was unprofitable. His search became a pursuit that rankled because he saw this rejection as a failure to recognize his past achievements.[1]

Hayden commented on two poems he planned to include in the volume. He revealed that he intended to title one of them "Ancestors" and said that it would be a "composite based on stories his mother told him about his grandfather and other men in the family" and that it would indicate the thrust of his present interest. The poem is included in *Angle* but is retitled "Beginnings." The other poem, "For a Young Artist," was inspired by the "fresh and exciting" approach used by certain young South American artists whom he had lately discovered.[2] In addition to this poem's intrinsic merit, it is Hayden's most significant statement on his poetic development and the artist's role.

Angle of Ascent is a collection of seventy-five poems. Eight of them are new and are to be found in the title section, which also includes a ninth poem. This poem, "Crispus Attucks," is a completely rewritten version of one of Hayden's earliest Afro-American history poems.

The remaining poems in the volume were culled from *The*

144

Night-blooming Cereus (1972), *Words in the Mourning Time* (1970), and *A Ballad of Remembrance* (1962). However, not all of the poems attributed to *A Ballad* are in that volume. The editor mistakenly attributed fourteen poems that are in *Selected Poems* (1966) to *A Ballad of Remembrance*, which preceded *Selected Poems* by four years. Hayden did not include in *Angle* any poems from *Heart-Shape in the Dust* (1940). Most of the poems in that early volume are topical. However, one of them, "Sunflowers: Beaubein Street," reveals poetic powers that would fully justify inclusion.

Although *Angle of Ascent* is not a complete representation of Hayden's canon, it is his most comprehensive collection. It includes all of the poems that the poet wished, in 1975, to preserve. Yet, there is a problem in that Hayden was constantly revising his poetry, and the "final" version often presents a more mature and experienced statement in the guise of an earlier poem. This is especially true of "Crispus Attucks" and of all of the poems selected from *A Ballad of Remembrance* that first appeared in *The Lion and the Archer* (1948) and *Figure of Time* (1955). Also it is true of certain poems included in the "Words in the Mourning Time" section of *Angle*. Therefore, although *Angle* is beautifully organic in arrangement, it does not demonstrate the total development of the poet.

Angle of Ascent makes available to the reader the best of the out-of-print poems, all of *A Ballad of Remembrance*, six of the eight poems in *The Night-blooming Cereus*, and all but one of the poems in the difficult to obtain *Words in the Mourning Time*. Since *Angle* includes poems Hayden first published in 1948 and the emended version of a 1942 poem, it does present a perspective, if limited, of the poet's canon.

Biographical materials inspired the first five poems in *Angle of Ascent*. Collectively, these poems outline the poet's angle of artistic ascent. It is an ascent, he reveals, that began in the experiences and deeds of his pre–Civil War forebears, includes his ghetto experiences, and pauses at the time of his then current poetic powers and attainments.

"Beginnings"[3] describes an American racial potpourri—his ancestors, who are the

Plowdens, Finns,
Sheffeys, Haydens,
Westerfields

Named in the first stanza are his natural mother's people (line 1); his natural parents, the Sheffeys; his adoptive parents, the Haydens (line 2); and his adoptive mother's people, the Westerfields (line 3). Each of these groups is characterized in stanza 2:

> Pennsylvania gothic
> Kentucky homespun
> Virginia baroque

Pennsylvania is the geographic locale of his natural mother's people, and their racial background may be described as "gothic" in the sense that the Plowdens were Pennsylvania Dutch and interracial in "legal unions," according to Hayden. The Finns were of Indian heritage, and the Plowdens white. Hence, "Pennsylvania gothic" is, perhaps, a commentary on these legal interracial unions that were uncommon enough during the 1860s, even in a free state, to be seen as fantastic, strange. The allusion in line 5 is to Hayden's adoptive father, who migrated from West Virginia to Detroit, where he became a common laborer. Before coming to Detroit he was a coal-miner. "Homespun," meaning hardy or plain, describes the kind of man Hayden said his adoptive father was. Hayden's natural father, Asa Sheffey, who migrated from Kentucky to Detroit, is the subject of line 6.

Hayden makes clear in part 2 of the poem that his heritage is deeply rooted in America's historic fight for freedom:

> Joe Finn came down from
> Alleghany wilderness
> to join Abe Lincoln's men

The poet's ancestor, committed to America's fight to freedom, leaves the comforts of his mountain home and joins the Union cause. He survives the "slaughter at the Crater. / Disappears into his name" (lines 14–15).

Additional information about the poet's natural father's people and a suggested explanation of "Virginia baroque" are given in part 3. Here it is revealed that Hayden's great grandparents on his father's side formed an interracial union; "Greatgrandma Easter" was Indian and her husband was a "Virginia freedman"—an Afro-American, according to the poet.

Part 4 is a composite of information about some of Hayden's other female ancestors and women he knew as a boy and now romanticizes. Among these are "Great-aunt Sally, great-aunt Melisse" (line 1). Their joie de vivre is suggested in the line "how they danced and sang in that hoo-rah's house" (line 2). Their heyday is fixed with references to sacrifices that they made in order to see Billy Kersands, a black entertainer who forced the "darky characterization to the limits of unction and denigration."[5] The poem is closed with a final allusion to Sally's and Melisse's racial identity. Thus, the speaker bids the

> calico curtain fall
> on Pocahontas and the Corncob Queen.
>
> (Lines 9–10)

Part 5 of "Beginnings" is subtitled "The Crystal Cave Elegy." If this section is an elegy to Floyd Collins, as it purports to be, it is also a tribute to the poet's adoptive father. The speaker, "Pa Hayden," recalls a "game loner," Collins, who was trapped in "Crystal Cave" and literally became a "loner" when he was unable to get out. His recollections trigger memories of a part of himself, his "greenhorn dreams," that is similarly trapped in the Kentucky coal mines where he once worked. Beyond his meditations on Collins, the biographical import in the poem develops in the poet's description of the speaker's painful involvement in his reflections on his own life. He "sighed" and was moved to "Extra trembling." Capitalization of "Extra" suggests a sense of the increased tremulousness in an old man whose memory brings the stark realization that he failed to do the things he dreamed of doing as a young man. The phrase "Extra trembling" may also be an ambiguous reference to press and media attention given a real-life incident, which might have inspired Hayden to write the poem. Floyd Collins was a real-life spelunker who was trapped in a sandstone wormhole near Marmouth Cave in Edmonton, Kentucky. The unsuccessful attempts of local coal miners to rescue him were the subject of press and media coverage. Like other writers who were exposed to the coverage and responded creatively, most likely Hayden, too, used the potential symbolic import of the entombment. The "Extra trembling" phrase, therefore, could be not only a reference to his adoptive father's agitated realization that his dreams were entombed with his lost youth and his empathy as a former miner with the spelunker's ordeal but also a reference to the Extra editions of newspapers that monitored Collins's drawn-out demise.[6]

In two previously written poems, Hayden wrote of his adoptive father in whose household he remained until he was twenty-seven years of age. It is this elegy, however, that reveals how deeply he came to empathize with his adoptive father's predicament as a victim of the ghetto that bound him.

Outside the Hayden household was the ghetto, and it is here Hayden focuses his attention in "Free Fantasia: Tiger Flowers."[7] Its significance lies partly in the fact that it affirms Hayden's 1973 avowal to draw upon his early Detroit ghetto experiences more heavily than he had in the past. The poem develops from the point of view of a speaker who, in retrospect, reviews certain of his boyhood pursuits and acquaintances.

The subject is the "sporting people" who lived in the heart of Detroit's old East Side black ghetto on St. Antoine Street. For these who live beyond the pale of the religious community as well as on the fringes of the law, the street is a "scufflers' paradise," a place of small-scale scrabbling, insecurities, strivings, and occasional triumphs. Included in this group are two prostitutes, "Miss Jackie" and "Eula Mae," and the provocatively named character, "Stack-o-Diamonds," Eula Mae's pimp.[8]

The speaker is with these ladies of the night when they speed through "cutglass dark" to see "macho angel" Tiger Flowers in a boxing match. The speaker takes care to inform the reader that Flowers is a "trick they'd never turn" (lines 19–20). That he denies those whom he has taken care to describe as exotically beautiful the pleasure of sexual intimacy with their idol is seemingly plausible. They are after all women of ill-repute: Flowers is a cultural hero. However, on a deeper level, the speaker's denial and his description of Flowers are, perhaps, sexually suggestive. Set up is the question, Who will turn the trick, if they will not? It is a question, even though it may be attributable to the speaker's fantasy, that turns the reader's attention back to the speaker as participant, frozen, perhaps, in a moment of sexual covetousness. It is a state hinted at in the phallic "bluesteel prowess" and "macho angel" images.

As in the earlier Beaubein Street poem " 'Summertime and the Living . . . ,' " in which Hayden's "mosiac-eyed elders" see in "big splendiferous" Jack Johnson a vision of "Ethiopia spreading forth her wings," likewise, in "Free Fantasia: Tiger Flowers," his "sporting people" of St. Antoine Street take pride in their "elegant avenger." Like Johnson, Flowers was a boxer, a middle-weight who fought between 1926 and 1931. In "Free Fantasia," Flowers's fans "amen'd the wreck" he makes of his opponent and see his victory as "God A'mighty's will" (lines 23–25). Their faith in divine intervention on his behalf and the "salty money" that they bet on him is eloquent testimony of their pride in him. The money is that rare windfall stashed away in a woman's perspiring bosom, or it is money that some man earned by the sweat of his brow—in a figurative sense, "salty," engagingly provocative, because these poor people even had the audacity to wager money that was best used for necessities.

This mood is broken and the milieu is banished with a significant disclaimer that ends stanza 4:

> I'd thought
> such gaiety could not
> die. Nor could our
> elegant avenger.

The first three lines allude to Yeats's line, "gaiety hiding all that dread" in "Lapis Lazuli."[9] It is a line that, in the full Yeatsian sense, Hayden had frequently and affirmatively used. That is, he espoused the Yeatsian precept that man, confronted with the transcience of life and the need to transcend death, should not give in to his dread of death but should maintain a tragic gaiety. Here, on the contrary, the past tense "had thought" and the conditional "could" serve to set aside what once was a strongly held tenet. The reader is left not only with a sense of the poet's loss of a happier way of life, but also with the sense that the poet has come to question his adherence to what had been a guiding artistic principle.

In the last stanza, the speaker calls the reader's attention to a painting by Henri Rousseau.[10] He explains that the painting was chosen as an elegy for Flowers. Three features of the painting are mentioned—the flowers, the dark figure, and the leopard—yet the entire painting is relevant to an understanding of the poem. One of the twenty-one paintings in the jungle series of Rousseau's late period, it is exemplary of the painter's characteristic arresting sky, in this instance a sky that is illuminated by a blood-red setting sun. Dazzling, luminous, larger-than-life lilies are cast in the central plane of the painting. The lilies are framed by Rousseau's intricately patterned verdure. In the foreground, dwarfed by the foliage, lilies included, is a dark male figure who is armed with a bladed weapon and locked in mortal combat with a leopard.

The flowers, the dark figure, and the leopard are central to meaning in the poem. The reader is reminded that elsewhere in his canon Hayden used the sunflower to symbolize the existentialism of the Afro-American ghetto dweller—that is, the Afro-American's ability to endure, to transcend alienation, dislocation, and oppression. "Fantasia," with a different choice of flowers, yet in a jungle as choked and teeming with life as is the ghetto, suggests an analogy between the towering, lucent lilies that dominate the painting and the "Creole babies," "Stack-o-Diamonds," and "Tiger Flowers." As much a "free fantasia" as are the lilies in the painting are these people of St. Antoine Street.

The "dark dream figure" of the poem alludes to the dark figure of the painting. In the painting, the subject heroically and effectively manages to plunge his blade through the upper torso of a leopard that is attacking him in a vital area. The dark figure, in his lethal effectiveness, even if he goes down, will leave the attacking beast a wreck—as Tiger Flowers leaves his opponent a wreck.

The third allusion is to the leopard of the painting. Rousseau's leopard suggests an unromanticized view of nature as a brute force that brings death, if unchecked by man. Accordingly, the leopard's instinctive drive is to slay the dark figure, but the figure, assisted by a product of technology, his bladed weapon, probably brings death to the leopard. In "Free Fantasia," Flowers makes a "wreck" of his opponent, probably gives him a knockout blow in Hayden's special use of Rousseau's "psychedelic flowers." Tiger is one of the symbolic referents—a sunflower that had "set [his] solid brightness in the air," the ghetto air of Detroit.

In real life, Flowers's boxing career spanned the period of Hayden's adolescence. It was also the time span that included the heyday and the demise of both the Harlem Renaissance and the Roaring Twenties, cultural periods that had some meaning for him. It is precisely this demise, including that of the sporting people of St. Antoine Street and the end of Tiger Flower's career—in short, the death of a milieu—that Hayden mourns in his dubious tribute to Yeats.

Not mentioned in the poem is the blood-red setting sun in the painting. It is the source of light that floods the sky, catches the lilies' faces, outlines the flora, fauna, and man. As a setting sun it strengthens the central metaphor in that it further suggests both the demise of the St. Antoine Street-Tiger Flowers milieu and the waning of the poet's own life.

Continuing his examination of his autobiographical and artistic angle of ascent, Hayden in "For a Young Artist" is concerned with the artist in relation to life and art, particularly his struggles to attain disciplined mastery over the creative process. Of the three poems he previously published on the poet, "For a Young Artist" is his most powerful.[11]

The fabulous situation in the allegory is based on a winged "naked old man" fallen into a "pigsty" (lines 1–3). "Sprawled" there, he became an object of the villagers' inhumanity. Throughout his ordeal, he suffers, searches for understanding of his predicament, and strains to achieve flight. In stanza 3, he "twists away" from the "cattle-prod" that his captors use to force response from him. In stanza 4, he avoids being the dupe of their "smiles" but is the object of their "threats," the target of their "dumbshow" and "lingua franca." In stanzas 5 and 6, he is offered "hand-me-downs" and is sent to sleep in the "chicken-house." In stanzas 8 and 9, he refuses their "left-overs" and is the object of their awe, curiosity, and derision.

That the poem is autobiographical is clearly hinted to the reader who has kept the facts of Hayden's life in mind. Stanza 2 reminds us that August is the poet's birth month. Also, if the reader recalls the circumstances of Hayden's separation from his natural parents and his quasi-adoption by the Haydens, the Daedalus "Fallen from the August sky" allusion carries a deeper than merely fabulous import. It connotes the sense of rootlessness, alienation, and of the haphazard. It is a sense that he had conveyed in two earlier poems. In " 'Summer-time and the Living . . . ,' " he poeticized the people of his Detroit ghetto neighborhood including the "vivid children," who, like himself, were "unplanned"; and in " 'Mystery Boy' Looks for Kin in Nashville," he describes an agonizing quest for identity.

Perhaps, then, it should not be surprising that the satire Hayden uses to carry the allegory beyond the fabulous to the deeper meaning is bitter. In language and images it is a satire directed against the society and environment in which the artist operates. Thus, in stanza 1, the "pigsty" image equates the artist's early environment with squalor, disorder, and filth. A lowly place, it is one to which the artist has "fallen." In stanza 2, the "cattle-prod" image reminds us of the civil rights marchers in Birmingham, Alabama, during the 1960s. Further developing the man's-inhumanity-to-man metaphor, the "smiles" and "threats" in stanza 4 recall similar images Hayden used in " 'Mystery Boy' Looks for Kin in Nashville' " to indict the beguilement and menace used to restrict the speaker to an insecure place. In "For a Young Artist," the "smiles" and "threats" are immediately followed by the "dumbshow" and "lingua franca," suggesting efforts to relegate Hayden's artist to a peripheral place, one that is not in the main play of action or in the main mode of communication. This also has to do with the difficulty society experiences in communicating with the artist. The artist and society have no common language. This sense of alienation and rejection is reinforced in stanza 7. Here the artist exchanges the "pigsty" for the "chicken-house," where the rooster pecks him. Behind "barbedwire," he is given "leftovers" to eat and becomes a commercial oddity that spectators worship as divine or abuse as a freak.

Transcending his physical, psychological, and spiritual ordeal, the artist maintains an unwavering quest. He directs his attention not to his plight, but particularly to discovering his tormentor's nature. He regards all with "searching eyes." Thus, he is engaged in sustained scrutiny in the effort to discern their humaneness. Inviolate, he is untouched by both their beguilement and menace and does not capitulate to their manifest intent in the charades they use to dupe him. What is more, he rejects their efforts to make him cover up his humanity. When they elevate him from the "pigsty" to the "chicken-house," graciously, he concedes their humaneness.

Not only does he maintain a human perspective, he finds in his situation content for subject matter. When he is given "leftovers" to eat, he eats "sunflowers" instead. The reader recalls the significance of this key image in Hayden's canon. Here, again, it suggests that the speaker makes a deliberate choice to take as his theme the existentialism of the Afro-American—that is, his historical alienation, dislocation, and oppression. In short, his theme is the Afro-American's ability to endure a hostile environment much like the sunflowers that black Southerners planted in the cold northern ghettos.

Even in the darkest moments, Hayden's artist engages in his solitary struggle to fly—to master his discipline:

> He leaps, board wings clum-
> sily flapping, big sex
> flopping, falls.
>
> (Lines 36–38)

These lines suggest that the young artist's endeavors to master his discipline will be hampered by ineptitude and awkward technique. His muse is a demanding mistress, and he remains in her service in old age. He does so even though, as suggested in the "flutter," "squawk" and "squeal" images, his audience lacks comprehension and appreciation. Instead, they respond to his effort with consternation and disquietude. Nevertheless, he transcends his "awkward patsy" status and seeks mastery of his art. At that point in his development, when he masters his art, he attains the metamorphosis. "Board wings" become "silken" and the "angle of ascent / achieved" (lines 46–47).

At the end of the poem the footnote, "After the story, 'A Very Old Man with Enormous Wings' by Gabriel García Márquez" leads the reader to the model. A careful reading of the story reveals how judiciously Hayden exercised his artistic privilege in drawing from the "coded records of successive impositions of the eminent domain" that is language and literature.[12]

Apart from the differences between poetry and prose, albeit highly imagistic prose, of major import is the difference in the kind of flight each subject attains. In the story the subject attains flight and simply disappears in space, while Elisenda, the peasant who became rich at his expense, feels "he is no longer an annoyance in her life but an imaginary dot on the horizon of the sea"; in the poem the subject attains an angle of flight that lifts him to an artistic zenith. Although the metaphor in both story and poem are similar, the resolve in the poem is uniquely Hayden's; even the devices mentioned are imbued with meaning that was undeniably in Hayden's consciousness of the Afro-American experience. Thus in being inspired by Márquez's story, he exercised his right to the "eminent domain" as his literary mentors, Auden, Eliot, and Yeats, had done before him.

Hayden was influenced equally by the South American writers' style and by the statements they make in treating the empirical reality of societies, not an accident in the twentieth century. These societies are represented by the scrabbling, stultifying poverty that characterizes Márquez's peasants and by José Donosco's let-out-to-pasture old women in *The Obscene Bird of Night* (1972).[13]

The end of the artistic quest is the subject of "Stars."[14] In this five-part poem, the speaker arrives light years from earth in the remoteness of space. The poem also suggests that in preparation for the ascent the artist developed powers as painstaking as those the ancient Greeks used in their astronomy, or those required by cosmologists to find the trigonometric parallax of the constellations mentioned in the poems. Also, "Stars" suggests that like the Afro-American freedom fighter Sojourner Truth, who held great abolitionists as her models and became stellar herself, so did the poet-speaker keep his mind on "stars" and, in attaining mastery of his art, likewise become star-like.

Part 1 is an allusion to the constellation Orion. It is here in the remoteness of space that Hayden's artist, upon mastery of his art, arrives at the apogee of his ascent. The symbolic import of this destination is suggested in at least three sources. According to Greek mythology, Orion, a celebrated warrior, was blinded by Chios and had his sight restored when he turned his face to the rising sun. Later, he was killed, and a compassionate goddess placed him in the western sky as the constellation that bears his name. Beautiful captor of man's imagination since antiquity, it is a celestial group to which Hesiod, Homer, and the Book of Job refer. According to cosmology, it is a constellation of first magnitude with its elements including white, blue, and red stars.[15] Third, and most important, in view of Hayden's deep commitment to the Bahá'i religion, is the symbolic meaning placed on stars as lesser luminaries than the sun. Baháism holds that while all things manifest the beauty of God, with greater or lesser clearness, the sun is the supreme source of light and is symbolic of God, the spiritual light. In this manner so were Moses for the Hebrews, Christ for Christians, Muhammed for Muslims supreme sources of light and direct manifestations of God. These "manifestations of God" were perfect mirrors by which the love and wisdom of

God are reflected to the rest of mankind. In this view, religious leaders, the genius, the poet, each a star and "higher in the ascent of life" than most of their fellowmen, are the means for helping those who are lower in their ascent. Attainment of ascent lies in the believer's perceiving his occupation as prayer to God. Also, if the believer is a poet, he knows he is accorded a special place of honor.[16] Accordingly, the arrival of Hayden's poet-speaker at Orion is fraught with meaning, not only in relation to his art and service to man but also because he has attained a spiritual plane that is revered in the Bahá'i religion, a plane that puts him closer to God.

Part 2 of the poem includes mention of nine other stars. Like Maia, for whom his only daughter is named, most of them figure in Greek mythology. However, cosmology and a key literary tenet are the referents that Hayden uses in developing the metaphor in the poem. While the speaker marvels at the spectacle these stars present, he is also cognizant that what he sees is actually light that has taken "eons" of years after it was made to reach the viewer. Thus, the speaker observes, a star is a "paradox," one by which the poet enjoins the artist to "keep" his mind "warm." Perhaps, also, he hints at the permanence of the written word long after the writer is dead. In accepting the power of the paradox, Hayden aligns himself with Auden, Yeats, and Rilke, who demonstrated that the paradox is, indeed, so much the language of poetry, the truth they uttered could only be approached in terms of paradox.[17]

Part 3 is a tribute to Sojourner Truth, freed slave, abolitionist, suffragette. A human "paradox," her accomplishments included the audience she obtained with Abraham Lincoln. At that time, reportedly, she argued that the president enlist freed slaves to fight in the Union Army.[18] It was an argument, she was perceptive enough to see, that was persuasive on the premise that the ultimate sacrifice the black would proffer in the service to his country was one that would earn him an undeniable place as a full citizen. Once she challenged a discouraged Frederick Douglass in Faneuil Hall.[19] She became a confederate of Harriet Beecher Stowe, Lyman Beecher, and Jim and Lucretia Mott, all prominent abolitionists.[20] When she followed these "stars," her mind became, the poet states, "a star." In part 4 Hayden's concern with cosmological phenomena is directed to "pulsars" and "quasars." He notes the "blue receding" aspects and the radiological qualities of both, concludes they are a "Cosmic

Ouija," then wonders what is the "mathematics" of their message. In fact, "pulsars" and "quasars" are highly luminous, blue, star-like objects, some of which emit radio waves detectable on earth.[21] Hayden, of course, was aware of the scientific explanation, and he was equally aware that in naming these a "Cosmic Ouija" he was attributing to them spiritual qualities. Thus, if he took poetic license, it is a license that strengthens the central metaphor of the "Stars" quintet. Both "pulsars" and "quasars" are parts of the Orion constellation, where Hayden's artist arrives upon mastery of his art, an attainment that moves him closer to God. Moreover, it is a vantage point from which he can more effectively illuminate the way—send poetic messages—for those not so far advanced as he is to God.

Part 5 of "Stars" concludes the series and is subtitled "The Nine-Pointed Star." The stripped, lyrical poem includes three short stanzas, each of which is a distinct thought division. The first stanza is an expression of purely scientific observation about stars; the second stanza is a statement of symbolic meaning about the particular star; and the third stanza is an affirmation of the premise set in part 1. In stanza 1, from a vantage point on earth, the speaker views an expanse of the cosmos and notes two kinds of stars, "stable stars" and "variable stars," as well as their astronomical properties. In stanza 2, the speaker gives his attention to a particular star in the expanse he described in part 2. It is a star that he distinguishes in importance in his incremental description of its significance—in this mode, a "Nine-Pointed Star," the "sun star" and a part of the "nuclear Will." Each of these descriptions carries symbolic import in the poet's religious belief. Whereas in astronomy, a sun star is a star of sun-like magnitude, in Baháism the sun star, the Nine-Pointed Star, symbolizes perfection and unity. Also, if "sun" is a play on son, and Jesus and Bahá'u'lláh referents of son, then each is an embodiment of God and each is a part of God's will, the "nuclear Will."

In stanza 3, hailing this "fixed star" and declaring its permanence, the speaker basks in its radiance. It is a star that he personifies. Not only does it project a radiance that lights both the "mind" and the "spirit," it points the way to "future light."

Further exploration of Hayden's cosmological theme is the major concern in "Two Egyptian Portrait Masks."[22] In these complementary poems he is concerned with man's quest to find God and the role man plays as God's precursor to other men not yet as advanced as he

is. The first poem is subtitled "Nefert-iti" and the other "Akhenaten," the subject matter being the controversial pharoah and his
exquisitely beautiful queen. "Nefert-iti" is a tribute to the legendary
queen. It praises her physical beauty and the artists who captured it
for posterity, as well as her spiritual beauty. She is "fair of face," and
her beauty is "carved on stelae" (line 2); she has "burntout / loveli-
ness" and it is "alive in stone" (lines 11–12). Complementing this
picture of her physical beauty is the one that Hayden gives of her
spiritual beauty. She was "Joyous," the "Mistress of Happiness," "a
Lady of Grace" who was "Great in Love." Emphasized by capital
letters, these qualities enhance her physical beauty and combine
with a "disposition" that "cheers her Lord." The allusions are, of
course, to the sparse facts that are known about Nefert-iti as Akhenaten's queen and the mother of their six daughters. Extant stelae do, in
fact, depict the royal family in revealing scenes of domestic tran-
quility. Nefert-iti is seen playing with two of their daughters on her
lap, Akhenaten kissing her. Another scene shows the pharoah giving
her a flower.[23]

However, the emphasis in the first stanza, as well as the paramount significance in the poem, is Nefert-iti's role as queen of the
pharoah who had rejected the Third Empire's traditional polytheistic,
sometimes henotheistic, religion to found its first monotheistic religion—a religion that included universal precepts. Accordingly, the
poet reveals that she was commemorated for posterity in the "city
that Akhenaten built for God" (line 3). In point of fact, not only do
stelae portrayals show Nefer-iti as a wife, mother, and lover, they
depict her standing by Akhenaten's side as his consort in the official
act of adoring the new god.[24] Therefore, in his portrayal mask of the
queen, Hayden suggests that her value to posterity lies not as much in
her exalted beauty as in her contribution as a coreformer in part-
nership with the pharoah, her husband Akhenaten, who held up for
the people of his empire worship of one God.

"Akhenaten" memorializes the visionary pharoah, and it is a
tribute to his role in the sweeping continuity of man's endeavors to
afix the meaning of his existence in terms of his creator's identity and
his relationship to the creator, to other men, and to nature. Thus, in
the first two stanzas, the omniscient speaker calls attention to Aten
(alternate name for Aton), the ancient sun-god that had risen from the
tangle of deities in the New Empire and in Akhenaten's conscious-

ness to become the supreme deity. In the pharoah's own words, Aten was "sole god like whom there is no other" and who had created "whatever is on earth and on high flying." More importantly, Akhenaten believed Aten to be a universal god whose rays fell on noble and commoner, Egyptian and Asian alike. It was by Aten's beneficence alone that man enjoyed the fruits of earth.[25] Hayden shows that, tradition and politics notwithstanding,[26] it was the awesome power of this god that set the "spirit moving"—the same spirit that moved the hearts of Afro-Americans to freedom and to God—in Akhenaten's heart.[27] That his was a noble heart we are reminded by the poet's emphasis on the pharoah's might as "Lord of Two Lands" in "Nefert-iti" and his rule as "Lord of every land" in "Akhenaten." Both declarations are allusions to the real pharoah's reign over Upper and Lower Egypt and the foreign lands of the New Empire in the 18th dynasty.[28]

In the third stanza the interest is in a highly symbolic description that establishes Aten's relationship to God. He is "multi-single like the sun," a play on Son (Jesus Christ), who is part of a trinity. Aten is characterized as "reflecting Him by Him / reflected" (lines 9–10). The dramatic fourth stanza indicates that Aten's might made Anubis howl, an allusion to the upheaval that Aten's ascendancy wrought in the Third Empire's henotheistic pantheon in which Amon-Re of Knark was supreme god and Anubis a jackal god of the necropolis.[29] Thus Anubis's response is a foil against which the speaker shows Akhenaten's response to and involvement in the vicissitudes of his visionary and unpopular reforms. Under the weight of those vicissitudes he "reeled." His populace considered him to be either "maddened" or "exalted." Certainly, Hayden also alludes to the Herculean endeavors Akhenaten wrought to assure Aten's ascendancy: he raised on a virgin site a new city for the worship of the new god; he relocated the center of government to the new site; he effaced all old gods; he rejected his old official name Amenhotep (Amon is satisfied) for Akhenaten (it pleases Aten).[30]

Stanza 5 concludes the poem with a crescendo of spiritual affirmation that reveals the depth and comprehensiveness of Hayden's "God consciousness." This affirmation is revealed in the speaker's sweep of the chronological high points in man's quest to find his creator—a quest, he shows, that began with Aten, progressed to "Javeh," includes "Allah," and ends with "God."

Another dimension of Hayden's celebration of the creative spirit is evident in the reverence for life that he reveals in "Butterfly Piece" and in "The Moose Wallow," two of the remaining new poems.[31] Both are nature poems. The first is a celebration of the beauty that nature possesses, as well as a criticism of its wanton destruction by man. The second is a perceptive observation of the life force in an unseen moose that, like the butterfly, is lowest in the "great chain of being."

In the first stanza of "Butterfly Piece," the speaker calls the reader's attention to his interest in the Brazilian Morpho butterfly. He describes its colors with characteristic accuracy for detail. Then a certain amount of tension is set up when he gives the reader to understand that what he admires is "static," indeed, is a "corpse."

In stanza 2, the speaker makes a second analogy. It is in relation to the Morpho's distinctive colors, and it serves to form a link between the human world and the Morpho's. The Morpho's "intense" colors caused it to "break," to be prized by men, caught by them and killed by them in much the same manner "human / colors in our inhuman world burden, break" (lines 6–7). It is possible that Hayden's allusion may be to more than one referent. He may be alluding to the Afro-American's color, a distinctive feature that played for him a similar role in an "inhuman world." On the biographical level, he may be alluding to the same personal referent that he used in "The Sphinx," in which he referred to those who "suffer" from a "cosmic joke."

In stanza 3, the speaker would have us visualize the "Jewel corpses fixed / in glass" that the giant Morpho now is and, at the same time, evoke a picture of the "Morpho . . . living." The reader should see that, living, it is not "static," "fixed," that its colors do not have the static regularity of being "banded" and "stripped." Rather, its colors have the movement of the "prismatic" and are so beautiful as to seem to belong to the "occult." It seems an unworldly creature that was summoned to the world by "magic." It is this "wild beauty" that man "killed," encapsulated in glass, and "sold to prettify."

Whereas Hayden creates an evocation of visual beauty in his aptly titled "Butterfly Piece," a verbal work of art that compliments the exquisite elfin delicacy of the Russian jeweler's creations, "The Moose Wallow" is interesting in its suggestion of an opposite viewpoint. The receptive speaker in "The Moose Wallow" has sympathy for the great moose that he "feared" yet "hoped" to see when he walked a path near their water hole. His role as a prospective spectator is reversed, ironically, when he senses it may be that they watch him—a circumstance that, theoretically, would please the speaker who was called to admire butterfly "corpses" in "Butterfly Piece."

Hayden closes part 1 of *Angle* with a poetic gesture reminiscent of the classic jazz player's musical signature, used to close a "set." This signature is a brief composition that is meant to encapsulate the musician's art. Accordingly, "Crispus Attucks" reaffirms Hayden's interest in the Afro-American culture-hero.[32] The four-line poem is a tribute to the Afro-American who, purportedly, was the first American to give his life in the Revolutionary War. In evaluation of Attucks's place in history, the speaker decries it as a peripheral place. Attucks's is a mere "Name in a footnote," a "Faceless name" that has no meaning. For white America, he is a debatable hero who is "shrouded" in the highly visible significance of Betsy Ross's contribution, the American flag. For black Americans he is equally debatable. His was a sacrifice wasted on a nation that was never to claim him as one of its own and "shrouded" in the black, green, and orange flag that served Marcus Garvey's back-to-Africa movement of the 1920s and, more recently, the black militants of the 1960s. That both flags are "propped up / by bayonets" is perhaps an allusion to both the numerous wars America fought since the Revolutionary War and the black nationalists' militancy of the 1960s. In both cases, it seems the poet suggests that flags are "forever falling." Certainly Attucks's image as a national hero remains in need of rhetorical propping up by his supporters.

The appropriateness of "Crispus Attucks" as a signature also lies in its stripped, economical four-line structure. The style sharply contrasts with that in the original, " 'Whereas in Freedom's Name. . .' (Boston Massacre)," a poem of six four-line stanzas that originally appeared in "The Black Spear":

> I choose him for preamble now
> To covenants of faith we've written here—
> Tall slaveborn Attucks, fugitive,
> Dying in Revolution's square. . . .
>
> He strides into the violent morning
> Of Yankee rage and Hessian gun,

A giant shouting, *Free men, rise*
And strike oppression down.

He stands, amid the patriot faces,
Encircling, echoing him,
In tallest allegory of
His kinsmen and their dream;

Bestows on Revolution's hour
A bitter emphasis;
They cheer, applaud, but cannot guess
The larger meaning he is.

How could they know on what harsh tracts
Of nettle and outcropping stone,
From what brave gropings in the dark,
He grew from slave to man? . . . .

Oh, let the bells of Boston toll
In sorrow and in praise
For Crispus Attucks, fugitive,
Who with his fellows dies.

An examination of some of the emended material is revealing. For example, the oblique "name in a footnote" and "faceless name" phrases in "Crispus Attucks" succinctly suggest his relegation to a place in history that is subordinate to the real drama of the Revolutionary War and to Betsy Ross's contribution. Also suggested is Attucks's anonymity and the obscurity of his background. The emended version sharply contrasts with the expository original. Attucks was first portrayed as "slave born Attucks / Dying in Revolutions' Square. . . ," "the tallest allegory of / His kinsmen and their dreams" (lines 3–4, 11–12), a man of whom the people "cannot guess / the larger meaning he is" (lines 15–16). A crucial addition is that of the poet's intervening voice, as may be seen in the italicized emphasis Hayden gives Attucks's war cry to the patriots, *"free men, rise up / And strike oppression down* (line 8); the poet's question, "How could they know. . ." (line 17); and the hortatory appeal that closes the poem, "Oh let the bells of Boston toll. . . For Crispus Attucks" (lines 21–23). In short, "Whereas in Freedom's Name. . ." is merely what Hayden refers to in other instances as his "armature" (repository of ascertainable facts and insights, impressions, poetical fancy) from which he drew to create "Crispus Attucks."

A second poem in *Angle* that is as severely emended as "Crispus Attucks" is the title poem of *Words in the Mourning Time.*[33] Of the original ten-part poem, only three parts remain. The seven deleted parts contained a criticism of America's role in the Vietnam War and the suffering that war inflicted on both Vietnamese and American soldiers, criticism of the oppressive forces in America and the domestic unrest that defined Afro-American life during the 1960s, and a passionate avowal of the Bahá'i religion that is given with greater impact elsewhere in the poem. The three parts that are retained as they appear in *Words* are a tribute to Martin Luther King and Robert Kennedy, a description of Lord Riot, and Hayden's most powerful statements on Baháism and an appeal for its acceptance as the way, through the power of love that it offers, for man's salvation.

Unlike the sweeping emendations in "Crispus Attucks" and "Words in the Mourning Time," the changes that Hayden makes elsewhere in the volume are the results of his successful efforts to hone. It is a honing that was done with the artistry that marked the culmination of his "angle of ascent." A comparison of the new versions with the originals reveals important indices of his growth. A textual analysis would reveal even more. It is an analysis, however, that lies outside the scope of this study.

To an appreciable extent, *Angle* is biographical. However, of greater importance than the use of personal information is Hayden's use of the material as a metaphor, as a set of images for his poetry. The importance of *Angle of Ascent* lies in its timeliness and relevance to modern life. It profoundly conveys the Afro-American experience; it is an expression of a modern man's search for God; and ultimately it is a testimony to Hayden's long trek to mastery of his art.

By turning the dials of his television set, which is now possibly equipped with world-wide satellite coverage, the reader of *Angle* can see the centers of the world—Vietnam, Africa, South America, Europe. What he sees and hears will be news of the agony of oppression and famine, civil strife and war, man's fight for freedom. Both the agony and the breadth of this experience are vivid examples of *Angle*'s direct relationship to the twentieth century. The full dimension of human misery and hope in these struggles is exhibited in this volume; the suffering and the indomitable will to transcend are very clear to any man who does not wish to deceive himself with systematic lies.

Angle is concerned not only with Hayden's attitude toward man and society, but also, we noted, with his attitude toward God. The book reveals his deepening attraction to the Bahá'i religion. It went far beyond its initial attraction to him of the vision of world brotherhood in which black, white, red, yellow would enjoy the millennium. To opt for Baháism was not only to reject a social hierarchy, an economic system, and a political government,[34] but to revolt against a moral order that was content to treat the black man, the red man, and the yellow man each as but half a man; and it meant to subordinate, if not to spurn, the theology in which the moral order claimed to be based. Accordingly, the key note in the title poem of *Words in the Mourning Time* praises Bahá'u'lláh: "logos, poet, cosmic-hero, surgeon, architect / of our hope of peace" (part 10, lines 17–18). By 1975, our poet pointed his reader to "The Nine-Pointed Star." This paramount Bahá'i religious symbol is the source in the poem that "signals future light" for man.

Moreover, Hayden's commitment gained for him not only temporal sanction and support for his art but also a valued place in the Bahá'i spiritual hierarchy alluded to in "For a Young Artist" and "Stars." In his personal faith and in his poetry Hayden demonstrated this precept: "To love God means to love everything and everybody, for all are of God . . . love everyone with a pure heart, fervently . . . hate no one . . . despise no one . . . love will know no limit of sect, nation, class or race."[35] To the end, it was this rock that succored him during the mental and physical anguish of his terminal illness.

Angle demonstrates the level of mastery Hayden had attained. Although his subject matter remained generally the same, as did his interests, by 1975 his style had evolved from heavily symbolic to spare: instead of a profuse symbolic effect, a specific lucid one; instead of many images, the precise observation and the precise word convey a specific emotion. The poet's initial gift for versifying, abundantly clear in his apprentice work, had become the power to examine verbal behavior, to effectively utilize diction and syntax, colloquial speech and rhythm, and to explore nuances of emotion.

Angle also demonstrates the extent of Hayden's mastery of "the tradition"—that is, both the Afro-American and the Euro-American traditions. It is a mastery that exploits his use of what T. S. Eliot called a "historical sense" and a "sense of its presence." In this view he had a historical sense that compelled him to write not merely with intimate knowledge of his own generation but with a feeling that the literature of Europe from Homer to Rilke and Yeats, the literature of Africa including Senghor, the literature of South America, including Márquez and Donosco, and the whole literature of his own country all have a simultaneous existence and comprise a simultaneous order.

Accordingly, *Angle* reveals Hayden's demonstration that his complete meaning is not to be seen alone. He makes clear in tributes and in allusions to his fellow artists that his significance, his appreciation, is the appreciation of his relation to poets and other artists both dead and alive. The result is a group of poems that will last as long as the English language lasts.

Epilogue:
American Journal (1978, 1982) and *Collected Poems* (1985)

Since this study was written, Hayden died. Plans were made for a posthumous collection of his verse to encompass the poems of the Effendi collection of *American Journal* (1978) and a volume of collected poems.[1] The posthumous volume, also titled *American Journal* (1982), was published by Liveright. This volume includes twenty-three poems: all of the poems from the Effendi edition, eight new poems, and two revised poems from earlier volumes. *Collected Poems* (1985) is a selected collection of Hayden's emended poems from selected volumes. In two instances it presents two separate volumes that were published by different companies, under the title of only one volume. The collection begins with *A Ballad of Remembrance*, which is assigned the years "(1962, 1966)." In 1962, under Paul Breman's Heritage Series label, the first edition of the volume was published in London. Four years later in 1966 the American company October House published a version of the volume under the title *Selected Poems*. Except for emendations and new additions, *Selected Poems* had enough similiarity to *A Ballad of Remembrance* to arouse Breman's displeasure. He did not like Hayden's American undertaking and he did not like the fact that Hayden had not informed him of his plans. However, the bothersome fact to a serious Hayden scholar is that *Collected Poems* does not indicate which poems appeared in which volume, and it does not distinguish the new additions. The volume includes " 'Lear is Gay,' " an early version of which appeared in *Figure of Time* (1955), was not included in *A Ballad of Remembrance* (1962) or in *Selected Poems* (1966), but was included in *Words in the Mourning Time* (1970). The presentation of *American Journal* provides the second instance. It, too, is assigned two years: 1978, the year of the Effendi publication and 1982, the year of the Liveright publication. *Collected Poems* includes all of the poems included in the Liveright edition, which does include the poems that make up the Effendi edition. However, again, it does not distinguish the new poems or the two poems carried over from earlier volumes. The collection presents all poems, including the substantially emended title poem, from *Words in the Mourning Time* (1970), with the exception of "The Mirages"; all poems from *The Nightblooming Cereus* (1962), with the exception of the prologue poem; and all poems from the title section of *Angle of Ascent* (1975). The collection does not include any of the poems from *Heart-Shape in the Dust* (1940) or other poems, some of which are important, that Hayden rejected as apprentice pieces.

The collection is an excellent compendium of Hayden's honed poems that gives the reader a sense of his powers at his zenith. This selectivity, however, lacks a rounded sense of the progression of Hayden's artistic struggles to attain the mastery he achieved at his zenith. Nor does it provide a sense of certain key influences, which captured his early concern and permanently shaped his poetic stance. One of these was his experience at the Writers Project, that led him to the necessity to tout Afro-American cultural heroes, to "correct the distortion of Afro-American history," and to embrace the idea of world brotherhood.

The Epilogue which follows completes this study, which was begun and virtually ended before either edition of *American Journal* was published. It treats most of the poems from the Effendi edition and key poems from the new pieces presented in the Liveright edition. These poems reveal Hayden's final embrace of the Detroit ghetto where he grew to manhood, the extent to which he plumbed the human psyche, especially his own, as he awaited the last curtain call, and his final salute to Afro-American cultural heroes, who had believed in "something they call the American dream."

One of these poems, "Elegies for Paradise Valley," is a poetic treatment of some slice-of-life ghetto characters he knew.[2] The poem alludes to the taproot of his personality. The eight-part elegy sets forth his meditations upon his life in Detroit during the twenties and thirties. In it, he reflects upon the end of a place, a time, a people. It was a place where, as a boy, he saw a junkie die in the maggot-infested alley beneath his "bedroom's window," and it was a place where he recognized the "hatred . . . glistening like tears in the policemen's eyes."[3] Instead of the planned and gentle introduction of children to the best in a cultural environment that is alluded to in the "Pestaloz-zi's fiorelli" phrase,[4] the children in his ghetto were dependent upon "shelter" that the ordinarily unusual alliance of "Godfearing elders" and "Godless grifters" jointly provided.

Among these "protectors" was his Aunt Roxie's friend, "Uncle Crip," who was a frequent visitor in the Hayden household.[5] Hayden recalls him as he was alien in death: a "waxwork" mummy laid out in his mahogany casket. In life, however, he was warm and fun-loving. He chose to "Ball-the-Jack"[6] with the boy rather than kiss him as the boy wished. Perhaps he already knew that his sexuality had been awakened by "taunted Christopher," who is sympathetically charac-terized as the "sad queen of night" in part 5.

If it is speculative that "Uncle Crip" knew the nature of Hay-den's sexuality, Hayden makes clear that he "knew" himself. In part 8, which carries a second reference to his dancing with "Uncle Crip," he writes that he was "precocious" in the "ways of guilt" and the "secret pain" that "guilt brings." His consciousness of his own pain was complemented by his awareness of pain in others. He sympathiz-es with "Tump the defeated artist," who daubed with "disconsolate blues," "Ray," the mulatto, who cursed and "crossed the color line," "Mel," who was a dopefiend, "Jim," who joked and left to become a soldier in France. Included also are the women who were neighbors and frequent visitors in the Hayden home: "Belle," who was a "classy dresser," "Nora," who was "stagestruck," and "Iola," who "loved to dance,"[7] "mad Miss Alice who ate from garbage cans." Like "van-ished rooms," "the gasoliers dimmed," the "streets," all of them, Hayden laments, are "dead."

Unlike these colorful, warmly human ghetto denizens elegized in "Paradise Valley," there were others who handled Hayden's sex-uality harshly. In "Names," he refers to the power of their words about him.[8] He disavows the folk aphorism's claim that words lack the power to do bodily harm. Here words are "sticks and stones" that "break (his) bones." The one example he could bring himself to give was "Old Four Eyes," a crude reference to the thick-lensed spectacles that his myopia forced him to wear and that drew derision from his

detractors until he died. In "From the Life: Some Remembrances,"
his autobiographical sketch, he details what "And Worse" means—
gross references to his sexuality. After a lifetime of rumors, when he
was in his "fortieth decade," he discovered that his "name was not
(his) name." He learned that Robert Earl Hayden was not the name
his biological parents had registered on his birth certificate. They
registered him as Asa Bundy Sheffey. He seriously considered legally
assuming this name and only refrained upon strong consul from his
lawyer and friends.[9] Adding to this biographical information is the
oblique reference to the "life his mother fled." It is an allusion to his
biological mother—Ruth Sheffey's youthful experience as a runaway
with a traveling show. She fled what were for her the stultifying and
hopeless restrictions of life for blacks in Altoona, Pennsylvania, a
major but mountain-locked railhead during the turn of this century.
"Names" reveals much about the pain that harrowed Hayden and the
cruelty directed against him in the course of his two-fold guest for
identity—sexual identity as well as legal identity.

If these epithets scarred Hayden's memory and brought him
pain, so did they also operate to drive him to the "danger zones" that
"Tom Swift" and "Kubla Kahn" traveled, an allusion to the adolescent novels of adventure and romance he read as a boy and to the
exotic realms of the imagination that attracted him in his effort to
escape the immediate "ugliness" that was his lot.

Beyond these personal concerns, the title poem, "American Journal," expresses Hayden's disappointment at the disparity between
the artist's life as it could be and as he actually found it. It is a
rejection of the "sometimes night mare facts" of the "american
dream" and a plea that Americans turn away from the "cruelties"
they direct against their fellow countrymen for the very quality that
distinguishes them—their variegations, racial as well as other. Yet,
he also saw what is positive in the country and took it as a basis for
hope. He pointed to the human resources, their diversity, "elan
vital," and "quiddity." Moreover, he saw that the people possess the
"ingenuity" to make the country "a damn sight better" than "good,"
which it already is.

Four poems in *American Journal* (1982) reaffirm Hayden's 1942
avowal to "correct the distortions of Afro-American history." The
poems widen his panoramic treatment of Afro-American heroes.

"A Letter from Phyllis Wheatley" is notable for the fresh insight it gives on what could have been the response of the colonial poet to her visit in England.[10] It belies the beliefs of some that she was a docile and gratified participant in her own slavery. Her voyage from America to England prompts her recollections of the "horrors" of the "middle passage," the voyage to America, and slavery. In England she was gratified when "the Countess," her patron, praised her poetry, but she resented the segregated dining area where she was seated. She learned that what seemed like "Eden" also had its "serpent" when she was called a "Cannibal Mockingbird" at the same time she was being feted at teas. Nevertheless, she kept her sense of humor when a young "Chimney Sweep" asked her if she, too, were a sweep. Her forbearance, a saving grace, came from her deeply religious faith.

In "from THE SNOW LAMP" his subject is Matthews H. Hensen, black co-discoverer of the North Pole with Admiral Richard Perry.[11] The poem, an excerpt from what was intended to be a longer piece, is developed by perceptive use of Eskimo folklore and common characteristics of the human race. It poeticizes the Eskimos' love and admiration of Hensen for his "festive speech" and his skills as a "whaler" and "builder." In praise they called him "Miypaluk" and believed that he, like them, too, was "Inouk." The poem is not only a tribute to Hensen, it is yet another example of Hayden's avowal of the "oneness of mankind." The third part of the poem, titled "(cairn)," memorializes the explorer's struggle to survive the hazards of the long polar winter night. Historically it was a struggle, as "(cairn)" also denotes, that was a benchmark in the anals of Artic discovery. In their struggle to overcome nature, to "exert the indomitable will to live," explorers and Eskimos alike are sustained through the "Demonic dark" by their human capacity to have and see visions. Also, they have faith in the "Angakok's" chant to summon food from the sea before they starve. The polar night was so inhuman that it was only by using the Eskimo women to "satiety" they know they were "men, not ghosts."

"Paul Lawrence Dunbar" salutes another Afro-American poet who was the object of negative criticism.[12] Wheatley has been disapproved because she totally embraced assimilation; Dunbar has been objected to because he wrote in Negro dialect and projected so-called Uncle Tom plantation stereotypes. In his tribute to Dunbar, Hayden perceptively acknowledges that the "beguiling" allure of Dunbar's "blackface lilt and croon" (line 13) was really a "cri du couer," albeit presented in a "broken tongue." Some seven decades after Dunbar's death, the poet-speaker and his companion in the poem acknowledge that, once under his poetic influence, they, too voiced Dunbar's "cri du couer." Dunbar's dialect and stereotypes, which, in fact, masked his own as well as the slaves' pain, are now seen to have been the "happy look" on the face of a "victim" who is dying—the smoothing out and relaxing of contorted features that death brings. The poem is, of course, an allusion to the dilemma Dunbar experienced when his publisher forced him to use Negro dialect rather than the Standard English and Romantic themes he preferred.

The fourth poem in this pastiche of Afro-American cultural nonconformists is a "Homage to Paul Robeson."[13] It is a short lyrical poem in tribute to the controversial, internationally famous baritone and political activist. Here he is evaluated with scathing criticism of communism. The party is seen to have "deluded," "betrayed," and made of him a "dupe." Notwithstanding, the poet can see Robeson in true perspective, where "all else fades" before the "power of his / compassionate art" (lines 4–5). Hayden knew well that "power." As a young music and drama critic for the *Detroit Chronicle*, he had reviewed Robeson's Detroit concert and came to know and admire him greatly.[14] The poem was first presented to the public at a memorial in Detroit by his friend and fellow poet Michael Harper.[15]

A corollary to Hayden's poetic endeavor to correct the distortions of Afro-American history was his interest in revealing the historic depth and international scope of black achievement. In *Angle of Ascent*, his complementary lyrics "Nefert-iti" and "Akhenaten" paid homage to the two Egyptian leaders who promoted monotheism; thus he acknowledged this African contribution to world civilization. It was his intention to continue this theme. About 1979 he was "having difficulties writing" an "important poem." His subject was Alessandro de' Medici (1510–47), who was the duke of Florence and an eminent member of the illustrious de' Medici family. The drafts of this poem indicate that his "difficulties" stemmed from determining whether to use Catherine de' Medici's or the omniscient poet's point of view.[16] Hayden did not live to complete this poem, which in all probability would have been included in the Liveright edition of *American Journal* (1982).

Hayden's conceptualization of Afro-American history included his cognizance of the cataclysmic role that John Brown, the white abolitionist, played in promoting freedom of the slaves. "John Brown" was first published as a collaborative work of the poet and Jacob Laurence, who did the accompanying silk-screen prints for the Founder's Society, Detroit Institute of Arts' 1978 publication and show. The elegy is an assessment of Brown's failed insurrection to free the slaves.[17] In the poem he is aligned with Gabriel Prosser and Nat Turner, bound blacks who also led unsuccessful attempts to free the slaves and who, like their successor Brown, were executed by the State for their attempts. The poem projects the ambiguity of Brown's position in American history. From the point of view of his captors, he was a destroyer, a traitor. From the point of view of the slaves, he was a savior. Ambiguity is emphasized through use of oxymora. Brown's acts were done out of "Love," yet, he was "feared hated." His insurrection was "angelic evil / demonic good." The "Axe" in "Jehovah's loving wrathful hand" (lines 7–8), though he failed at Harper's Ferry, he achieved the "prophetic task."

Hayden created this poem out of his personal experience of the milieu of John Brown's Detroit connection with the Underground Railroad. John Brown, Frederick Douglass, and church elders periodically rendezvoused at Second Baptist Church, where Hayden received his first poetic patronage and grew to manhood.[18] Hayden remained with this church for nearly thirty years. No doubt its historical ambience influenced the compelling and awesome grandeur that imbues this elegy.

One of the few poems Hayden wrote about children is "The Year of the Child," a poignant tribute to Michael, his grandson.[19] Its subject matter includes not only the young victims of the Warsaw ghetto and the "Biafran / child with swollen belly," but also those who are the victims of human gullibillity—"the children in Guyana slain by hands they trusted." Confronted with these horrors, the poet declares that modern man has made a "world that is no place for a child," yet he prays that the spirit that compelled Huckleberry Finn's deliberate rejection of the enslavement of his fellow man and Jim's active quest for freedom will attend Michael. He prays that Bahá'u'lláh "keep him His concern."

A revised version of "Double Feature," a poem that was first published in 1950, was included in the volume.[20] Its theme is reminiscent of "Homage to the Empress of the Blues." The speaker in both poems uses the world of the theater to escape momentarily the harshness of ghetto existence. "Feature," however, lacks the dramatic power of "Empress."

Seven new poems open up the deepest recesses of the poet-speaker's psyche. They were written during the evening of his life and probe to the very quick of his being experiences related to his "condition" and the spiritual trauma he suffered leading to his demise.

As noted previously, "Names" alludes to the trauma inflicted upon Hayden by the insensitive about his sexuality even when he was a youth. "The Dogwood Trees" (p. 37) is faintly reminiscent of Whitman's Calamus poems in its use of phallic symbols, especially trees, and the male comradeship theme.[21] The dramatic action in this poem is set against the backdrop of violence that took place in this country during the sixties. As the speaker and his companion drive to their rendezvous, they do so with "bitter knowledge" of the "odds against comradeship." Nonetheless determined, they "dared and were at one." The note of ambiguity introduced by the phrase "crooked crosses flared" cautions against a too-strict promotion of the Whitman-like theme. Given the violent backdrop and the tenor of black-white relations, the implication would be different.

Originally Hayden planned to include in the volume a homoerotic poem titled "Boneflower Elegy." In an interview with the author, Michael Harper said that Hayden reconsidered and made a late decision to omit the poem. The setting is a deserted theater, a cavern-like place with Freudian overtones. In this setting the speaker evokes scenes, images, and personae reminiscent of those pictured in "The Diver." Projected is a voluptuous "beast-angel-angel-beast" which "traps and holds" the speaker to "rend" and "redeem" him.

The "beast-angel-angel-beast" theme is continued in "Letter."[22] Here it has "for a life time nurtured and tormented" him. In "old age" it makes him "desperate still." The short lyric communication is directed to one who has "freely given," risked "pain," engaged in heroic effort to "save" him and is yet "compassionate." The speaker observes that though it is the "elegy time" of his life, when he should be experiencing a sense of "shores receding," he is "desperate still." Now, he determines, he "will no longer ask for more" (line 13). Reminiscent of Matthew Arnold's "Dover Beach," "Letter" likewise makes its point about faith, about the love two people have for each other. It does not seem to force the imagination to see this as a thank-you note to the poet's wife of forty years, who kept her faith in him, notwithstanding he was "desperate."

A fundamentalist sense of sin and guilt, punishment and retribution, colors certain of Hayden's last poems. They reveal a poet partly freed from life-long restraints and strong enough to confront more candidly than ever before his own human "condition." In his heart of hearts, Hayden believed his homoerotic tendencies to be aberrant, sinfully aberrant. He believed his was a state contrary to the laws of God that were impressed upon him in his early black Baptist fundamentalism that governed him for almost three decades and the Bahá'i precepts that influenced him thereafter. To the end of his life, he believed it was a condition that had called down upon him the harshly chastising, but cleansing, wrath of God—a wrath he saw in the nature of his terminal disease.[23]

Three of the poems in this group poignantly reveal the poet's last thoughts about his own mortality. "The Tattooed Man" is reminiscent of "For a Young Artist" in that it repeats the estrangement of the artist from society and the environment in which he works.[24] The caged tattooed man is as much of a "grotesque outsider" to society (those who came to "gawk") as the "naked old man with bloodstained wings" who lived in the "chicken-house" and whom the "curious paid" to see. However, whereas in "For a Young Artist" Hayden's emphasis is on the naked old man's attainment of metamorphosis through art (and this too is a consideration in "The Tattooed Man"), it is the tattooed man's metamorphosis through death that is given the dominant focus. Hayden wrote this poem knowing that he had cancer and that it was terminal. Detailing his demise, he equates the nature of his illness to the "Black Widow." He embellishes the analogy with images that evoke lurking malignancy and surveillance and spinning and spreading encroachment. In graphic detail, the speaker locates his cancerous web in his "belly to groin." Deploring the physical deterioration of his sexual prowess, he bemoans that what were once his "pride" now "repell." Clutching a picture of "Da Vinci's Last Supper" to his breast, the tattooed man "clenches" his "teeth in pain." Hayden's pain, which he objectifies in the poem, is induced by the trauma of his cancer, which he compares with the pain related to his life's work, the artistic process. "All art is pain / suffered and outlived" (lines 19–20), he observes. Thus he answers the question

> Ars Longa   Which is crueller
> Vita Brevis   life or art?

which he posed earlier in "The Peacock Room." The poem closes
with an affirmation of self: "I am I."

"As my blood was drawn" expresses the poet's post-operative
reflection upon medical experiences he endured during his terminal
illness.[25] It reveals his struggles to relate these failed endeavors to a
larger social context and to attain spiritual significance from his
trauma. The speaker begins with reference to a blood test and to being
subjected to a bone scan. He compares the psychological agony he
suffered to the trauma inflicted on the "People of Bahá," who "were
savaged were slain"—so many of them that their "skeletons were
gleaning famine fields." Death, symbolized by innumerable "skeletons" which "multiplied like cancer cells," was stripping the Bahá'i
populace and making fallow the "fields" (lands) where they lived.
"Horrors multiplied like cancer cells," the speaker observes, thus
rounding out his analogy. In pressing consciousness of his condition,
he compares his metastasis to "spreading oilslicks [that burn] the
seas." He asks if it is the "evil," the "sickness" of the world that has
"invaded his body's world." It is a world he "loved / and loving hated"
(lines 25–26). Repeatedly, he calls upon Bahá'ulláh, the "irradiant
One." The speaker's fears, revulsion, and keen awareness of the
insidious nature of his illness, over which he keeps his faith, speaks
poignantly of the common human condition.

The last published poem in this group is "Ice Storm," a lyric
underlined with pathos.[26] In the still of night, "Unable to sleep, or
pray" (line 1), the speaker stands at his window peering out at the
effects of a winter storm. He notes that the "Maple and mountain ash
bend" under the weight of the ice. Reflecting on this scene, which he
has witnessed in winters past, he knows that although the tree
boughs will be "cracked," they will not only "survive," but will
"thrive." He knows that he, too, is "cracked" in the sense of his
terminal illness. With touching human wavering in his faith, he asks
God, "am I less to you?"

The dominant concern and mood in *American Journal* (1982) is
richly elegiac. The volume is compassionate in its perceptive praise
of important people—the Afro-American artists and cultural heroes
of the past who were subjected to negative criticism from society.

Related to this theme are the poems which treat Hayden's reaffirmation of his theme on the artist's alienation from society. In earlier
volumes he wrote of this separation, and here, as before, he avows his
faith in the power and permanence of art. Art is "the birds of paradise / perched on [his] thighs." By implication art can transport the
soul to paradise—yet another elegiac convention. The volume laments the poet's departed youth during the twenties and thirties and
the "vanished" gusty people of Paradise Valley. However, the harsh
realities it pictures remove it from elegiac nostalgia. In its meditations on the poet's own mortality, which links his plight to man's
common lot, again it is elegiac. Likewise it is elegiac in its testimony
of the poet's faith. Although he questions it, in the final analysis his
faith is firmly based in God, in America, and in the future—children
for whom man must make a "safe" world. Also in the elegiac tradition, it is this avowal of faith in the Supreme Being, in the face of
personal adversity and the great social problems, he speaks of in
"Year of the child," "Killing the Calves," and "American Journal,"
that eases the burden he places on the reader in this volume and
reassures him all will be well.

His work thus ended, it now seems appropriate that we turn to
the matter of Hayden's poetic achievement and its value to posterity.
He believed that his poetic career really began in 1966. His belief was
based on the attention and opportunities that the Grand Prix de
Poesie award and the well-received publication of *Selected Poems*
(1966) brought him. Lifting him out of relative obscurity, these attainments resulted in a growing demand for his poetry and services as
visiting professor and poet-in-residence at prestigious colleges and
universities (see the chronology in Appendix D). A watershed year for
the poet, 1966 divides twenty-six years of uneven productivity and
quality from the succeeding fourteen years of increased productivity
and high quality that culminated in *Angle of Ascent* (1975) and
American Journal (1978).

An assessment of Hayden's career may be made through examination of his place as a member of a literate society possessed of a
specific status, the degree of social recognition and reward he received, and the nature of the "publics" he addressed. The body of this
study treats the first two areas, but something remains to be said
about the poet's audience.

Hayden was an editor and contributor to widely used anthologies. One of these is Scott Foresman's *America in Literature*, a high school anthology. His contributions to it include not only several of his poems but the essay on modern literature. He was a contributor to *The Norton Anthology of Poetry* and *The Norton Anthology of Modern Poetry*, widely used college and university textbooks. He was editor of and contributor to *Kaleidoscope*, an anthology of poems by American Negroes. Other anthologies, too numerous to be listed here, appear in the Bibliography. It seems logical to assume that he had a large and widespread public in the thousands of young people who use the Foresman text. In addition, it was possible for their exposure to his written poetry to be reinforced through use of Foresman's "Living Poets" recording of his readings. If it is the young who are most receptive to the efforts of the tastemakers, and if the school does play the principal part—at the least an important part—we may assume that a large and widespread portion of young adults make up one of Hayden's publics.

An examination of the tributes sent to the testimonial that the University of Michigan and the Ann Arbor Bahá'i community jointly held in Hayden's honor reveals much more about his audience and possibly indicates the nature of his value for posterity.[27] The respective authors of the tributes conform very closely to Russell Lynes's "intellectual pyramid."[28] At the top level of the pyramid are the critics, poets, university professors, and foundation administrators. One of these, Arthur P. Davis, who is also the University Professor at Howard University, held Hayden to be one of the "few outstanding poets of our generation," and he noted his "refusal to confine (and therefore prostitute) his great poetic talent solely to the cause of black literature." Darwin Turner, like Davis also an author, critic, and educator, in an appraisal that is complementary to Davis's, praised Hayden's "exercise of the right to choose any subject and his choice of Afro-American . . . heroes." Because Davis and Turner are also authors of widely used Afro-American anthologies in which Hayden is treated, from their vantage point they not only expose Hayden's art to their publics, they shape taste for it as well.

Included in the testimonial are tributes from many of Hayden's fellow poets. Margaret Walker, whose friendship with Hayden began at a poetry reading that featured them both in the 1930s, elegized him as "the magician with legerdemain" who had a "multiplicity of words." Poet Laureate of Illinois, Gwendolyn Brooks, wrote that

Hayden's work is "a staple of our times." The poet William Meridith, poetry consultant at the Library of Congress, observed that his "poems and service to poetry have been deeply felt in this country for twenty-five years." Beyond the gratification these tributes may have caused Hayden to feel, there is value to posterity in these statements from those who possess an unusual grasp of poetry and language— fine poets who are also, in a sense, critics. In the latter capacity they serve as important tastemakers in their evaluations.

Representing yet another important public are college and university presidents. Their view of Hayden was shaped by the value they placed on him as a poet and teacher. Ironically, in view of the circumstances that led to Hayden's departure from Fisk University, President Walter W. Leonard wrote, "There are those young men and women who prefer artists that have stood the test of time and who still command the attention and respect of all eyes." He included in his letter details of his effort to get Hayden back at Fisk, even if only briefly. However, Harold T. Shapiro, president of the University of Michigan, wrote that Hayden was a most valued and important member of his faculty. In praise of his poetry he wrote, "It helps define the landscape of our existence," and he noted that he had "remained responsible to his art, to his people, and to mankind." B. E. Frye, dean of the University of Michigan, praised Hayden for "bringing to life a poet we should not forget and also teaching us to recognize our common humanity." In a similar vein, Stephen Dunning wrote, "We know your poems are among the handful that will go forward from our time."

Early in the year, Hayden had received recognition that held special significance for him and that he had the opportunity to savor. He was one of the American poets honored by President and Mrs. Carter at a reception held in the Executive Mansion. The warm attention they gave him during the course of the evening's festivities was a pleasant and unexpected bonus. Hayden regretted that there seemed not to be a place in government for the artist, the poet. The irony is that less than two months later, his demise occasioned the president's next communication with the Hayden household, the note of condolence that he sent to Mrs. Hayden.[29]

Hayden himself, as we have seen, treated the death of the artist in relation to his art. In "The Peacock Room" he posed the thesis "Ars Longa . . . Vita Brevis" and developed it by using Whistler's painting, from which he borrowed the title of the poem. He showed that while this work of art, as well as the bronze statue of Bodhisattva, endures, like Betsy Graves Reyneau, whom he mourns in the poem, the artists are dead. Likewise dead are the compelling emotions that drove them and prompted his consideration of the question, "Which is crueller . . . life or art?"

Hayden's life, likewise, was "short." If his art is to be "long," it will confront the test of time based on his use of language, the keystone in his poetic architectonics. It is a keystone that he used, as we have seen, to create metaphors that express the anguish of his experience and the perils in the human condition.

Robert Frost once noted that a poem "begins in delight and ends in wisdom"[30]—that it finds its origin in a state of initial emotion and divarication, then out of its own internal momentum assumes a shape or order, and eventually ends in a momentary vivification of life. Dylan Thomas argued that a poem is hewn out of an internal war of inevitable conflicting imagery within the poet himself, resulting in a momentary peace.[31] C. Day Lewis maintained that a poet initiates a poem through a series of myopic discoveries—snagging recollections, images and phrases drawn from a visionary expanse—and then uncovers the explanations and themes within those discoveries.[32] It is obvious that in all three of the definitions above there exists one identical concept. The poet attempts to create, in one form or another, some design out of disorder, whether he calls that design "delight," "war," or "myopic discovery."

Robert Hayden also believed that poetry was a method by which men could momentarily come to live with chaos—with disorder. He, too, believed that a poem takes shape out of chaos—out of what he called "ugliness." Like Yeats, he felt the poet "must lie down where the ladders start / In the rag-and-bone shop of the heart," and, like Thomas, he recognized the destructive capabilities of poetry. In a paper he prepared for his final presentation at the Library of Congress in 1978, he wrote: "Once I might have thought of my poetry as a release from tension, as catharsis, which it sometimes is. And once the writing of a poem might have provided me an escape from the ugliness I had to endure—but now I think of poetry as a way of discovery and definition."[33] All of this is not to say, however, that the reader should be capable of relegating Hayden's poetic process to a mere vehicle of ideas and order. To do so would be to separate

Hayden's poetic details from his poetic meaning—something we cannot do if we are to allow Hayden or any poet his world. His best poems unfold not by design alone but by an internal network of words that are consciously aligned and methodically arranged in an organic fashion. These details appear in a calculated sequence, an order which defies any singular transformation from one abstraction to another. He made a conscious effort to choose just the right word, the right image for his purpose. His best poems spring from his kaleidoscopic experiences and knowledge, his recollections and sensibilities. While it is true that all poetry is created out of words, the symbolic value attached to an individual's choice of words alters from poet to poet. We have seen Hayden's distinctive use of "sunflower." Elsewhere in his poetry and in the deepest level of his psyche, he used words "to exorcise demons . . . gross names he could not repeat."[34]

Criticism must be a double-edged sword that seeks the truth. In Hayden's case it will acknowledge his early excesses of diction, substitutions of sentimental and horatory rhetoric for ideas, a tendency toward obscurantism, a fondness for the exotic. Hayden took risks, including the risk of topicality. Like many of his virtues, his faults are expected in a poet whose aim was often to envision Utopian precepts and to create a noble race memory. But a poet is known for his successes, not for his failures. Hayden succeeded, whether his materials are statement, commentary, meditation, or celebration. He succeeded when his inspiration gave him subtlety in technique and the powers of imagination to make his "armature" serve his powers. He is one of the true poets of our century, one whom his audience will keep on reading as it keeps on listening to a Leontyne Price or Billie Holiday, or looking at a Jacob Laurence or Richard Hunt. His best poems are the work of a man fully human, who passionately cared about justice and who loved his fellow man—Eskimo, Indian, Vietnamese, European, American, white as well as black, and are both deeply and brightly intelligent. They treat existence with mastery and with sadness, or with delight and impassioned hope. An intellect of this quality, breadth, and delicacy of understanding is, indeed, a link between all of us and the past. This is true because he was, for us, the past made present, and he is our surest link with the future since it is that part of us the future will know.

A good poet is like a good dhow diver, who, in a lifetime of searching, manages to find a few good pearls. But a poet who retrieves from the sea of experience a dozen or more pearls of flawless quality may justly be considered great. In his sonnet to Frederick Douglass, Hayden honors greatness in another. But the words apply with equal justice to himself:

> this man, superb in love and logic, this man
> shall be remembered.

Bibliography

Published Works by Robert Hayden

Poetry Books

"Heart-Shape in the Dust." The Jules and Avery Hopwood Summer Award Collection. Ann Arbor: University of Michigan, 1938.
Heart-Shape in the Dust. Detroit: Falcon Press, 1940.
"The Black Spear." The Jules and Avery Hopwood Award, First Prize Collection. Ann Arbor: University of Michigan, 1942.
The Lion and the Archer. Nashville, Tenn.: Hemphill Press, 1948.
Figure of Time. Nashville, Tenn.: Hemphill Press, 1955.
A Ballad of Remembrance. London: Paul Breman, 1962.
Selected Poems. New York: October House, 1966.
Words in the Mourning Time. New York: October House, 1970.
The Night-blooming Cereus. London: Paul Breman, 1972.
Angle of Ascent. New York: Liveright, 1975.
American Journal. Taunton, Mass.: Effendi Press, 1978.
The Legend of John Brown. Detroit, Mich.: Detroit Institute of Arts, 1978.
American Journal. New York: Liveright, 1982.
Collected Poems. Edited by Frederick Glaysher. New York: Liveright, 1985.

Anthologies and Essays

Afro-American Literature: An Introduction. Edited by Robert E. Hayden and others. New York: Harcourt Brace Jovanovich, Inc., 1971.
Beyond the Blues. Edited by Rosey E. Pool (Kent, England: Hand and Flower Press, 1962.
Collected Prose. Edited by Frederick Glaysher. Ann Arbor: University of Michigan Press, 1984.
Counterpoise 3. Nashville, Tenn.: Hemphill Press, 1968.

181

"The History of 'Punchinello,' a Baroque Play in One Act." *SADSA: Encore.* Nashville, Tenn.: Fisk University, 1948, 30–33.

"The John Dancy Papers (Calendar of the John C. Dancy correspondence, 1898–1910)." Compiled by Robert E. Hayden and others. Prepared by the Michigan Historical Records Survey Project, Division of Community Service Programs, Work Projects Administration. Detroit: The Michigan Historical Records Survey Project, 1941.

Kaleidoscope: Poems by American Negro Poets. Edited by Robert Hayden. New York: Harcourt Brace and World, 1967.

"The Poet and His Art: A Conversation." In *How I Write.* Judson Phillips, Lawson Carter, and Robert Hayden. New York: Harcourt, Brace, Jovanovich, Inc., 1972.

"20th Century American Poetry." In *The United States in Literature.* Edited by James E. Miller, Jr., Robert Hayden, and Robert O'Neal. Glenview, Ill.: Scott Foresman and Co., 1973.

"The becoming of a poet—the becoming of poetry." An Interview with Robert Hayden by Maxine Pinson. In *English Highlights* (Scott Foresman's news periodical), Winter, 1972.

Sound Recordings

Robert Hayden. *"From the Life: Some Remembrances"* and *"The Inquisitor."* Library of Congress Tape LWO 12201, May 8, 1978.

——. *Selected Poems.* Washington, D.C.: Library of Congress, 1968.

——. *Spectrum in Black.* New York: Scott Foresman and Co., 1971.

Today's Poets: Their Poems, Their Voices. Vol. 4: Phillip Booth, Adrienne Rich, Gary Snyder, Robert Hayden. Compiled by Stephen Dunning. Scholastic Magazine, Inc., 1968.

References

Abrams, M. H., ed. *The Norton Anthology of English Literature.* Vol. 2. New York: W. W. Norton and Co., 1968.

——, ed. *English Romantic Poets: Modern Essays in Criticism.* 2d ed. New York: Oxford University Press, 1975.

American Stuff: An Anthology of Prose and Verse by Members of the Federal Writers Project. New York: Viking Press, 1937.

Aptheker, Herbert. *American Negro Slave Revolts.* New York: International Publishers, 1943.

——. *Nat Turner's Slave Rebellion* (Including the Full Text of Nat Turner's 1831 "Confession.") First Evergreen Black Cat Edition. New York: Grove Press, Inc., 1968.

Auden, W. H. *The Dyer's Hand.* New York: Random House, 1948.

Barksdale, Richard, and Keneth Kinnamon, eds. *Black Writers of America.* New York: Macmillan Co., 1972.

Benét, Stephen Vincent. *John Brown's Body.* New York: Rhinehart and Co., 1928.

Bone, Robert. *The Negro Novel in America.* New Haven: Yale University Press, 1965.

Bontemps, Arna. Review of *A Ballad of Remembrance. Fisk News* 37, no. 1 (Fall, 1962): 12.

Bradley, Sculley, and others. *The American Tradition in Literature.* Vol. 2. New York: W. W. Norton and Co., 1967.

Breton, André. "Manifesto on Surrealism," 1924 and 1920. Cited in *The Encyclopedia of World Art,* Vol. 13.

———. *Manifesto in Surrealism.* Paris: Pauvert, 1962.

Brooks, Cleanth. *The Well Wrought Urn: Studies in the Structure of Poetry.* New York: Reynal and Hitchcock, 1947.

Brooks, Gwendolyn. Review of *Selected Poems.* In "Books Noted." *Negro Digest,* October, 1966, 51–52.

———. *Negro Poetry and Drama and the Negro in American Fiction: Studies in American Life.* New York: Atheneum Press, 1969.

Brown, Sterling. *Negro Poetry and Drama and the Negro in American Fiction: Studies in American Life.* New York: Atheneum Press, 1969.

———. "The New Negro in Literature (1925–1955)." In *The New Negro Thirty Years Afterwards.* Edited by Rayford W. Logan, Eugene C. Holmes, and G. Franklin Edward. Washington, D.C.: Howard University Press, 1955.

Calderwood, James L., and Harold E. Toliver. "The Poet's Method." In *Perspectives on Poetry.* New York: Oxford University Press, 1968.

Carey, William. *Brothers Under the Skin.* Boston: Little, Brown and Co., 1964.

Cash, W. J. *The Mind of the South.* New York: Alfred A. Knopf, 1970.

Chapman, Abraham, ed. *Black Voices.* New York: New American Library, 1968.

Conot, Robert. *American Odyssey.* Bantam Edition. New York: William A. Morrison and Co., 1974.

Crane, Hart. *The Letters of Hart Crane.* Edited by Brom Weber. New York: Hermitage House, 1952.

Crossman, Richard, ed. *The God That Failed.* New York: Harper and Brothers, 1949.

Cullen, Countee. *Copper Sun.* New York: Harper and Brothers, 1929.

———. *On These I Stand: An Anthology of the Best Poems of Countee Cullen.* New York: Harper and Row, 1947.

Davenport, Walter. "Detroit Strains at the Federal Leash." *Colliers,* October 31, 1942, 15–16, 39.

Davis, Arthur P. *From the Dark Tower: Afro-American Writers—1900 to 1960.* Washington, D.C.: Howard University Press, 1974.

————, and Saunders Redding, eds. *Cavalcade: Negro American Writing from 1760 to the Present.* Boston: Houghton Mifflin Co., 1971.

Davis, Charles. "Robert Hayden's Use of History." In *Black Is the Color of the Cosmos: Essays on Afro-American Literature 1942–1981.* Edited by Henry Louis Gates. New York: Garland Publishing Co., 1982.

de Coy, Robert H. *The Nigger Bible.* Los Angeles: Holloway Publishing Co., 1967.

Donoso, José. *The Obscene Bird of Night.* New York: Alfred A. Knopf, 1973.

Douglass, Frederick. *Life and Times of Frederick Douglass.* Reprinted from the revised edition of 1892. New York: Collier Books, 1962.

Drew, Elizabeth. *T. S. Eliot: The Design of His Poetry.* New York: Scribner's Sons, 1949.

Eastman, Arthur M., ed. *The Norton Anthology of Poetry.* New York: W. W. Norton and Co., 1970.

Eliot, T. S. *The Sacred Wood.* London: Methuen and Co., 1920.

Ellison, Ralph. "A Very Stern Discipline." *Harpers,* March, 1967, 80.

————. "Richard Wright's Blues." *Black Expression.* Edited by Addison Gayle, Jr. New York: Weybright and Talley, 1969.

Ellman, Richard. *Eminent Domain.* New York: Oxford University Press, 1967.

Emanuel, James A., and Theodore L. Gross, eds. *Dark Symphony: Negro Literature in America.* New York: The Free Press, 1968.

Esselemmont, J. E., ed. *Bahá'u'lláh and the New Era.* 3rd ed. rev. New York: Pyramid Books, 1970.

Fetrow, Fred M. "Robert Hayden's 'Frederick Douglass': Form and Meaning in a Modern Sonnet." *College Language Association Journal* 17, no. 1 (September, 1973): 79–84.

Fogel, Robert W. *Time on the Cross: The Economics of American Negro Slavery.* New York: Little, Brown and Co., 1974.

Franklin, John Hope, and Isidore Starr, eds. *The Negro in 20th Century America.* New York: Vintage Books, Random House, 1967.

Frost, Robert. "The Figure a Poem Makes." *American Poetry and Poetics.* Edited by Daniel G. Hoffman. Anchor Books. New York: Doubleday and Co., 1962.

Galler, David. "Three Recent Volumes." *Poetry* 110, no. 4 (July, 1967): 267–68.

Gayle, Addison, Jr., ed. *Black Expression.* New York: Weybright and Talley, 1969.

————. *The Black Aesthetic.* Anchor Books. New York: Doubleday and Co., 1972.

Genovese, Eugene D. *Roll, Jordan, Roll: The World the Slaves Made.* Pantheon Books. New York: Random House, 1974.

Grebstein, Sheldon Norman, ed. *Perspectives in Contemporary Criticism.* New York: Harper and Row, 1968.

Gross, Seymour, and John Edward Hardy. *Images of the Negro in American Literature.* Chicago: University of Chicago Press, 1966.

Harper, Michael S. *Images of Kin.* Urbana: University of Illinois Press, 1977.
———. "A symbolist poet struggling with historical fact." *New York Times Book Review,* February 22, 1976, 34–35.
Harrison, William. "A New Negro Voice." *Opportunity* 19, no. 3 (March, 1941): 91.
Hart, Henry, ed. *American Writers' Congress.* New York: International Publishers, 1935.
Hayes, George Edmund, and Sterling Brown. *The Negro in Detroit and Washington.* For the Federal Writers Project. Reprinted. New York: Arno Press and the *New York Times,* 1969.
Higginson, Thomas Wentworth. "Gabriel's Defeat." *Atlantic Monthly* 10 (September, 1862): 338–41.
Huggins, Nathan Irvin. *Harlem Renaissance.* New York: Oxford University Press, 1971.
Hoyle, Fred. *Astronomy and Cosmology, A Modern Course.* San Francisco: W. H. Freeman and Co., 1975.
Hughes, Langston. *Book of Negro Folklore.* New York: Dodd Mead and Co., 1958.
———. "The Negro Artist and the Racial Mountain." *The Nation* 122, no. 3181 (June 23, 1926): 692–94.
———. *Shakespeare in Harlem.* New York: Alfred A. Knopf, 1942.
———, and Arna Bontemps, eds. *The Poetry of the Negro.* Garden City, N.Y.: Doubleday and Co., 1949.
Ivy, James W. "Concerning a Poet and a Critic." "*Crisis*" 48, no. 4 (April, 1941): 128.
Johnson, James Weldon. "Detroit." *Crisis* 32, no. 3 (July, 1926): 117–20.
Kinney, Herbert A. "Words That Leap from the Pages." *Boston Sunday Globe* (Books), December 11, 1966, p. A–32.
Lester, Julius. "For a World Where a Man." *New York Times Book Review,* January 24, 1972, pp. 4–5, 22.
Levine, Judson. "Poetry How and Why." *Writers Digest* 52, no. 2 (February, 1972): 39–43.
Lewalski, Barbara K., and Andrew J. Sabol, eds. *Major Poets of the Earlier Seventeenth Century.* New York: The Odyssey Press, 1973.
Lincoln, C. Eric. *The Black Muslims in America.* Boston: Beacon Press, 1963.
Loftis, N. J. *Black Anima.* New York: Liveright, 1973.
Lynes, Russell. *A Surfeit of Honey.* New York: Harper and Brothers, 1957.
Malcolm X. *Autobiography of Malcolm X.* New York: Grove Press, Random House, 1966.
Mangione, Jerre. *The Dream and the Deal: The Federal Writers Project 1935–1943.* Boston: Little, Brown and Co., 1972.
Márquez, Gabriel García. *Leaf Storm and Other Stories.* Translated by Gregory Rabasa. New York: Harper and Row, 1972.
Martin, Ralph G. "Detroit Danger Area," *The New Republic,* Nov. 26, 1945, p. 703.
Mayer, Brantz. *Adventures of an African Slaver.* New York: A. C. Boni, 1928.

Meltzer, Milton. *Langston Hughes, A Biography.* New York: Thomas Y. Cromwell Co., 1968.

Mills, Ralph, Jr. Review of Book Review. *The Christian Scholar* 45, no. 3 (Fall, 1962): 337–40.

Moore, Gerald. "Poetry in the Harlem Renaissance." The *Black American Writer.* Vol. 2: *Poetry and Drama.* Edited by C. W. E. Bigsby. Baltimore: Penguin Books, Inc., 1969.

Murray, Albert. *Stomping the Blues.* New York: McGraw Hill, 1976.

The Negro Heritage Library. *Profiles of Negro Womanhood, 1619–1900.* Vol. 1. Yonkers, New York: Educational Heritage, Inc., 1964.

O'Brien, John, ed. *Interviews with Black Writers.* New York: Liveright, 1973.

O'Sullivan, Maurice J. "The Mask of Allusion in Robert Hayden's 'The Diver.'" *College Language Association Journal* 17, no. 1 (September, 1973): 85–92.

Owens, William A. *Black Mutiny: The Revolt of the Schooner* Amistad. Boston: Pilgrim Press, 1968.

Pierson, George Wilson, ed. *Tocqueville in America.* Abridged by Dudley C. Lunt from *Tocqueville and Beaumont in America.* Anchor Books. Garden City, N.Y.: Doubleday and Co., 1959.

Pritchard, J. B. *Ancient Near Eastern Texts Relating to the Old Testament.* 2nd ed. Princeton, N.J.: Princeton University Press, 1955.

Record, Wilson. *The Negro and the Communist Party.* Chapel Hill: University of North Carolina Press, 1951.

Rilke, Rainer Maria. *Sonnets to Orpheus.* Translated by M. D. Herter Norton. New York: W. W. Norton and Co., 1942.

Rodman, Selden. "Negro Poets." *New York Times Book Review,* October 10, 1948, 27.

Rourke, Constance. *American Humor: A Study of National Character.* New York: Harcourt, Brace and Co., 1931.

Rukeyser, Muriel. "The Amistad Mutiny." In *Primer for White Folk.* Edited by Bucklin Moon. New York: Doubleday, Doran and Co., 1945.

Schwartz, Delmore. *Selected Essays of Delmore Schwartz.* Edited by Donald A. Dike and David H. Zucker. Chicago: University of Chicago Press, 1970.

Skeeter, Sharyn J. "Poetry Collections." *ESSENCE,* January, 1973, p. 70.

Spiller, Robert E., and others. *Literary History of the United States.* 3d ed. rev. New York: Macmillan, 1963.

Stanford, Donald E. "W. B. Yeats: Critical Perspectives." *The Southern Review* 5, no. 3 (Summer, 1969): 831–32.

Starke, Catherine Juanita. *Black Portraiture in American Fiction.* New York: Basic Books, Inc., 1971.

Stephenchev, Stephen. *American Poetry Since 1945.* New York: Harper and Row, 1965.

Stevenson, Burton. *The Home Book of Quotations.* 10th ed. New York: Dodd Mead and Co., 1967.

"The Three Civil Rights Workers—How They Were Murdered." *Mississippi Eye Witness.* Special issue of *Ramparts.* 1964.

Treece, Henry. *Dylan Thomas: "Dog Among the Fairies."* London: Ernest Benn, Ltd., 1956.

Turner, Darwin. *Black American Literature: Poetry.* Columbus, Ohio: Charles E. Merrill Publishing Co., 1977.

Vassa, Gustavus. *The Interesting Narrative of the Life of Olaudah Equiano or Gustavus Vassa, The African.* London: Printed and published by the author, 1789.

Veja (Rio de Janeiro) 600 (March 5, 1980): 78.

Vendler, Helen Hennessy. *Yeats' Vision and the Later Plays.* Cambridge, Mass.: Harvard University Press, 1963.

Wagner, Jean. *Black Poets of the United States from Paul Laurence Dunbar to Langston Hughes.* Translated by Kenneth Douglass. Urbana: University of Illinois Press, 1973.

Walker, Margaret. "New Poets." *Phylon* 11, no. 4 (Fourth Quarter): 345–54.

Wallace, Anthony F. D. "Revitalization Movements." *American Anthropologist* 58 (April, 1956): 264–81.

Warnke, F. J. "Baroque Once More: More Notes on a Literary Period." *New Literary History* 1, no. 2 (Winter, 1970): 145–62.

Warnock, Robert, and George K. Anderson. *The World in Literature.* Glenview, Ill.: Scott Foresman and Co., 1967.

Wasserman, Earl R. *The Finer Tone: Keats' Major Poems.* Baltimore: The Johns Hopkins Press, 1967.

Who's Who Among Black Americans. 4th ed. Lake Forest, Ill.: Educational Communications, Inc., 1985.

Williams, Carey. *Brothers Under the Skin.* Boston: Little, Brown and Co., 1964.

Wordsworth, William. "The Simplon Pass." In *The Poetical Works of Wordsworth.* Cambridge Edition. Boston: Houghton Mifflin Co., 1982.

Wright, Richard. "Between the World and Me." *Partisan Review* 2, no. 8 (July-August, 1935): 18–19.

———. "Blueprint for Negro Writing." *New Challenge* (Fall, 1937): 53–65.

———. *Uncle Tom's Children.* New York: Harper and Brothers, 1940.

Wylie, Elinor. *Collected Poems of Elinor Wylie.* New York: Alfred A. Knopf, 1932.

Yeats, William Butler. *The Collected Poems of W. B. Yeats.* New York: Macmillan Co., 1956.

———. *On the Boiler.* Rathmines, Dublin, Ireland: Cuala Press, 1939.

Other Sources

Unpublished Manuscripts and Lectures

Bone, Robert. Lecture at Columbia University, Teachers College. February 5, 1973.

———. "Phase II, The Negro Awakening." 1972. Typescript in author's possession.
Hayden, Robert. "Final Presentation at the Library of Congress." 1978. Typescript in author's possession.
———. "From the Life: Some Remembrances" and "The Inquisitor." pp. 1, 5, 11. Typescript in author's possession.

Personal Communications

Carter, President and Mrs. Jimmy. Letter of condolence to Erma Hayden on Robert Hayden's death, undated. Robert Hayden's private papers.
Hayden, Robert. Correspondence with Paul Breman, 1952 to 1972. Robert Hayden File, Vivian G. Harsh Collection, Carter G. Woodson Library, Chicago, Ill.
———. Correspondence with Rosey Pool, 1961 to 1966. Rosey Pool Papers, University of Sussex Library, Sussex, England.
———. Letter to author, October 25, 1979.
———. Telephone conversations with author, October 17, 1972, October 20, 1972, November 5, 1978, February 9, 1979, February 12, 1979, November 12, 1979.
Pool, Rosey E. Letter to Robert Hayden, undated. Hayden's private collection.
Tate, Allen. Letter to Robert Hayden, December 19, 1967. Hayden's private collection.

Interviews with Author

Anderson, Leroy. Charleston, S.C., May 6, 1979.
Breman, Paul. New York, N.Y., May 9, 1979.
Brown, Sterling. Washington, D.C., December 10, 1979.
Butler, Broadus N. Robert R. Moton Memorial Institute. Capahosic, Gloucester, Va., February 25, 1979.
Cooper, Alvin. New York, N.Y., May 9, 1979.
Davis, Arthur P. Washington, D.C., December, 1979.
Demby, William. New York, N.Y., October 7, 1972.
———. New York, N.Y., May 6, 1979.
Ford, Gladys. Fisk University. Nashville, Tenn., April 25, 1979.
Hayden, Robert. New York, N.Y., October 31, 1972.
———. New York, N.Y., July 3 and 4, 1973.
———. Ann Arbor, Mich., August 14, 1973.
———. Ann Arbor, Mich., April 7, 1979.
Hemphill, George. Hemphill Press. Nashville, Tenn., April 25, 1979.
Jackson, Blyden. Robert R. Moton Memorial Institute. Cepahosic, Gloucester, Va., April 20, 1979.
Lawson, James. Washington, D.C., November 7, 1978.

Palmer, Grace B. Columbia, S.C., May 7, 1979.
Randall, Dudley. Detroit, Mich., April 8, 1979.

Selected Letters and Tributes:
Testimonial for Robert Hayden

University of Michigan, February 24, 1980, Robert Hayden File, Schomburg Center of Afro-American Studies, New York City Public Library.

Alexander, Margaret Walker. "Tribute to Robert Hayden," February, 1980.

Collier, Eugenia W. "A Tribute to Robert Hayden," February 21, 1980.

Davis, Arthur P. Tribute, February 6, 1980.

Dunning, Stephen. Letter to Robert Hayden, no date.

Frye, B. E. Letter to Niara Sudarkasa, February 20, 1980.

Giovanni, Nikki. Letter to Niara Sudarkasa, February 7, 1980.

Leonard, Walter J. Letter to Robert Hayden, February 6, 1980.

Lindsay, J. Rikee. Letter to Niara Sudarkasa, February 7, 1980.

Meredith, William. Letter to Niara Sudarkasa, February 5, 1980.

Shapiro, Harold T. "A Tribute to Robert Hayden," February 20, 1980.

Turner, Darwin. "Ode to Robert Hayden," no date.

Major Poems by Robert Hayden Discussed in Text

MAGNOLIAS IN SNOW
from *The Lion and the Archer* (1948)

Snow alters and elaborates perspectives,
confuses South with North and would deceive
me into what egregious error
but for these trees that keep their summer-green
and like a certain hue of speech mean South.

Magnolias stand for South, as every copy-
reader knows, and snow means North to me,
means home and friends I walked with under boughs
of hemlock when the cold of winter
was a carilloneur that played on china bells.

But still, snow-shine upon magnolia leaves
that wither into shapes of abstract sculpture
when brought inside for garnishment,
does compensate for things I must forego
if I would safely walk beneath these trees:

These dazzleclustered trees that stand in heaped
and startling ornaments of snow, a baroque
surprise. O South, how beautiful is change.

A BALLAD OF REMEMBRANCE
from *The Lion and the Archer* (1948)

Quadroon mermaids, Afro angels, saints
blackgilt balanced upon the switchblades of that air
and sang. Tight streets unfolding to the eye
like fans of corrosion and elegiac lace
crackled with their singing: Shadow of time. Shadow of blood.

Shadow, echoed the zulu king, dangling
from a cluster of balloons. Blood,
whined the gunmetal priestess, floating
out from the courtyard where dead men sat at dice.

What will you have? she inquired, the sallow vendeuse
of prepared tarnishes and jokes of nacre and ormolu.
What but those gleamings, oldrose graces,
manners like scented gloves? Contrived ghosts
rapped to metronome clack of lavalieres.

Contrived illuminations riding a threat
of river, masked Negroes wearing chameleon
satins gaudy now as an undertaker's dream
of disaster, lighted the crazy flopping dance
of my heart, dance of love and hate among joys, rejections.

Accommodate, muttered the zulu king, throned
like a copper toad in a glaucous poison jewel.
Love, chimed the saints and the angels and the mermaids.
Hate, shrieked the gunmetal priestess
from her spiked bellcollar curved like a fleur-de-lys:

As well have a talon as a finger, a muzzle
as a mouth. As well have a hollow as a heart.
And she pinwheeled away in coruscations
of laughter, scattering those others before her.

But my heart continued its dance—now among
metaphorical doors, decors of illusion,
coffeecups floating poised hysterias:
now among mazurka dolls offering
deaths-heads of peppermint roses and real violets.

Then you arrived, meditative, ironic,
richly human. And your presence was shore where my heart
rested, released, from the hoodoo of that dance,
where I spoke with my human voice again and saw
the minotaurs of edict dwindle feckless, foolish.

And this is not only, therefore, a ballad
of remembrance for the down-South arcane city
with death in its jaws like gold teeth and archaic
cusswords; not only a token
for Bernice and Grady, for Mentor, for George and Oscar,
held in the schizoid fists of that city like flowers,
but also, Mark Van Doren,
a poem of remembrance, a gift, a souvenir for you.

HOMAGE TO THE EMPRESS OF THE BLUES
from *The Lion and the Archer* (1948)

Because there was a man in a candystripe silk shirt,
gracile and dangerous as a jaguar and because a woman
    moaned
for him in sixty-watt gloom and mourned him Faithless Love
Twotiming Love Oh Love Oh Careless Aggravating Love,
    She came out on the stage in yards of pearls, emerging like
    a favorite scenic view, flashed her golden smile and sang.

Because grey laths began to show from underneath
torn hurdygurdy lithographs of dollfaced heaven,
because there were those who feared alarming fists of snow
    upon
the door and those who feared the riot squad of statistics;
    She came out on the stage in ostrich feathers, beaded satin,
    and shone that smile on us and put the lights to shame and
    sang.

EINE KLEINE NACHTMUSIK
from *The Lion and the Archer* (1948)

I.

The siren cries that ran like mad and naked screaming women
with hair ablaze all over Europe, that like ventriloquists
made steel and stone speak out in the wild idiom of the
      damned—
oh now they have ceased but have created a groaning after-
      silence.

And the mended ferris wheel turns to a tune again
in nevermore Alt Wien and poltergeists in imperials
and eau de cologne go up and up on the ferris wheel la la
in contagious dark where only the dead are relaxed and warm.

II.

Anton the student hunches in a cold-starred room and reads
      and hears
the clawfoot sarabande, the knucklebone passacaglia coming
      close:
he has put on the requisite ancestral blue,
and his hair would glister festive as opals if the girandole

Had its way. A single prism is left to exclaim at the dear
iota of warmth and light a burntdown candle salvages.
Anton aching reads re-reads the dimming lines,
warms his fingers at the candleshine and turns the page.

III.

Now as the ferris wheel revolves to extrovert neomusic
and soldiers pay with cigarettes and candybars
for rides for rides with the famished girls whose colloquies
with death have taught them how to play at being whores:

Now as skin-and-bones Europe hurts all over from the
      swastika's

hexentanz: oh think of Anton, Anton brittle, Anton
    crystalline;
think what the winter moon, the leper beauty of a Gothic tale,
    must see:
the ice-azure likeness of a young man reading, carved most
    craftily.

"SUMMERTIME AND THE LIVING . . ."
from *Figure of Time* (1955)

Nobody planted roses, he recalls,
but sunflowers gangled there
sometimes, tough-stalked and bold
and like the vivid children there unplanned.

There circus-poster horses curveted
in trees-of-heaven above
the quarrels and shattered glass
and he was daredevil rider of them all.

No roses there in summer—oh never roses
except when people died—
and no vacations for
his elders so harshened after each unrelenting day

That they were shouting-angry. But summer was,
they said, the poor folks' time
of year. And he remembers
how they would sit on broken steps amid

Jactations of the dusk, the dark, wafting
hearsay with funeral-parlor fans
or making evening solemn
by their quietness. Feels their Mosaic eyes

Upon him, though long since the florist roses
that only sorrow could
afford have bidden them
God-speed.

                  Oh summer summer summertime

When wild street-preachers shook their tambourines
and Bibles in the face
of tolerant wickedness;
when Elks parades and big splendiferous

Jack Johnson in his limousine made all
the ghetto bloom
with fantasies
of Ethiopia spreading gorgeous wings.

MIDDLE PASSAGE
As Published in *A Ballad of Remembrance*

I.

Jesús,   Estrella,   Esperanza,   Mercy:

Sails flashing to the wind like weapons,
sharks following the moans the fever and the dying;
horror the corposant and compass-rose.

Middle Passage:
                    voyage through death
                                    to life upon these shores.

'10 April 1800—
Blacks rebellious. Crew uneasy. Our linguist says
their moaning is a prayer for death,
ours and their own. Some try to starve themselves.
Lost three this morning leaped with crazy laughter
to the waiting sharks, sang as they went under.'

Desire,   Adventure,   Tartar,   Ann:

Standing to America, bringing home
black gold, black ivory, black seed.

  Deep in the festering hold thy father lies,
  of his bones New England pews are made,
  those are altar lights that were his eyes.

Jesus   Saviour   Pilot   Me
Over   Life's   Tempestuous   Sea

We pray that Thou wilt grant, o Lord,
safe passage to our vessels bringing
heathen souls unto Thy chastening.

Jesus   Saviour

'8 bells. I cannot sleep, for I am sick
with fear, but writing eases fear a little
since still my eyes can see these words take shape
upon the page & so I write, as one
would turn to exorcism. 4 days scudding,

but now the sea is calm again. Misfortune
follows in our wake like sharks (our grinning
tutelary gods). Which one of us
has killed an albatross? A plague among
our blacks—Ophthalmia: blindness—& we
have jettisoned the blind to no avail.
It spreads, the terrifying sickness spreads.
Its claws have scratched sight from the Capt.'s eyes
& there is blindness in the fo'c'sle
& we must sail 3 weeks before we come
to port.'

What port awaits us, Davy Jones'
or home? I've heard of slavers drifting, drifting,
playthings of wind and storm and chance, their crews
gone blind, the jungle hatred
crawling up on deck.

Thou   Who   Walked   On   Galilee

'Deponent further sayeth The Bella J
left the Guinea Coast
with cargo of five hundred blacks and odd
for the barracoons of Florida:

'that there was hardly room 'tween-decks for half
the sweltering cattle stowed spoon-fashion there;
that some went mad of thirst and tore their flesh
and sucked the blood:

'that Crew and Captain lusted with the comeliest
of the savage girls kept naked in the cabins;
that there was one they called the Guinea Rose
and they cast lots and fought to lie with her:

'that when the Bo's'n piped all hands, the flames
spreading from starboard already were beyond
control, the negroes howling and their chains
entangled with the flames:

'that the burning blacks could not be reached,
that the crew abandoned ship,
leaving their shrieking negresses behind;
that the Captain perished drunken with the wenches:

'further Deponent sayeth not.'

Pilot   Oh   Pilot   Me

II.

Aye, lad, and I have seen those factories,
Gambia, Rio Pongo, Calabar;
have watched the artful mongos baiting traps
of war wherein the victor and the vanquished

were caught as prizes for our barracoons.
Have seen the nigger kings whose vanity
and greed turned wild black hides of Fellatah,
Mandingo, Ibo, Kru to gold for us.

And there was one—King Anthracite we named him—
fetish face beneath French parasols
of brass and orange velvet, impudent mouth
whose cups were carven skulls of enemies:

he'd honor us with drum and feast and conjo
and palm-oil-glistening wenches deft in love,
and for tin crowns that shone with paste,
red calico and German-silver trinkets

would have the drums talk war and send
his warriors to burn the sleeping villages
and kill the sick and old and lead the young
in coffles to our factories.

Twenty years a trader, twenty years,
for there was wealth aplenty to be harvested
from those black fields, and I'd be trading still
but for the fevers melting down my bones.

III.

Shuttles in the rocking loom of history,
the dark ships move, the dark ships move,
their bright ironical names
like jests of kindness on a murderer's mouth;
plough through thrashing glister toward
fata morgana's lucent melting shore,

weave toward New World littorals that are
mirage and myth and actual shore.

Voyage through death,
                    voyage whose chartings are unlove.

A charnel stench, effluvium of living death,
spreads outward from the hold,
where the living and the dead, the horribly dying,
lie interlocked, lie foul with blood and excrement.

Deep in the festering hold thy father lies,
the corpse of mercy rots with him,
rats eat love's rotten gelid eyes.

But oh the living look at you
with human eyes whose suffering accuses you,
whose hatred reaches through the swill of dark
to strike you like a leper's claw.
You cannot stare that hatred down
or chain the fear that stalks the watches
and breathes on you its fetid scorching breath;
cannot kill the deep immortal human wish,
the timeless will.

'But for the storm that flung up barriers
of wind and wave, The Amistad, señores,
would have reached the port of Principe in two,
three days at most; but for the storm we should
have been prepared for what befell.
Swift as the puma's leap it came. There was
that interval of moonless calm filled only
with the water's and the rigging's usual sounds,
then sudden movement, blows and snarling cries
and they had fallen on us with machete
and marlin-spike. It was as though the very
air, the night itself were striking us.
Exhausted by the rigors of the storm,
we were no match for them. Our men went down
before the murderous Africans. Our loyal
Celestino ran from below with gun
and lantern and I saw, before the cane-
knife's wounding flash, Cinquez,

that surly brute who calls himself a prince,
directing, urging on the ghastly work.
He hacked the poor mulatto down, and then
he turned on me. The decks were slippery
when daylight finally came. It sickens me
to think of what I saw, of how these apes
threw overboard the butchered bodies of
our men, true Christians all, like so much jetsam.
Enough, enough. The rest is quickly told:
Cinquez was forced to spare the two of us
you see to steer the ship to Africa,
and we like phantoms doomed to rove the sea
sailed east by day and west by night,
deceiving them, hoping for rescue,
prisoners on our own vessel, till
at length we drifted to the shores of this
your land, America, where we were freed
from our unspeakable misery. Now we
demand, good sirs, the extradition of
Cinquez and his accomplices to La
Havana. And it distresses us to know
there are so many here who seem inclined
to justify the mutiny of these blacks.
We find it paradoxical indeed
that you whose wealth, whose tree of liberty
are rooted in the labor of your slaves
should suffer the august John Quincy Adams
to speak with so much passion of the right
of chattel slaves to kill their lawful masters
and with his Roman rhetoric weave a hero's
garland for Cinquez. I tell you that
we are determined to return to Cuba
with our slaves and there see justice done. Cinquez—
or let us say 'the Prince'—Cinquez shall die.'

The deep immortal human wish,
the timeless will:

Cinquez its deathless primaveral image,
life that transfigures many lives.

Voyage through death
                    to life upon these shores.

THE DIVER
from *Selected Poems* (1966)

Sank through easeful
azure. Flower
creatures flashed and
shimmered there—
lost images
fadingly remembered.
Swiftly descended
into canyon of cold
nightgreen emptiness.
Freefalling, weightless
as in dreams of
wingless flight,
plunged through infra-
space and came to
the dead ship,
carcass that swarmed with
voracious life.
Angelfish, their
lively blue and
yellow prised from
darkness by the
flashlight's beam,
thronged her portholes.
Moss of bryozoans
blurred, obscured her
metal. Snappers,
gold groupers explored her,
fearless of bubbling
manfish. I entered
the wreck, awed by her silence
feeling more keenly
the iron cold.
With flashlight probing
fogs of water
saw the sad slow
dance of gilded
chairs, the ectoplasmic
swirl of garments,
drowned instruments

of buoyancy,
drunken shoes. Then
livid gesturings,
eldritch hide and
seek of laughing
faces. I yearned to
find those hidden
ones, to fling aside
the mask and call to them,
yield to rapturous
whisperings, have
done with self and
every dinning
vain complexity.
Yet in languid
frenzy strove, as
one freezing fights off
sleep desiring sleep;
strove against the
cancelling arms that
suddenly surrounded
me, fled the numbing
kisses that I craved.
Reflex of life-wish?
Respirator's brittle
belling? Swam from
the ship somehow;
somehow began the
measured rise.

Chronology of Robert Hayden's Life

1913   Born in Detroit, Michigan, to Asa Sheffey and Ruth (Gladys) Finn Sheffey, August 4; named Asa Sheffey, Jr. Mother moved to Buffalo, New York, father to Gary, Indiana. "Adopted" by Mr. and Mrs. Robert Hayden after parents separated.

1919   Joined the Second Baptist Church of adoptive father's faith. Experienced what he believed was a genuine conversion.

1930   Graduated from Northern High School, Detroit, Michigan.

1931   "Africa" published in *Abbott's Monthly.*
       Submitted poems to Harper and Brothers—rejected.

1932   Entered Detroit City College (Wayne State University).

1936   Ended matriculation one credit hour short of needed hours for graduation.

       Published "Equinox" in the *Detroit Collegian*, Detroit City College.

       Met Langston Hughes about this time.

       Began tenure as writer and researcher for the Detroit Writers Project, Works Project Administration.

       Awarded UAW award and citation as "People's Poet" (exact date unknown).

1937   "Autumnal" published in *American Stuff.*

1938   Began studies at the University of Michigan (summer school).

Adoptive father died.

Won Jules and Avery Hopwood summer award for "Heart-Shape in the Dust" Collection, the University of Michigan.

Became writer, radio station CKLW: wrote radio scripts based on Afro-American history subject matter.

1939   Wrote news stories for the Negro Progress Exposition in Detroit, "75 Years of Negro Progress."

Became Director of Negro Research, Detroit Federal Writers Project.

1940   Ceased work at Detroit Federal Writers Project.

Published *Heart-Shape in the Dust.*

Married Erma Inez Morris.

Became staff writer for the *Michigan Chronicle.*

Studied under W. H. Auden at the University of Michigan.

1941   Adoptive mother died.

Resumed graduate studies at the University of Michigan.

Studied under W. H. Auden.

1942   Won Jules and Avery Hopwood major award for "The Black Spear" Collection, the University of Michigan.

Daughter, Maia, was born, October 5.

Granted B.A. degree, Detroit City College.

1943   Became a member of the Bahá'i religion.

Published "O Daedalus, Fly Away Home" in *Poetry.*

1944   Appointed teaching assistant at the University of Michigan, Department of English.

Awarded M.A. degree, the University of Michigan.

Elected to Phi Kappa Phi

1945   Maternal grandfather Joseph Finn died.

1946   Resigned assistantship at the University of Michigan.

Appointed assistant professor in English, Fisk University, Nashville, Tennessee, and began a 23-year tenure.

Met Arna Bontemps. Friendship began.

Met Mark Van Doren. Got inspiration for "A Ballad of Remembrance."

1947   Awarded Rosenwald Fellowship in Creative Writing.

1948   Published "Counterpoise 3," a position statement.

Published *The Lion and the Archer* in collaboration with Myron O'Higgins.

1950–55   Natural father died, exact date unknown.

1950   Granted leave of absence from Fisk University.

1951   Returned with family to Fisk University.

1953–54   Discovered that the Haydens did not legally adopt him and that his natural parents had named him Asa Sheffey.

1954   Promoted to associate professor at Fisk University.

1954–55   Awarded Ford Foundation Fellowship for travel and creative writing in Mexico.

1955   Published *Figure of Time* (Counterpoise Series).

1957   January: natural mother died.

1962   Published *A Ballad of Remembrance.*

1963   Met Rosey Pool, European publisher, critic, and fellow Bahá'í.

1966   Awarded Grand Prix de la Poesie, First World Festival of Negro Arts, Dakar, Senegal

Became Poet Laureate of Senegal.

Published *Selected Poems.*

1968   Appointed poetry editor, *World Order.* Published *Kaleidoscope: Poems by American Negro Poets.*

Confronted black militants at the first Black Writers Conference, Fisk University.

Recorded poetry for *Today's Poets,* Scholastic Folkways.

Promoted to professor of English at Fisk University.

Participated in "Middle Passage and Beyond," television film (with Derek Alcott), WETA.

Recorded poems for the Library of Congress Archives.

1969   Presented Mayor's Bronze Medal for distinguished achievement for a native scholar (Detroit).

Appointed Bingham Professor at the University of Louisville.

Resigned from Fisk University.

Appointed visiting poet at the University of Washington, Seattle, Washington.

Awarded citation by the Pan-American Association, Washington, D.C., November 21, 22, 23.

1970   Published *Words in the Mourning Time.*

Awarded Russell Loins Award for Poetry for distinguished poetic achievement: National Institute of Arts and Letters.

1971   Appointed visiting poet, University of Connecticut, February.

Served as co-editor, *Afro American Literature: An Introduction.*

Served as visiting poet, Dennison University, April.

Recorded *Spectrum in Black.*

1972   Published *The Night-blooming Cereus.*

Appointed staff member, Breadloaf Writers Conference, Middlebury College, August.

Edited modern American poetry section, *The United States in Literature*, Scott Foresman and Co.

1974   Served as visiting poet, Connecticut College.

1975   Elected Fellow of the American Academy of Poets, citation and $10,000 award.

Appointed consultant in poetry at the Library of Congress, 1976–77.

1976   Assumed post at the Library of Congress.

1977   Reappointed consultant in poetry at the Library of Congress, 1977–78.

1978   Published *American Journal*, Effendi Press edition.

"John Brown" published by Founders' Society, Detroit Institute of Arts, in portfolio: *The Legend of John Brown* with
screen prints by Jacob Lawrence.

1980   Included in a group of American poets President Jimmy Carter
and his wife, Rosalyn Carter, honored at the Executive Mansion, January 4, 1980.

Died February 25, 1980.

1982   Published *American Journal*, Liveright Corporation edition
(volume published posthumously, contracted before his
death).

Chronological Listing of Robert Hayden's Poetry, Including Reprints and Revised Works

1931

"Africa," *Abbott's Monthly* 3, no. 1 (July, 1931): 40, not included in any of Hayden's volumes.

1936

"Equinox," *Detroit Collegian* (January 13, 1936), n/p, not included in any of Hayden's volumes.

1937

"Autumnal," in *American Stuff: An Anthology of Prose and Verse by Members of the Federal Writers Project* (New York: Viking Press), included in *Heart-Shape in the Dust* (1940).

"Flying Shadow," "Confessional," (not included in any of Hayden's volumes), "Leaves in the Wind," "To a Young Negro Dancer," (included in *Heart-Shape in the Dust* (1940), all included in *The Phenix*, 3, no. 2 (March, 1937), 19.

The "Heart-Shape in the Dust" Collection, Jules and Avery Hopwood Summer Award Collection, University of Michigan: " 'He is Foredoomed,' " "Words this Spring," "Monody," "Sonnet to E.," "This Grief," "Allegory," "Dedication," "Religioso," " 'We Have not Forgotten,' " "Old Woman with Violets," reprinted in *Heart-Shape in the Dust* (1940), and "It is not all Night," not included.

1940

"The Mountains," *Kaleidograph* 12, no. 1 (May 1940): 9, revised and reprinted in *Heart-Shape in the Dust* (1940), and "It is not all Night," not included.

"To a Young Negro Poet," *Opportunity* 18, no. 4 (April, 1940): 116; "Sunflowers: Beaubien Street," *Opportunity* 17, no. 7 (July, 1940): 245; "We Have not Forgotten," *New York Herald Tribune*, April 7, 1940, p. 11. All poems reprinted in *Heart-Shape in the Dust* (1940).

1941

"Prophecy," "Gabriel," "Speech," "Obituary," in *The Negro Caravan*, ed. Sterling Brown, Arthur P. Davis, and Ulysses Lee (New York: Dryden Press), pp. 405–8, included in *Heart-Shape in the Dust* (1940).

1942

"The Black Spear," with Additional Poems, Collection, Jules and Avery Hopwood Major Award Collection, University of Michigan, 1942. I: "Prologue," " 'Whereas in Freedom's name . . . ,' " "Spiritual," " 'They are sitting by the Cumberland, The Sewanee,' " " 'I am the secret midnight voice you do not hear,' " "O Daedalus, Fly Away Home," "Go Down Moses," " 'And now, the word for which the fathers bled,' " "Fire Image," " 'Vigil Strange I Kept on the Field One Night,' " "He had no time for pulling at his pipe," "The caissons roll . . ."; II: "Incidental Numbers," "Schizophrenia," "Beethoven," "Address to the Mind." None of these poems were included in any of Hayden's volumes.

1943

"O Daedalus, Fly Away Home," *Poetry* 62, no. 2 (April-September, 1943): 192–93, published in *A Ballad of Remembrance* (1962).

1945

"Middle Passage," *Phylon* 6, no. 3 (Third Quarter, 1945): 247–53; "Middle Passage," in *Cross Section* (New York: L. A. Fischer, pp. 153–61, revised and reprinted in *A Ballad of Remembrance* (1962).

"Frederick Douglass," *Atlanta Monthly* (February, 1947): 124, revised and reprinted in *A Ballad of Remembrance* (1962).

1948

"The Lion," *Voices: A Quarterly of Poetry* 4 (Summer, 1948): 15–16. "Homage to the Empress of the Blues," *The Tiger's Eye* 1, no. 4

(June 15, 1948): 7; "Invisible Circus," all revised and reprinted in
The Lion and the Archer (1948).
The Lion and the Archer. Nashville, Tenn.: Hemphill Press.
"The History of Punchinello, A Baroque Play in One Act," *SADSA: Encore*, (Nashville, Tenn.: Fisk University), pp. 30–33.

1949

"O Daedalus, Fly Away Home," "Homage to the Empress of the Blues," "A Ballad of Remembrance," "Eine Kleine Nachtmusik," "Runagate Runagate," "Frederick Douglass" (included in various volumes of Hayden's canon), "Letter to the South," "A Photograph of Isadora Duncan" (not included in any of Hayden's volumes), all included in *The Poetry of the Negro*, ed. Langston Hughes and Arna Bontemps (New York: Doubleday), pp. 163–71.
"Mourning Poem for the Queen of Sunday," *12th Street: A Quarterly* 3, no. 1 (December, 1949): 7–8, reprinted and revised in *A Ballad of Remembrance* (1962).

1950

"Double Feature" and "Noel Noel," *Voices: A Quarterly of Poetry* 160 (Winter, 1950): 23, not included in any of Hayden's volumes.

1951

"A Ballad of Remembrance," in *American Sampler: A Selection of New Poetry*, ed. Francis Coleman Rosenberger (Iowa City: The Prairie Press), pp. 47–48.

1954

"Locus," "Incense to a Lucky Virgin," "A Road in Kentucky," all revised and reprinted in *Figure of Time* (1955); "Bert Williams, Comedian," *The Midwest Journal* 6, no. 2 (Summer, 1954): 410–43, not included in any of Hayden's volumes.

1955

Figure of Time. Nashville, Tenn.: The Hemphill Press.

1958

"Runagate Runagate," in *Black and Unknown Bards: A Collection of Negro Poetry* (Kent, England: The Hand and Flower Press), pp. 33–34, revised and reprinted in *Selected Poems* (1966).
"Speech" and "Figure," in *I Saw How Black I Was: An Anthology of Poetry by American Negroes*, ed. Rosey E. Pool and Paul Breman.

MSS of Poetry Reading, Schomburg Collection, New York City Public Library.

1959

"Corrida de Toros," Etc.: A Review of General Semantics (December, 1959): 7–8, revised and reprinted in A Ballad of Remembrance (1962).

1960

"Incense of the Lucky Virgin," "Homage to the Empress of the Blues," "Corrido de Toros," "Eine Kleine Nachtmusik," The Fisk University Herald, 48, no. 2 (January, 1960), special section.

1962

"Full Moon," "Belsen, Day of Liberation," "The Diver" (revised and reprinted in Selected Poems [1966]), "School Integration Riot" (not included in any of the volumes), in Beyond the Blues, ed. Rosey E. Pool (Kent, England: Hand and Flower Press).

1963

"Veracruz," "Full Moon" (revised and reprinted in Selected Poems [1966]), in Soon, One Morning: New Writing by American Negroes, 1940–1962 (New York: Alfred A. Knopf), pp. 579–81.

1967

"El-Hajj Malik El-Shabazz (For Malcolm X)," in For Malcolm, ed. Dudley Randall and Margaret G. Burroughs. (Detroit, Mich.: Broadside Press), pp. 14–16, revised and reprinted in Words in the Mourning Time (1970).

"And All the Atoms Cry Aloud," read at the Bahá'i Centennial Celebration, Chicago, Illinois, October, and published in World Order 9 (Winter, 1967): n/p; revised and reprinted in Words in the Mourning Time (1970).

1968

"Night, Death, Mississippi," included in Angle of Ascent (1976).

1969

"Monet's 'Waterlilies,'" in "Today's Poets," Chicago Tribune Sunday Magazine, February 16, 1969, 16, revised and reprinted in Words in the Mourning Time (1970).

"The Mirages," "Sphinx," "'Mystery Boy' Looks for Kin in Nashville," Thoroughbred 1 Magazine (University of Louisville, Belknap Campus, Louisville, Kentucky), p. 14.

1970

"Zeus Over Redeye," in *Anon*, pp. 56–57, reprinted in *Words in the Mourning Time* (1970).

"A Plague of Starlings," "Soledad," *Generation* 21, no. 2 (Winter, 1970): 44–46, revised and reprinted in *Words in the Mourning Time* (1970).

"Aunt Jemima of the Ocean Waves," *Confrontation: A Journal of Third World Literature*, no. 1 (Summer, 1970): 8–9, a revised reprint from *Figure of Time*, reprinted in *Words in the Mourning Time* (1970).

1971

"Night-blooming Cereus," "The Peacock Room," *Concerning Poetry*, no. 2 (Fall, 1971): 58–61. (Phi Beta Kappa poem, 1970.)

"from 'Words in the Mourning Time,'" *World Order* (Spring, 1971): 42–43, revised and reprinted in *The Night-blooming Cereus* (1972).

1973

"For a Young Artist," *Anon*, pp. 106–8.

"Free Fantasia," "Tiger Flowers," "The Virgin Forest," all unpublished manuscripts.

1975

Read *American Journal* for Michigan Chapter of Phi Beta Kappa.

"John Brown," in *The Legend of John Brown* (Detroit: Detroit Institution of Arts).

1980

American Journal, Taunton, Mass.: Effendi Press.

1982

American Journal, New York: Liveright (published posthumously).

Readings

Albion College, Albion, Michigan
Atlanta University, Atlanta, Georgia
Ball State University, Muncie, Indiana
Beloit College, Beloit, Wisconsin
Colorado College, Colorado Springs, Colorado
Columbia University, New York, New York
Fisk University, Nashville, Tennessee
Hampton Institute, Hampton, Virginia
Howard University, Washington, D.C.
Lehigh University, Bethlehem, Pennsylvania
Mills College, New York, New York
Oakland University, Oakland, California
Ohio State University, Columbus, Ohio
Pennsylvania State College, University Park, Pennsylvania
Rockford College, Rockford, Illinois
Stephens College, Columbia, Missouri
University of Chicago, Chicago, Illinois
University of Colorado, Boulder, Colorado
University of Dayton, Dayton, Ohio
University of Kansas, Lawrence, Kansas
University of Michigan, Ann Arbor, Michigan
University of Missouri, Columbia, Missouri
Western Reserve University, Cleveland, Ohio
Western Washington State University, Bollingham, Washington
Jackson State University, Jackson, Mississippi
United States Bond rally, New Orleans, Louisiana
Bahai National Spiritual Assembly Convention, Wilmette, Illinois

YMHA Poetry Center, New York, New York
Virginia Union University, Richmond, Virginia
College of William and Mary, Williamsburg, Virginia
Roanoke College, Salem, Virginia
Randolph-Macon Woman's College, Lynchburg, Virginia
Hampton Institute, Hampton, Virginia
Benedict College, Columbia, South Carolina

Notes

Chapter 1   A Biographical Sketch

1. Robert Hayden, interview with author, October 31, 1972.

2. Ibid.

3. Ibid.

4. Ibid. Robert Hayden died February 25, 1980.

5. Ibid.

6. Hayden, "The Poet and His Art," *How I Write*, p. 136.

7. Ibid. p. 148.

8. Hayden, "Homage to the Empress of the Blues," *Selected Poems*, p. 44, *Angle of Ascent*, p. 104, *Collected Poems*, p. 32.

9. Hayden, "Those Winter Sundays," *A Ballad of Remembrance*, p. 29, *Angle of Ascent*, p. 113, *Collected Poems*, p. 41.

10. Hayden, interview, 1972; "Those Winter Sundays," *A Ballad of Remembrance*, p. 29, *Angle of Ascent*, p. 113, *Collected Poems*, p. 41.

11. Ibid. Sue Ellen Hayden's maiden name was, in fact, Westerfield. See also Hayden, "The Ballad of Sue Ellen Westerfield," *Selected Poems*, p. 21, *Angle of Ascent*, p. 85, *Collected Poems*, pp. 13–14.

12. Hayden, "The Poet and His Art," p. 142.

13. Hayden, interview with author, July 3, 4, 1973.

14. Hayden, "The Poet and His Art," p. 142.

15. Hayden, interview, 1972.

16. Hayden, telephone conversation with author, February, 1979.

17. Hayden, "The Whipping," *A Ballad of Remembrance*, p. 140, *Selected Poems*, p. 54, *Angle of Ascent*, p. 112, *Collected Poems*, p. 40.

18. George Edmund Hayes, "Negro Newcomers in Detroit," *The Negro in Detroit, and Washington*, ed. George E. Hayes and Sterling Brown, p. 8.

19. Hayden, interview, 1972.

20. Hayden, "Homage to the Empress of the Blues," lines 9–10.

21. Hayden, "Summertime and the Living . . . ," *Selected Poems*, p. 53, *Angle of Ascent*, p. 111, *Collected Poems*, p. 39.

22. Hayden, "Incense of the Lucky Virgin," *Selected Poems*, p. 46, *Angle of Ascent*, p. 106, *Collected Poems*, p. 34.

23. Hayden, "Mourning Poem for the Queen of Sunday," *Selected Poems*, p. 50, *Angle of Ascent*, p. 110, *Collected Poems*, p. 38.

24. Hayden, "Summertime and the Living . . . ," line 29. Jack Johnson (John Arthur Johnson) was the first American Negro to hold the world heavyweight boxing championship.

25. Hayden, "The Rabbi," *Selected Poems*, p. 17, *Angle of Ascent*, p. 81, *Collected Poems*, p. 9.

26. Hayden, interview, July 3, 1973.

27. Hayden, telephone conversation, February, 1979.

28. Hayden, interview, 1972.

29. Hayes, "Negro Newcomers in Detroit," p. 8.

30. Hayden, interview, 1972.

31. Ibid.

32. Hayden, "The Poet and His Art," p. 152.

33. Hayden, telephone conversation, February, 1979.

34. Hayden, interview, 1972.

35. Ibid.

36. Hayden, interview, 1972; "The Poet and His Art," pp. 136–37.

37. Robert Hayden, "Beethoven," "The Black Spear," The Jules and Avery Hopwood Award, First Prize Collection, University of Michigan, 1942, unnumbered.

38. Hayden, interview, 1972.

39. Hayden, telephone conversation, February, 1979.

40. Hayden, interview, July 3, 1973.

41. Hayden, interview, July 4, 1973.

42. Hayden, interview, 1973.

43. Robert Hayden, "Africa," *Abbott's Monthly* 3 (July, 1931): 40.

44. Countee Cullen, "Heritage," *On These I Stand: An Anthology of the Best Poems of Countee Cullen*, pp. 24–28.

45. James A. Emanuel and Theodore L. Gross, *Dark Symphony: Negro Literature in America*, pp. 173–75.

46. Hayden, interview, 1972.

47. Hayden, "Flying Shadows," "Confessional," "Leaves in the Winds," "To a Young Dancer," *Phenix* (March, 1937): 19.

48. Hayden, "The Poet and His Art," p. 138.

49. Countee Cullen, *Copper Sun*.

50. Hayden, "Epilogue," *Detroit Collegian*, January 13, 1936.

51. Hayden, "The Poet and His Art," pp. 139–40.

52. Richard Wright, "Blueprint for Negro Writing"; Langston Hughes, "To Negro Writers," *American Writers' Congress*, ed. Henry Hart, pp. 139–41.

53. Hayden, "The Poet and His Art," p. 141.

54. Ibid.

55. Hayden, interview, July 3, 1973.

56. Jerre Mangione, *The Dream and the Deal: The Federal Writers Project 1935–1943*, p. 9.

57. Ibid., pp. 258–59. Mangione states that Henry G. Alsberg, national director of The Writers Project, ordered state directors to hire as many blacks as possible. He appointed Sterling A. Brown national editor of Negro Affairs. To compensate for the sketchy treatment in the individual guidebooks, Brown instigated a series of field projects conducted by blacks who, working under his direction, investigated the story of the American black in depth. It was such a project that Hayden attempted.

58. Hayden, interview, July 3, 1973, telephone conversation, February, 1979.

59. John C. Dancy (1857–1920) was the son of a slave, a skilled carpenter, and a successful builder and contractor after the Emancipation Proclamation. He attended Howard University for three years and while in Washington he served in the United States Treasury Department briefly. Upon his return to North Carolina, he became a prominent Republican. From 1891 to 1895, and 1897 to 1902, appointed by President Benjamin Harrison and reappointed by President William McKinley, he was Collector of Customs at Wilmington, N.C. In 1902 President Theodore Roosevelt appointed him Recorder of Deeds for the District of Columbia, a post he held until 1910.

Dancy's powerful oratory distinguished his political, civic, and religious services, particularly as he was a spokesman for the African Methodist Episcopal Lion Church and the Republican party.

During his early years in North Carolina he was an apprentice of the Tarboro *Southerner*. He built on the experience to begin a second career when he became a journalist. He began his career with editorship of the North Carolina *Sentinel*; later, he became editor of the A.M.E. *Star of Lion and Lion Quarterly Review*.

Dancy met Booker T. Washington (1865–1915) sometime during the 1890s and became a member of the coterie of Afro-American businessmen and leaders who supported Washington and from whom stemmed the National Negro Business Association. The preserved Dancy–Washington correspondence is the valuable feature of the Calendar. See Robert Hayden, ed., "Calendar of the John C. Dancy Correspondence 1898–1910," passim.

60. Hayden, "What Is Precious Is Never to Forget," *Heart-Shape in the Dust*, p. 52.

61. Robert Bone, unpublished manuscript, 1972, p. 6 and passim.

62. Carey Williams cites more than thirty-three riots over widely dispersed areas in the United States, 1917–19, and over 600 deaths of Negroes (*Brothers Under the Skin*, pp. 5–6). John Hope Franklin and Isidore Starr give a summary of lynchings of Negroes by state from 1882 to 1951 (*The Negro in 20th Century America*, pp. 3, 186–87, 437).

63. Franklin and Starr, *The Negro in 20th Century America*, pp. 380–91.

64. Hayden, interview, 1972.

65. Hayden, interview, 1972.

66. Wilson Record, *The Negro and the Communist Party*, pp. 11–113.

67. See "Richard Wright," in *The God That Failed*, ed. Richard Crossman, pp. 115–62.

68. Hayden, interview, 1972, telephone conversation, February, 1979.

69. Wright, *Uncle Tom's Children*, especially "Fire and Cloud" and "Bright and Morning Star."

70. Hayden, "These Are My People," *Heart-Shape in the Dust*, pp. 56–63.

71. Robert Bone, *The Negro Novel in America*, p. 95.

72. Mangione, *The Dream and the Deal*, p. 255.

73. Robert Hayden, "Autumnal," *American Stuff*, p. 9, *Heart-Shape in the Dust*, p. 9.

74. Hayden, interview, 1972.

75. "Protest from Labor Bars Parole to Black Legion," *Daily Worker*, July 6, 1945, p. 6; "Liberties Union Writer Says Racist Lies Flood Detroit," *New York Post*, November 1, 1943, p. 38; Ralph G. Martin, "Detroit Danger Area," *The New Republic*, November 26, 1945, p. 703; Walter Davenport, "Detroit Strains at Federal Leash," *Colliers*, October 31, 1942, pp. 15–16, 39. See also Robert Conot, *American Odyssey*, pp. 416–18, 481, 482–98.

76. Hayden interview, 1972, interview, July 3, 1973; James Weldon Johnson, "Detroit," *Crisis* 32, no. 3 (July, 1926): 117–20. Dr. Ossian Sweet was an Afro-American medical doctor who, in defense of his family and his own life, confronted a mob that tried to oust him from a home that he purchased in a middle-class white neighborhood. He was twice brought to trial; in the second trial, he was defended successfully by Clarence Darrow.

77. Hayden, interview, July 4, 1973.

78. Hayden, interview, 1972.

79. Hayden, interview, 1972.

80. Hayden, interview, 1972.

81. Hayden, "Middle Passage," *Selected Poems*, pp. 65–70, *Angle of Ascent*, pp. 118–23, *Collected Poems*, pp. 48–54.

82. Hayden, interview, 1972.

83. Hayden, ibid., interview with author, April 9, 1979.

84. Hayden, interview, 1972.

85. Hayden won his second Jules-Avery Hopwood First Prize Award at the University of Michigan in 1942.

86. Hayden, "The Poet and His Art," p. 140.

87. Arthur P. Davis, "Integration and Race Literature," *Black Voices*, ed. Abraham Chapman, pp. 606–11.

88. Before the decade ended, Frank Marshall Davis, a pioneer poet in the Wright Protest School, had written his last volume, *47th Street* (Detroit: Black Cat Press, 1948); Owen Dodson had not followed his volume of poetry,

Powerful Long Ladder (New York: Farrar, Strauss, 1946), with another; Margaret Walker published only one volume, *For My People* (New Haven: Yale University Press, 1942), and Frank Yerby, who started out as a poet and short story writer, defected from the group to become a writer of popular fiction.

89. Hayden, "The Poet and His Art," p. 162, interview, October 31, 1973.

90. W. H. Auden, "The Virgin and the Dynamo," *The Dyer's Hand,* pp. 61–71.

91. Hayden, "Frederick Douglass," *Selected Poems,* p. 78, *Angle of Ascent,* p. 131, *Collected Poems,* p. 62.

92. W. H. Auden, "In Memory of W. B. Yeats," *Another Time: Poems by W. H. Auden* (New York: Random House, 1940), pp. 93–96.

93. Hayden, interview, July 4, 1973.

94. Hayden, " 'Lear Is Gay,' " *Words in the Mourning Time,* p. 62, *Angle of Ascent,* p. 70, *Collected Poems,* p. 108; W. B. Yeats, "Lapis Lazuli," *The Collected Poems of W. B. Yeats,* pp. 291–93.

95. Hayden, "Kodachromes of the Islands," *Words in the Mourning Time,* pp. 27–29, *Angle of Ascent,* pp. 47–49, *Collected Poems,* pp. 78–80; W. B. Yeats, "The Circus Animal's Desertion," *The Collected Poems of W. B. Yeats,* pp. 335–36.

96. Donald E. Stanford, "W. B. Yeats: Critical Perspectives," *The Southern Review* 5, no. 3 (Summer, 1969): 831–32.

97. Darwin Turner, *Black American Literature: Poetry,* p. 89.

98. Hayden, "The Poet and His Art," pp. 139–40.

99. Hayden, "Dance the Orange," *The Night-blooming Cereus,* p. 13, *Angle of Ascent,* p. 31, *Collected Poems,* p. 121; Rainer Maria Rilke, "Sonnet 15," *Sonnets to Orpheus,* p. 45.

100. J. E. Esselemont, ed., *Bahá'u'lláh and the New Era,* passim. The Bahá'i faith originated in Persia in 1844. At that time a young man who called himself the Bab ("Gate") began to teach that God would soon "make manifest" a world teacher to unite men and women and usher in a new age of peace. The growth in numbers of his followers so alarmed the Persian government and the Islamic clergy that they united to kill him and in the attempt massacred twenty thousand of his followers. In 1883 Bahá'u'lláh announced to the remaining followers of the Bab that he was the chosen manifestation of God for the age. He called upon the people to unite and outlined in his teachings the principles of his mission: one world, one people, one God, who manifests himself from age to age. The religious leaders of Islam reacted to the increase in his followers by forcing him into exile—first to Baghdad, then to Constantinople, to Adrianople, and finally to 'Akka, Palestine. There he died still in exile and in prison in 1892. Whereupon 'Abdu'l-Baha, his eldest grandson, Shongi Effendi, became the First Guardian of the Faith and interpreter of the teachings. The Bahá'i faith now has adherents in most countries.

101. Hayden, interview, August 14, 1973.

102. David Galler, "Three Recent Volumes," *Poetry* 110, no. 4 (July, 1967): 267–68.

103. Stephen Stephenchev, *American Poetry Since 1945*, pp. 2–3; Robert E. Spiller and others, *Literary History of the United States*, p. 1412.

104. Hayden, interview, August, 1973. The writers are William Demby, novelist; C. Eric Lincoln, social philosopher; Lonnie Elder, playwright; Julius Lester; Betty Latimer; Norman Loftis; Vilma Howard; and Al Cooper.

105. Julius Lester, "For a World Where a Man," *New York Times Book Review*, January 24, 1972, pp. 4–5, 22; Hayden, interview, August, 1973.

106. Hayden and others, "Counterpoise 3" n.p.

107. Esselemont, *Bahá'u'lláh*, pp. 59, 90.

108. Hayden, "The Poet and His Art," p. 141. The other writers were Sterling Brown, Owen Dodson, Margaret Walker, and Melvin Tolson.

109. Hayden, "The Poet and His Art," p. 162, interview, 1972, interview, October, 1973.

110. Hayden, "A Ballad of Remembrance" and "Tour 5," *Selected Poems*, pp. 39–40, 41, *Angle of Ascent*, pp. 99–100, 101, *Collected Poems*, pp. 27–28.

111. Hayden, interview, July, 1973.

112. Hayden, interview, July 4, 1973.

113. Hayden, interview, 1972.

114. Ron Karenga, "Black Cultural Nationalism," *The Black Aesthetic*, ed. Addison Gayle, Jr., pp. 31–37.

115. Hayden, interview, 1972.

116. Hayden, telephone conversation, February, 1979.

117. In fact, Fisk did not have its own funded chair for either a writer-in-residence or a poet-in-residence. Killens was brought to the university through a grant from the Ford Foundation, and it was thought that to grant Hayden a full professorship would represent greater security to him.

118. Hayden, interviews (all undertaken through 1973).

119. Hayden, interview, July 4, 1973.

120. Hayden, "Words in the Mourning Time," *Words in the Mourning Time*, pp. 41–51. Three of the original ten stanzas appear in *Angle of Ascent*, pp. 59–62, *Collected Poems*, pp. 90–100.

121. Hayden, "Traveling through Fog," *The Night-blooming Cereus*, p. 15, *Angle of Ascent*, p. 32, *Collected Poems*, p. 122.

122. Hayden, "The Peacock Room," *The Night-blooming Cereus*, pp. 10–11, *Angle of Ascent*, pp. 28–29, *Collected Poems*, p. 117.

123. Hayden, interview, July 4, 1973.

124. Hayden, interview, July 4, 1973; Hayden, "Beginnings," *Angle of Ascent*, pp. 1–5, *Collected Poems*, pp. 125–28.

125. Hayden, interview, 1972; Hayden, "For a Young Artist," *Angle of Ascent*, pp. 8–10, *Collected Poems*, pp. 132–33.

126. Michael S. Harper, "A symbolist poet struggling with historical fact," *The New York Times Review of Books*, February 22, 1976, pp. 34–35.

127. William Meridith, Consultant in Poetry, Library of Congress, to Dr. Niara Sudarkasa, February, 1980.

128. Arthur P. Davis, University Professor at Howard University, to Dr. Niara Sudarkasa, University of Michigan, February 1980.

129. Robert Hayden, statement made at the Library of Congress, April, 1977.

130. See Chronology, p. 208.

131. See Chronology.

132. Hayden, conversations with the author, April, 1977, February 9, 25, 1979, April 7, 1979.

133. Hayden to author, October 20, 1979.

134. Erma Hayden, telephone conversations with author, February 27 and March 9, 1980.

135. Hayden, "Stars," *Angle of Ascent*, pp. 11–15, *Collected Poems*, pp. 134–38.

Chapter 2   The Apprenticeship: *Heart-Shape in the Dust*

1. William Harrison, "A New Negro Voice," *Opportunity* 19, no. 3 (March, 1941): 91.

2. James W. Ivy, "Concerning a Poet and a Critic," *Crisis* 48, no. 4 (April, 1941): 128.

3. Arthur P. Davis, *From the Dark Tower: Afro-American Writers— 1900 to 1960*, pp. 174–80; Turner, *Black American Literature: Poetry*, p. 6; Arthur P. Davis and Saunders Redding, eds., *Cavalcade: Negro American Writing from 1760 to the Present*, p. 385.

4. See the Chronological Bibliography of Hayden's work at the end of this volume.

5. Hayden's *Selected Poems* contains poems about Cinquez ("Middle Passage," pp. 65–70), and Harriet Tubman ("Runagate Runagate," pp. 75–77) as well as "The Ballad of Nat Turner," pp. 72–73, and "Frederick Douglass," p. 78. Hayden's *Words in the Mourning Time* contains "El-Hajj Malix El-Shabazz," which is about Malcolm X. All these poems also appear in *Angle of Ascent* and *Collected Poems*.

6. Thomas Wentworth Higginson, "Gabriel's Defeat," *Atlantic Monthly* 10 (September, 1862): pp. 338–41.

7. W. J. Cash, *The Mind of the South*, pp. 84–86, 115–17, 128. Cash bases the centrality of the white woman in gyneolatry on (1) the fear conquered people entertain of their women being raped, (2) southern white woman being identified with the South itself—the belief in her enormous remoteness from the black man, and (3) the fact that the abolition of slavery opened up in the minds of all white southerners a vista at the end of which was the right of their sons in the legitimate line to be born to a pure white heritage.

8. Hayden, interview, July 4, 1973.

9. Seymour Gross and John Edward Hardy, *Images of the Negro in American Literature*, p. 16.

10. Hayden, interview, August 14, 1973.

11. Ralph Ellison, "Richard Wright's Blues," *Black Expression*, ed. Addison Gayle, Jr., pp. 311–25.

12. Harrison, "A New Negro Voice": 91.

13. Langston Hughes, "Evening Air Blues," in Emanuel and Gross, *Dark Symphony*, p. 207. See also Hughes, *Shakespeare in Harlem*, p. 40, especially "Out of Work."

14. Hayden, "The Dream," *Words in the Mourning Time*, pp. 12–13, *Angle of Ascent*, pp. 36–37, *Collected Poems*, pp. 66–67. Intending only to approximate what they perceived to be black idiom, both poets use phonological spelling—that is, omission of /g/s, simplification of consonant clusters, loss of /r/ sounds in final position, and the redundant use of the pronoun *me* to establish possession.

15. Langston Hughes and Arna Bontemps, eds., *Book of Negro Folklore*, p. 300.

16. Sterling Brown, *Negro Poetry and Drama and the Negro in American Fiction: Studies in American Life*, pp. 18–19.

17. Elinor Wylie, "Hospes Comesque Coparis," *Collected Poems of Elinor Wylie*, p. 124; see also p. viii for the poet's own explanation. The stanza follows:

> And the small soul's dissolving ghost
> Must leave a heart-shape in the dust
> Before it is inspired and lost
> In God: I hope it must.

Wylie based her lyric on the Latin original, which, according to Burton Stevenson (*The Home Book of Quotations*), is taken from the life of Emperor Hadrian: "Gentle little soul, hastening away, my body's guest and comrade, wither goest thou now, pale, fearful, pensive, not jesting as of old?" The title of Wylie's poem was translated by Howard D. Langford.

18. Spiller, *Literary History of the United States*, pp. 1253–62.

19. One of the first of these "reflective men," of course, was Ernest Hemingway, who became journalistically involved on behalf of the Spanish Loyalists in 1936. See Sculley Bradley and others, *The American Tradition in Literature* 2:1453–55.

20. Mangione, *The Dream and the Deal*, pp. 128–31, 176–78.

21. Milton Meltzer, *Langston Hughes, A Biography*, pp. 207–17.

22. F. R. Leavis, "Shelley," *English Romantic Poets: Modern Essays in Criticism*, ed. M. H. Abrams, pp. 345–65.

23. William Wordsworth, "The Simplon Pass," in *The Poetical Works of Wordsworth*, pp. 109–10; Percy Bysshe Shelley, "Mont Blanc," *The Complete Works of Shelley*, Cambridge ed. (Boston: Houghton Mifflin Co., 1901), pp. 347–49.

Chapter 3   The Exploratory Works

1. W. H. Auden, "The Virgin and the Dynamo," *The Dyer's Hand*, pp. 61–71.

2. Hayden, interview, 1972; William Demby, conversation with author, October 7, 1972.

3. Selden Rodman, "Negro Poets," *New York Times Book Review,* October 10, 1948, p. 27.

4. Margaret Walker, "New Poets," *Phylon* 11, no. 4 (Fourth Quarter): 345–54.

5. Sterling Brown, "The New Negro in Literature (1925–1955)."

6. Auden expounds that the arithmetical deals with the real, the actual, with recollected occasions of feelings. In translating these into poetry, the poet attempts to transfer them into a "society," a verbal society governed by laws of prosody and of "society" in order to produce the "community" which the successful poem is—a concept of potentiality (*The Dyer's Hand*, pp. 63–69).

7. Hayden, interview, July 4, 1973.

8. Hayden, telephone conversation, March, 1974.

9. *The Lion and the Archer* is unpaginated; poems are numbered. "Magnolias in the Snow" is number 1. The complete text of the poem is given in Appendix A at the end of this volume. Subsequent references to poems in *The Lion and the Archer* will be by number.

10. Barbara K. Lewalski and Andrew J. Sabol, eds., *Major Poets of the Earlier Seventeenth Century*, pp. 611–21.

11. F. J. Warnke, "Baroque Once More: More Notes on a Literary Period," *New Literary History* 1, no. 2 (Winter, 1970): 145–62.

12. Richard Barksdale, "Robert Hayden, 1913–," in *Black Writers of America*, ed. Richard Barksdale and Keneth Kinnamon, p. 676.

13. George Wilson Pierson, ed., *Tocqueville in America*, pp. 397–99; Robert W. Fogel, *Time on the Cross: The Economics of American Negro Slavery*, pp. 130–31, 135; Robert H. de Coy, *The Nigger Bible*, pp. 215–50. See also Eugene D. Genovese, *Roll, Jordan, Roll: The World the Slaves Made*, pp. 413–31, for a discussion of the extent, causes, nature, scope, and results of miscegenation in the antebellum South.

14. Constance Rourke, *American Humor: A Study of National Character*, pp. 75–82.

15. de Coy, *The Nigger Bible*, pp. 246–47, cites violent harrassment directed by the police against black spectators at the carnival for any real or imagined infraction of the law.

16. Ibid., p. 242. Participant described as follows: he wears tar-black makeup, clown-white circles around mouth and eyes, a crown with a jewel-studded band and purple peak atop which is a grinning human skull, a royal mantle of velvet trimmed in metallic gold and colorfully set with flashing rhinestones, a vest of leopard skin with a hula skirt of frilly, rustling, shredded strips of red cellophane which separate to show his contour-fitting black tights underneath.

17. Catherine Juanita Starke, *Black Portraiture in American Fiction*, pp. 30–35, 65–84. For another interpretation, see Albert Murray, *Stomping the Blues*, p. 190. Murray states that "the specific traditional ritual function of the outrageous costume and conduct of the King of the Zulus is to ridicule the whole idea of Mardi Gras and the Lenten season."

18. Robert Bone, lecture presented at Columbia University Teachers College, February 5, 1973.

19. Hayden, "The Poet and His Art," pp. 160–61.

20. Warnke, "Baroque Once More," pp. 145–62.

21. André Breton, "Manifesto on Surrealism," 1924 and 1930.

22. A revised version of "Homage to the Empress of the Blues" appears in *Angle of Ascent*, p. 104, and in *Collected Poems*, p. 32.

23. Hayden, "The Poet and His Art," pp. 148–49.

24. Lionel Trilling, cited in *Perspectives in Contemporary Criticism*, ed. Sheldon Norman Grebstein, p. 7.

25. Somewhere a lion trainer did, in fact, wear a "parakeet panache" in a cage (Hayden, telephone conversation, March, 1974). On another level, this recalls a passage in the farewell speech of Cyrano de Bergerac: "Hollow death, All my laurels you will take away. All my roses too. Everything except my panache." The "parakeet panache" of the lion-tamer seems to represent his style, his manner of facing the lion and the world, in much the same sense as Cyrano's *style*, for which he was most famous, and by reason of which he became, as a dramatic character, most memorable. "The Lion," severely revised, appears in *Angle of Ascent*, p. 64, and in *Collected Poems*, p. 102.

26. See the Chronological Bibliography for titles of previously published poems.

27. Hayden, telephone conversation, March 1974.

28. Hayden, "In Light half nightmare . . . ," slightly revised and retitled "From the Corpse Woodpiles, from the Ashes," is in *Angle of Ascent*, p. 116, *Collected Poems*, p. 46.

29. Hayden, "Locus," *Words in the Mourning Time*, p. 25, *Angle of Ascent*, p. 45, *Collected Poems*, p. 76.

30. Hayden, " 'Summertime and the Living . . . ,' " *Angle of Ascent*, p. 111, *Collected Poems*, p. 39.

31. Hayden, "The Poet and His Art," p. 143.

32. Hayden, "Incense of a Lucky Virgin," *Selected Poems*, p. 46, *Angle of Ascent*, p. 106, *Collected Poems*, p. 34; "The burly faded one," *Angle of Ascent*, p. 105, *Collected Poems*, p. 33.

33. Hayden, " 'Lear Is Gay,' " *Angle of Ascent*, p. 70, *Collected Poems*, p. 108.

34. W. B. Yeats, "Lapis Lazuli," *The Collected Poems of W. B. Yeats*, p. 296.

35. Yeats, *On the Boiler*, p. 35.

36. Yeats, *The Collected Poems*, pp. 184–85.

37. Yeats, "Upon a Dying Lady," *The Collected Poems*, pp. 155–57.

Chapter 4   *A Ballad of Remembrance*

1. Arna Bontemps, "A Ballad of Remembrance," review in the *Fisk News* 37, no. 1 (Fall, 1962): 12.

2. Ralph Mills, Jr., review in the *Christian Scholar* 45, no. 3 (Fall, 1962): 337–40.

3. Rosey E. Pool to Robert Hayden, undated note on copy of press release, Hayden's private papers.

4. Ibid.

5. Hayden, "The Poet and His Art," p. 196.

6. Benét, *John Brown's Body*, p. 308.

7. Although Hayden did not complete his projected Black Spear volume, in 1942 he entered the poems he had finished in the University of Michigan's Jules-Avery Hopwood competition. He gave that collection of poems the title he had intended to give his projected volume, and it won him first prize.

8. Anthony F. C. Wallace, "Revitalization Movements," *American Anthropologist* 58 (April, 1956): 264–81; Herbert Aptheker, *American Negro Slave Revolts*, pp. 162–292. According to Wallace, a revitalization movement is a deliberate, conscious effort by members of a society to construct a more satisfying culture. The process of revitalization involves four stages that are analogous to the parenthetical statements of Afro-American history: (1) Steady State (life in Africa); (2) Period of Individual Stress (forceful displacement from Africa); (3) Period of Cultural Discoloration (bondage in America); (4) Period of Revitalization (the numerous slave revolts in English America that began as early as 1663 and included subsequently Turner's, Gabriel Prosser's, and Denmark Vesey's).

9. Hayden, "Middle Passage," A Ballad of Remembrance, pp. 60–66, *Angle of Ascent*, pp. 118–23, *Collected Poems*, pp. 48–54. The complete poem is given in Appendix A.

10. Hayden, "The Poet and His Art," pp. 179–80.

11. Ibid.

12. Muriel Rukeyser, "The Amistad Mutiny," *Primer for White Folk*, pp. 23–50.

13. Hayden, "The Poet and His Art," p. 178.

14. Charles Davis, "Robert Hayden's Use of History," in *Black Is the Color of the Cosmos: Essays on Afro-American Literature and Culture 1942–1981*, pp. 255–64.

15. Elizabeth Drew, *T. S. Eliot: The Design of His Poetry*, pp. 21, 31, 72–77.

16. Hart Crane, *The Letters of Hart Crane*, p. 90.

17. Hayden, interview, July 3, 1973.

18. Allen Tate to Hayden, December 19, 1967, Hayden's private papers.

19. Hayden, "The Ballad of Nat Turner," *A Ballad of Remembrance*, pp. 68–70, *Angle of Ascent*, pp. 125–27, *Collected Poems*, pp. 56–58.

20. Herbert Aptheker, *Nat Turner's Slave Rebellion*, pp. 132–51.

21. The swamp is located in southeastern Virginia and northeastern North Carolina, extending from near Suffolk, Va., to Elizabeth City, N.C. It is partially located in Southampton County, Va., the site of the Turner revolt. In Turner's time, it was six times as large as it is now. *Encyclopedia Americana*, International ed., s.v. "Dismal Swamp."

22. This part of the discussion is based on Ezechiel 1:15–21; *Encyclopedia Americana*, International ed., s.v. "Ezekiel" and "Book of Ezekiel."

23. Aptheker, *Nat Turner's Slave Rebellion*, pp. 132–51.

24. Hayden, "Frederick Douglass," *A Ballad of Remembrance*, p. 71, *Angle of Ascent*, p. 131, *Collected Poems*, p. 62.

25. Frederick Douglass, *Life and Times of Frederick Douglass*, passim.

26. This last, Hayden makes clear, is his intention in his *Selected Poems* emendation of the "our children" phrase to simply "all."

27. Hayden, "O Daedalus, Fly Away Home," *A Ballad of Remembrance*, p. 67, *Angle of Ascent*, p. 124, *Collected Poems*, p. 55. See also the Chronological Bibliography.

28. Hughes and Bontemps, *Book of Negro Folklore*, pp. 62–65.

29. Hayden, "Witch Doctor," *A Ballad of Remembrance*, pp. 18–22, *Angle of Ascent*, pp. 107–9, *Collected Poems*, pp. 35–37.

30. Hughes and Bontemps, *Book of Negro Folklore*, pp. 62–63.

31. Ralph Ellison, "A Very Stern Discipline," *Harpers* (March, 1967): 80.

32. Hayden, interview, July 3, 1973.

33. Ibid.

34. Hayden, "Obituary," *Heart-Shape in the Dust*, p. 28, "This Grief," ibid., p. 34.

35. Hayden, "Rosemary," ibid., p. 37.

36. Hayden, "Those Winter Sundays," *A Ballad of Remembrance*, p. 29, *Angle of Ascent*, p. 113, *Collected Poems*, p. 41.

37. Hayden, "The Whipping," *A Ballad of Remembrance*, p. 28, *Angle of Ascent*, p. 112, *Collected Poems*, p. 40.

38. Hayden, "The Poet and His Art," pp. 147, 149.

39. Hayden, "An Inference of Mexico," *A Ballad of Remembrance*, pp. 45–57, *Angle of Ascent*, pp. 89–98, *Collected Poems*, pp. 17–26.

40. For an explanation of the system of *repartimentas*, under which the Indians were to supply labor for gold mines and plantations in return for instruction in the Spanish language and acceptance into the Christian religion, see "Tears of the Indies," *The American Heritage Book of Indians*, p. 99.

Chapter 5   *Selected Poems*

1. Galler, "Three Recent Volumes": 267–68.

2. Robert Moore Allen, "Hayden—True Artist and Skilled Craftsman," *Tennessean*, September 4, 1966, p. D-8.

3. Gwendolyn Brooks, "Books Noted," *Negro Digest* (October, 1966): 51–52.

4. Herbert A. Kinney, "Words That Leap from the Pages," *Boston Sunday Globe*, December 11, 1966, p. A-32; Cynthia Sinderis, "Poet Demonstrates the Logic of Love," *Kansas City Times*, December 9, 1970, editorial page.

5. Allen Tate to Hayden. Later Tate recommended Hayden for the Russell Loins Award, which he was given.

6. Hayden, interview, July 3, 1973. Hayden further stated that it was in 1966 that demand for his services as a poet began; for example, he was made poetry editor of *World Order*, the official organ for the Bahá'í faith. Moreover, upon publication of *Selected Poems*, his earnings from royalties, readings, fees, and visits as poet-in-residence were to exceed $10 thousand per year, once a princely sum for an English teacher whose salary was less than $5 thousand per year.

7. "Runagate Runagate," "Full Moon," "Belson, Day of Liberation," "Witch Doctor," and "Mourning Poem for the Queen of Sunday" had been previously published. See the Chronological Bibliography for publication information.

8. Hayden, "The Rabbi," *Selected Poems*, p. 17, *Angle of Ascent*, p. 81, *Collected Poems*, p. 9.

9. Hayden, "The Ballad of Sue Ellen Westerfield," *Selected Poems*, pp. 21–22, *Angle of Ascent*, pp. 85–86, *Collected Poems*, pp. 13–14.

10. Hayden, "Night, Death, Mississippi," *Selected Poems*, pp. 23–24, *Angle of Ascent*, pp. 87–88, *Collected Poems*, pp. 15–16.

11. Hayden, interview, July 3, 1973. The poet stated that he was motivated to write "Night, Death, Mississippi" when the Freedom Riders were lynched in Mississippi. He referred, of course, to the June 21, 1964, lynching of Andrew Goodman, Michael Schwerner, and James Chaney in Philadelphia, Mississippi. See "The Three Civil Rights Workers—How They Were Murdered," in *Mississippi Eye Witness*, a *Ramparts* Special Issue, 1964.

12. Hayden, "Runagate Runagate," *The Poetry of the Negro*, ed. Hughes and Bontemps, pp. 168–71, *Selected Poems*, pp. 75–77, *Angle of Ascent*, pp. 128–30, *Collected Poems*, pp. 59–61.

13. Hayden, "Kid," *Selected Poems*, p. 35, *Angle of Ascent*, p. 97, *Collected Poems*, p. 25.

14. Hayden, "Electrical Storm," *Selected Poems*, p. 13, *Collected Poems*, p. 5. The poem is dedicated to Arna and Alberta (Bontemps).

15. Hayden, "Full Moon," *Selected Poems*, p. 15, *Angle of Ascent*, p. 79, *Collected Poems*, p. 7.

16. Hayden, "Approximations," *Selected Poems*, p. 19, *Angle of Ascent*, p. 83, *Collected Poems*, p. 11.

17. Hayden, interview, July 3, 1973. Hayden's adoptive father died in 1938, his natural father in the early 1950s, his adoptive mother in 1941, and his natural mother in 1957.

18. Hayden, "The Diver," *Selected Poems*, p. 11, *Angle of Ascent*, pp. 75–76, *Collected Poems*, pp. 3–4. The complete poem is given in Appendix A.

19. Hayden, interview, July 3, 1973. Hayden stated that he read books by Jacques Cousteau and other authorities on marine life and deep-sea diving.

20. Maurice J. O'Sullivan, "The Mask of Allusion in Robert Hayden's 'The Diver,'" *College Language Association Journal* 17, no. 1 (September, 1973): 85–92. In his interesting analysis of "The Diver," O'Sullivan at-

tributes some of the allusions to Yeats and Dunbar. O'Sullivan correctly sees Hayden's line "have done with self and / every dinning / vain complexity" as an allusion to Yeats's Byzantium poems and to their confession of a desire to escape from "all mere complexities, / and the fury and mire of human veins." He does not, however, point out the older Keatsean precedent or Yeats's interest in Keats. The critic sees even Hayden's mode of escape conceived by the diver as an allusion to Yeats, whose ideal paradigm for transcendence exists in the dancer's physical transformation of self into artistic expression—a state apotheosized in his phrase "dying into a dance." O'Sullivan feels that like Yeats, who defected from the Irish Nationalist cause and embraced a concept of transcendence through art, so Hayden was tempted to defect from the complexities of the racial awakening that took place in mid-twentieth-century America. Strongly attracted to the Yeatsean ideal, Hayden' nevertheless repudiates the Irish poet's transcendence-through-art stance—that is, his "arcane historical prophecies and hypothesis combined with acute longing to transcend the affairs of men." Instead, O'Sullivan continues, Hayden favors the survival strategy that is implicit in what he sees as Dunbar's mask—now an artificial one—that he was tempted to fling away but does not in the poem. Clearly, crucial issues destroy credibility here: (1) O'Sullivan's debatable assessment of the meaning of Yeats's art—a meaning that even O'Sullivan finally admits Hayden rejects; (2) the critic's questionable interpretation of Dunbar's poetic interest as it may relate to Hayden's art and poetic intent; (3) O'Sullivan's ill-founded suggestion that Hayden is tempted to assume a literary stance—transcendence through art, precisely what Hayden had been about since his introduction and commitment to Yeats in the early forties—and the charge that he has instead adopted a "survival mask"—one that, by definition, he would fling aside once the millenium arrived.

21. John Keats, "Ode to a Nightingale," *The Norton Anthology of Poetry*, ed. Arthur M. Eastman, p. 696.

22. Earl R. Wasserman, *The Finer Tone: Keats' Major Poems*, pp. 178–223.

23. Hayden, interview, July 3, 1973, "The Poet and His Art," p. 166.

24. Hayden, Notebook, 1960, Robert Hayden Collection, Bahá'í National Center Archives, Wilmette, Illinois.

25. At the time Hayden wrote this poem, he had come under the influence of a Dutch woman, Rosey Pool, educator, scholar, and.editor. Hayden, interview, April 7, 1979.

Chapter 6   *Words in the Mourning Time*

1. Hayden, interview, July 3, 1973.

2. Barksdale and Kinnamon, "The Present Generation: Since 1945," in *Black Writers of America*, p. 676.

3. Lester, "For a World Where a Man," pp. 4–5, 22.

4. Chad Walsh to Hayden, March 4, 1971, sent with a copy of Walsh's review of *Words in the Mourning Time* for *Book World*. Hayden's private papers.

5. Hayden, "El-Hajj Malix El-Shabazz (Malcolm X)," *Words in the Mourning Time*, pp. 37–41, *Angle of Ascent*, pp. 55–57, *Collected Poems*, pp. 86–89.

6. Malcolm X (with the assistance of Alex Haley), *The Autobiography of Malcolm X*.

7. C. Eric Lincoln, *The Black Muslims in America*, pp. 76–77, citing Elija-Muhammed: "Out of the weak of the Black Nation, the present Caucasian race was created . . . by Yakub, a black scientist in rebellion against Allah."

8. Ibid., pp. 199–203. Lincoln gives a detailed account of the Fruit of Islam's function as the nucleus of the Black Muslim Secret Army.

9. Malcolm X, *Autobiography*, pp. 338–39. The leader writes that "the *color-blindness* of the Muslim world's religious society and the *color-blindness* of the Muslim world's human society . . . the *brotherhood*" impressed him most about the Hajj he undertook.

10. Malcolm X, *Autobiography*, p. 323.

11. According to Radman Ali, Ph.D., an Arabian, a Muslim, and a professional colleague of the author's.

12. Dudley Randall and Margaret G. Burroughs, eds., *For Malcolm* (Detroit: Broadside Press, 1967), p. 14.

13. Conrad Kent Rivers, "If Blood Is Black then Spirit Neglects My Unborn Son," in *A Broadside Treasury*, ed. Gwendolyn Brooks (Detroit: Broadside Press, 1971), p. 24.

14. Hayden, "Words in the Mourning Time," *Words in the Mourning Time*, pp. 41–51. The poem also appears, considerably emended, in *Angle of Ascent*, pp. 59–62, and in *Collected Poems*, pp. 90–100.

15. Esselemont, *Bahá'u'lláh*, pp. 105–7, 164–65.

16. Hayden, "The Web," *A Ballad of Remembrance*, p. 30, and "The Wheel," *A Ballad of Remembrance*, p. 33.

17. Hayden, "The Diver," *Beyond the Blues*, ed. Rosey E. Pool (Kent, England: Hand and Flower Press, 1962).

18. Hayden, Notebook, undated, Robert Hayden Collection, Bahá'i National Center.

19. Hayden, Notebook, unpaged.

20. Hayden, "The Sphinx," *Words in the Mourning Time*, p. 11, *Angle of Ascent*, p. 35, *Collected Poems*, p. 65.

21. Hayden, interview, July 3, 1973.

22. Hayden, interview, April 7, 1979.

23. The Sphinx at Giza, Egypt, is a male figure; in Greece and in Asia, the Sphinx is most commonly depicted as female. *Encyclopedia Britannica*, 15th ed.

24. Hayden, " 'Mystery Boy' Looks for Kin in Nashville," *Words in the Mourning Time*, p. 14, *Angle of Ascent*, p. 38, *Collected Poems*, p. 68.

25. Hayden, interview, April 7, 1979.

26. Hayden, "The Mirages," *Words in the Mourning Time*, p. 16, *Collected Poems*, p. 70.

27. Hayden, "The Broken Dark," *Words in the Mourning Time*, p. 15, *Angle of Ascent*, p. 39, *Collected Poems*, p. 69.

28. Hayden, "Aunt Jemima of the Ocean Waves," *Words in the Mourning Time*, pp. 18–21, *Angle of Ascent*, pp. 41–44, *Collected Poems*, pp. 72–75.

29. Benét, *John Brown's Body*, p. 138.

The matriarch of the weak and young,
The lazy crooning, comforting tongue
She has children of her own
But the white-skinned ones are bone of her bone.
They may not be hers, but she is theirs,

Half a nuisance and half a mother
And legally neither one nor the other.

30. Hayden, "The Dream," *Words in the Mourning Time*, pp. 13–14, *Angle of Ascent*, pp. 36–37, *Collected Poems*, pp. 66–67.

31. T. H. Dickinson cited in *A Handbook to Literature*, ed. William F. Thrall and Addison Hibbard, rev. C. Hugh Holman (New York: The Odyssey Press, 1960), pp. 280–81.

32. Hayden, "Locus," *Figure of Time*, p. 4, *Words in the Mourning Time*, p. 25, *Angle of Ascent*, p. 45, *Collected Poems*, p. 76. For a fuller discussion, see pp. 67–69 in this volume.

33. Hayden, "On Lookout Mountain," *Words in the Mourning Time*, p. 26, *Angle of Ascent*, p. 46, *Collected Poems*, p. 77.

34. Hayden, "Zeus Over Redeye," *Words in the Mourning Time*, pp. 30–31, *Angle of Ascent*, pp. 50–51, *Collected Poems*, pp. 81–82.

35. Hayden, "Kodachromes of the Island," *Words in the Mourning Time*, pp. 27–29, *Angle of Ascent*, pp. 47–49, *Collected Poems*, pp. 78–80.

36. Hayden, "Unidentified Flying Object," *Words in the Mourning Time*, pp. 32–34, *Angle of Ascent*, pp. 52–54, *Collected Poems*, pp. 83–85.

37. Hayden, "Monet's 'Waterlilies,'" *Words in the Mourning Time*, p. 55, *Angle of Ascent*, p. 63, *Collected Poems*, p. 101.

38. Hayden, "The Lion," *Words in the Mourning Time*, p. 56, *Angle of Ascent*, p. 64, *Collected Poems*, p. 102. For a detailed discussion, see pp. 63–65 in this volume.

39. Hayden, "The Return," *Words in the Mourning Time*, p. 61, *Angle of Ascent*, p. 69, *Collected Poems*, p. 107.

40. Hayden, "'Lear Is Gay,'" *Words in the Mourning Time*, p. 62, *Angle of Ascent*, p. 70, *Collected Poems*, p. 108. For a detailed discussion, see pp. 71–73 in this volume.

41. Hayden, "A Plague of Starlings," *Words in the Mourning Time*, p. 64, *Angle of Ascent*, pp. 71–72, *Collected Poems*, pp. 109–10.

Chapter 7   *The Night-blooming Cereus*

1. Hayden, interview, July 3, 1973.

2. Sharyn J. Skeeter, "Poetry Collections," *Essence*, January, 1973, p. 70.

3. Hayden, interview, July 3, 1973.

4. Skeeter, "Poetry Collections."

5. Hayden, "Traveling through Fog," *The Night-blooming Cereus*, p. 15, *Angle of Ascent*, p. 32, *Collected Poems*, p. 122.

6. Plato, "The Parable of the Cave," in G. M. A. Grube, *Plato's Thought* (Boston: Beacon Press, 1966).

7. Hayden, "The Ballad of the True Beast," *The Night-blooming Cereus*, p. 14.

8. Hayden, "Richard Hunt's 'Arachne,'" *The Night-blooming Cereus*, p. 5, *Angle of Ascent*, p. 23, *Collected Poems*, p. 113. Hunt's statue is displayed in the Museum of Modern Art, New York City. The young sculptor was one of Hayden's friends. Arachne is the mythological Greek girl who was skilled in weaving. Out of her vanity, she satirized the gods in her weavings. As a result, Minerva destroyed her web and shuttle, and Arachne hung herself. Minerva pitied her, however, and caused her and each of her descendants to live as a spider. Thomas Bulfinch, *The Age of Mythology*, Mentor Classics (New York: The New American Library of World Literature, Inc., 1962), pp. 142–46.

9. Hayden, "The Night-blooming Cereus," *The Night-blooming Cereus*, pp. 6–8, *Angle of Ascent*, pp. 24–26, *Collected Poems*, pp. 114–16.

10. Hayden, "The Peacock Room," *The Night-blooming Cereus*, pp. 10–11, *Angle of Ascent*, pp. 28–29, *Collected Poems*, pp. 118–19.

11. According to Hayden, a few years before Betsy Graves Reyneau died, she told him about a birthday party that a rich Detroiter gave for her in this room when she was twelve years old. The room was originally in the house of a rich English connoisseur, who first commissioned a young artist to design it. His design did not please the patron, and after he was fired he went insane. Whistler replaced him, but Whistler and the patron quarreled over both the fee and Whistler's artistic theories. As an act of spite, Whistler painted golden peacocks pecking at golden coins on the walls and doors. When the owner of the room died, the room was dismantled and sold to Charles Lang Freer, the Detroiter who was a friend of the Reyneau family. Years later, Hayden visited the room in the Freer gallery of the Smithsonian Institution and was inspired to write the poem.

12. O'Brien, "Robert Hayden," *Interviews with Black Writers*, p. 121.

13. Hayden, "The Performers," *The Night-blooming Cereus*, p. 9, *Angle of Ascent*, p. 27, *Collected Poems*, p. 117.

14. Hayden, "Smelt Fishing," *The Night-blooming Cereus*, p. 12, *Angle of Ascent*, p. 30, *Collected Poems*, p. 120.

15. Hayden, "Dance the Orange," *The Night-blooming Cereus*, p. 13, *Angle of Ascent*, p. 31, *Collected Poems*, p. 121.

16. Rilke, "Sonnet 15," *Sonnets to Orpheus*, p. 45.

17. J. R. Von Salis, *Rainer Maria Rilke: The Years in Switzerland*, trans. N. K. Cruickshank (Berkeley: University of California Press, 1966), pp. 217, 175–76.

18. Ibid., pp. 139–41. See Rilke's "The Willow of Saleeng," a ballad based on an actual three-hundred-year-old willow tree that regenerated itself when its decayed trunk sent a shoot down its interior, emerged again, formed a bark, and became itself a new trunk.

19. Vendler, *Yeats' Vision and the Later Plays*, pp. 79–81.

20. O'Brien, "Robert Hayden," *Interviews with Black Writers*, p. 113.

Chapter 8 *Angle of Ascent: New and Selected Poems*

1. Hayden, interview, October 31, 1973.

2. Ibid.

3. Hayden, "Beginnings," *Angle of Ascent*, pp. 1–5, *Collected Poems*, pp. 125–29.

4. Hayden, telephone conversation, February 9, 1979.

5. Nathan A. Huggins, *Harlem Renaissance* (New York: Oxford University Press, 1971), pp. 258–59.

6. Archie Green, *Only a Miner: Studies in Recorded Coal-Mining Songs* (Urbana: University of Illinois Press, 1972), pp. 125–26.

7. Hayden, "Free Fantasia: Tiger Flowers," *Angle of Ascent*, pp. 6–7, *Collected Poems*, pp. 130–31.

8. Hayden, interview, July 4, 1973. Hayden said he once worked as an errand boy in a house of ill repute.

9. Yeats, "Lapis Lazuli," *The Collected Poems of W. B. Yeats*, pp. 291–93.

10. Henri Rousseau, *Virgin Forest at Sunset*, in the Kunstmuseum, Basel, Switzerland.

11. Hayden, "For a Young Artist," *Angle of Ascent*, pp. 8–11, *Collected Poems*, pp. 132–33. For further discussion, see chapter 2, pp. 38–39 and chapter 3, pp. 64–65 in this volume.

12. Gabriel García Márquez, "A Very Old Man with Enormous Wings," *Leaf Storm and Other Stories*. In both the poem and the story the subject is characterized as an old man with bedraggled wings who has fallen from the sky. In the poem he falls into a pigsty; in the story he falls onto a beach covered with dead crabs. In the poem the villagers move him from a pigsty to a chicken-house; in the story a peasant couple carry him from the beach to their chicken coop. There, after fencing in their yard, they commercialize their find. Later, they improve his situation by putting him in a shed. In the poem he is "chunked at," derided, worshipped, and commercialized in a "barbedwire pen." In the story the subject is threatened with death by clubbing, is stoned, burned with a branding iron used for steers, is derided, worshipped, and commercialized. In the poem the old man is given "hand-me-downs" to wear and "leftovers" to eat; he eats, instead, sunflowers. In the story the old man is given mothballs to eat; he eats, instead, eggplant mush.

In the poem the old man is impervious to his captors' abuse and does not respond to their ploys. In the story the old man is impassive, regards his captors with antique eyes, and is the only one who does not take a part in his own act. In the poem the old man's surreptitious "flapping" effort to fly elicits "flutter[s]" and "squeal[s]." In the story, when it is dark, the old man gains flight by awkwardly clawing the dirt and flapping, causing a "whirlwind of chicken dung, lunar dust and a gale of panic." Quote from Richard Ellman, *Eminent Domain*, p. 8.

13. Hayden, interview, October 31, 1973.

14. Hayden, "Stars," *Angle of Ascent*, pp. 11–15, *Collected Poems*, pp. 134–38.

15. J. E. Zimmerman, *Dictionary of Classical Mythology* (New York: Harper and Row, 1964), pp. 184–85; Fred Hoyle, *Astronomy and Cosmology, A Modern Course* (San Francisco: W. H. Freeman and Company, 1975), pp. 601–2.

16. Esslemont, *Bahá'u'lláh*, pp. 2–7, 90, 110, 150, 208, 231.

17. Cleanth Brooks, "The Language of the Paradox," *The Well Wrought Urn*, pp. 3–21.

18. Sojourner Truth (née Isabela Baunfred) was born a slave in Ulster County, New York, and freed under the New York Emancipation Act of 1807. See Davis and Redding, *Cavalcade*, pp. 78–81.

19. At a protest rally in Faneuil Hall in Boston, Frederick Douglass addressed a large gathering. His attitude was pessimistic and defeatist concerning the future of the Negroes. "They have no hope of justice from the whites," he said, "no possible hope except in their own right arms." It was then that Sojourner Truth rose and challenged Douglass: "Is God dead?" *Profiles of Negro Womanhood*, vol. 1, *1619–1940*, The Negro Heritage Library, (New York, 1964).

20. The Negro Heritage Library, *Profiles of Negro Womanhood* I: 94–101.

21. Hoyle, *Astronomy and Cosmology*, pp. 601–2, 612–26, 654.

22. Hayden, "Two Egyptian Portrait Masks," *Angle of Ascent*, pp. 16–17, *Collected Poems*, pp. 139–40.

23. *Encyclopedia Britannica*, 15th ed., s.v. "Egypt: History: Ancient Period."

24. *Encyclopedia Britannica*, 15th ed., s.v. "Ikhnaton."

25. J. B. Pritchard, *Ancient Near Eastern Texts*, pp. 370–71.

26. *Encyclopedia Britannica*, 15th ed., s.v. "Ikhnaton."

27. Hayden, telephone conversation, February 9, 1979. Mr. Hayden stated that he intended a tie-in with the same spirit referred to in the Afro-American spiritual, "Every Time I Feel the Spirit."

28. *Encyclopedia Britannica, Macropedia*, 15th ed., s.v. "The New Kingdom."

29. Ibid.

30. Ibid.

31. Hayden, "Butterfly Piece," *Angle of Ascent,* p. 18, *Collected Poems,* p. 141, "Moose Wallow," *Angle of Ascent,* p. 19, *Collected Poems,* p. 142.

32. Hayden, "Crispus Attucks," *Angle of Ascent,* p. 20, *Collected Poems,* p. 143.

33. Hayden, "Words in the Mourning Time," *Words in the Mourning Time,* pp. 41–51, *Angle of Ascent,* pp. 59–62, *Collected Poems,* pp. 90–100.

34. Erma Hayden, interview with author, August, 1980. Mrs. Hayden said that, in accordance with the Bahá'í religion, her husband did not belong to a political party, Democratic, Republican, or otherwise.

35. Esslemont, *Bahá'u'lláh,* p. 87.

Epilogue

1. Erma Hayden, interview with author, August 20, 1980.

2. Hayden, "Elegies for Paradise Valley," *American Journal,* pp. 25–32, *Collected Poems,* pp. 132–33.

3. Conot, *American Odyssey,* pp. 417–18. During the thirties the entire social body of Detroit, including many of the policemen and even police chiefs, were members of the Black Legion, an organization that was violently active against Afro-Americans, Jews, and others. See also chapter 1 of this volume.

4. Johann Heinrich Pestalozzi was a Swiss educational reformer. He developed a plan for education of neglected children that integrated home and farm, industry, social morality, basic language, arithmetic, music, and recreation.

5. Hayden, interview, April 7, 1979.

6. "Ball-the-Jack" was a dance that was done to one of Jelly Roll Morton's blues songs. Jelly Roll Morton (né Fred) was a blues artist who was popular from the turn of the century through the thirties. He played solo piano at the Fairfax Hotel in Detroit between 1915 and 1917. Johnny Chilton, "Jelly Roll Morton," *Who's Who of Jazz* (Alexandra, Va.: Time-Life, 1978), pp. 233–34.

7. Hayden, telephone conversation, February, 1979.

8. Hayden, "Names," *American Journal,* p. 35, *Collected Poems,* p. 171.

9. Hayden, interview, 1979.

10. Hayden, "A Letter from Phyllis Wheatley," *American Journal,* pp. 3–4, *Collected Poems,* pp. 147–48.

11. Hayden, "from THE SNOW LAMP," *American Journal,* pp. 51–54, *Collected Poems,* pp. 186–89.

12. Hayden, "Paul Lawrence Dunbar," *American Journal,* p. 15, *Collected Poems,* p. 156.

13. Hayden, "Homage to Paul Robeson," *American Journal,* p. 16, *Collected Poems,* p. 157.

14. Hayden, undocumented clipping from the *Detroit Chronicle,* Hayden Collection.

15. Memorial service for Robert Hayden sponsored by the Ann Arbor Bahá'í community and the University of Michigan English Department, April 5, 1980.

16. Hayden, telephone conversation, 1979. Drafts for the poem about Alessandro de' Medici are in the Hayden Collection.

17. Hayden, "John Brown," *American Journal,* pp. 5–9, *Collected Poems,* pp. 149–53.

18. Information about John Brown's connection with the Underground Railroad in Detroit from a historical note in a program for a Sunday service in the files of the Second Baptist Church, Detroit, Michigan.

19. Hayden, "The Year of the Child," *American Journal,* pp. 43–44, *Collected Poems,* pp. 179–80.

20. Hayden, "Double Feature," *Voices: A Quarterly of Poetry* 140 (Winter, 1950): 23. *American Journal,* p. 36, *Collected Poems,* p. 172.

21. Hayden, "The Dogwood Trees," *American Journal,* p. 37, *Collected Poems,* p. 173.

22. Hayden, "Letter," *American Journal,* p. 38, *Collected Poems,* p. 174.

23. Hayden, interview, April 7, 1979.

24. Hayden, "The Tatooed Man," *American Journal,* pp. 19–21, *Collected Poems,* pp. 160–62.

25. Hayden, "As my blood was drawn," *American Journal,* pp. 40–41, *Collected Poems,* pp. 176–77.

26. Hayden, "Ice Storm," *American Journal,* p. 39, *Collected Poems,* p. 175.

27. Testimonial in honor of Robert Hayden, University of Michigan, February 24, 1980. Hayden was too ill to attend the testimonial; he died the next day. A folder of thirty tributes, including those cited in the text, is available at the Schomburg Center for Afro-American Studies, New York City Public Library.

28. Russell Lynes, *A Surfeit of Honey,* pp. 12–21, 29–30.

29. "Honor Roll of American Poets Read at White House," *New York Times,* January 4, 1980, p. C14; Erma Hayden, interview, August 20, 1980; Hayden, unpublished manuscript, Hayden Collection; President Jimmy Carter to Erma Hayden, read at memorial service, April 5, 1980.

30. Robert Frost, "The Figure a Poem Makes," *Perspectives on Poetry,* ed. Calderwood and Toliver, p. 350.

31. Henry Treece, *Dylan Thomas: "Dog Among the Fairies,"* pp. 37, 71–79.

32. C. Day Lewis, "The Poet's Way to Knowledge," *Perspectives on Poetry,* pp. 290–305.

33. Hayden, "From the Life: Some Remembrances," manuscript in the author's collection.

34. Ibid.

Index

Note on the Author

PONTHEOLLA T. WILLIAMS holds a B.A. from Johnson C. Smith University and M.A. and Ed.D. degrees from Columbia University Teachers College. She has been chairman of the Department of English and the Humanities Division at Morris College, from which she was a presidential appointee, 1984–86, serving as a special assistant in the Adult Literacy Initiative in the United States Department of Education in Washington, D.C.